For Whom God Calls
By
Michael H. Sands

PUBLISHED by PARABLES
Earthly Stories with a Heavenly Meaning

For Whom God Calls
By Michael H. Sands

Published By Parables
June, 2021

All Rights Reserved. No part of this book may be reproduced or utilized in any form or by any means, electronic or mechanical, including photocopying, **recording, or by any information storage and retrieval system, without permission in writing from the author.**

Printed in the United States of America

Readers should be aware that Internet Web sites offered as citations and/or sources for further information may have been changed or disappeared between the time this was written and the time it is read.

For Whom God Calls
By
Michael H. Sands

PUBLISHED by PARABLES
Earthly Stories with a Heavenly Meaning

TABLE OF CONTENTS

I. Dedication

II. Featured Authors

III. Inspirational Reading
The Sound of the Genuine
    Howard Thurman

IV. Preface
    Michael H. Sands

V. Introduction
    Michael H. Sands

Part One – The Why
The Black Church and the People Within

Chapter 1 – Origins
Reading: *The Black Church and Black Reconstruction: The Emergence of Independent Black Churches and Preachers*
    Henry Love Whelchel

Chapter 2 – Contemporary Black Preaching: What Cost the Amen?
Reading: *Teaching Preaching A Critique of Contemporary Preaching*
    Katie Geneva Cannon

Chapter 3 – The Black Congregation and the People Within
Reading: *Liberation From Mental Slavery*
    Na'im Akbar

Part Two – The What
Ministry and the African American Community

Chapter 4 – Expectations and Misconceptions of Ministry
Reading: *What To Expect In Seminary: Theological Education as Spiritual Formation - The Call To Ministry*
    Virginia Samuel Cetuk

Chapter 5 – Is There A Need For An Edified Ministry?
Reading: *"A Stutter and a Stick" The (Non-)Value of Educational Credentialing*
    Richard N. Pitt

Part Three – The How
The Ministry Declaration – "The Call" Paper

Chapter 6 – Reflections of the Self
Reading: *Recalling Our Own Stories (Spiritual Renewal for Religious Caregivers) - Suzanne: Allowing The True Self To Surface*
    Edward P. Wimberly

Chapter 7 – Becoming the Authentic Me
Reading: *Let Your Life Speak: Listening for the Voice of Vocation - Now I Become Myself*
    Parker J. Palmer

Chapter 8 – An Exercise In Self – Exposing Your Fears
    Michael H. Sands

Chapter 9 – Conclusion: The Call Paper
    Michael H. Sands

Chapter 10 – Your Personal Library

Chapter 11 – Next Steps
    Michael H. Sands

Attachment 1 - Sample Call Paper

Notes

Bibliographies

For Whom God Calls

I. Dedication

This book is dedicated to all Black Baptist ministers of the Gospel who never had nor ever will have the opportunity to obtain any formal religious education from an accredited Seminary or Bible College. It is to you, those who dare to follow their calling despite the challenges of the establishment and traditions of the Black Baptist Church, the content of this book herein addresses.

To my mother, Rosetta F. Sands, PhD., and my auntie, Mrs. Alva Maull, my cheerleaders from the beginning, I will forever love and appreciate you for never giving up on me, even in my darkest moments.

To my son, Michael H Sands, Jr., May you find joy in the life God has given you. Don't let the past interfere with your blessings in the present and future.

To Rev. Dr. Calvin Edmonds, the depth of your guidance and inspiration has been an immeasurable positive influence on my spiritual maturity. As my father in the ministry, you are and always will be the man of God whose example I aspire to follow.

Finally, none of this would have been possible without the love, support, and input of my lovely wife and best friend, Minister Rayetta Holts-Sands. Your unbridled love for God and your endless search for truth inspires me to make you proud and always to strive to do what God has called me to do to the best of my ability, no matter the struggle.

I Love You.

Michael H Sands

For

Stevie, Nycole
Gabrielle, and Jordan

Russell, Kimberlee
Kaeden, Ava Raye, and Russell, Jr.

Tamara and Faith

Jasmyne Renee Barnes
(Born into Heaven September 13, 2005)

*I(you) can do all things through Christ who strengthens me(you).
Philippians 4:13*

For Whom God Calls

II. Featured Authors

Howard Washington Thurman (1899–1981), was an American author, philosopher, theologian, educator, and civil rights leader. As a prominent religious figure, he played a leading role in many social justice movements and organizations of the twentieth century.

Na'im Akbar, is a clinical psychologist well known for his Afrocentric approach to psychology. He is a distinguished scholar, public speaker, and author. Akbar entered the world of Black psychology in the 1960s, as the Black Power Movement was gaining momentum.

Katie Geneva Cannon (1950–2018), was an American Christian theologian and ethicist associated with womanist theology and black theology. She was the first African-American woman ordained in the United Presbyterian Church (USA), which occurred in 1974.

L.H. Whelchel, Jr., is a respected scholar, university professor, and civil rights activist. A successful church pastor for 25 years, he brings meticulous research skills of the scholar together with first hand experiences as a minister and the passion of an activist. Dr. Whelchel was Professor of Church History at the Interdenominational Theological Center in Atlanta.

Virginia Samuel Cetuk, is Associate Dean for Contextual Learning and Director of Supervised Ministry, The Theological School of Drew University and an Ordained Elder in The United Methodist Church, Northern New Jersey Conference.

Edward P. Wimberly, served as the Interdenominational Theological Center's Ninth President. His role as theological educator in the area of pastoral psychology and care extends four decades. He is a licensed Marriage and Family therapist and has authored of an extensive list of publications including seventeen books.

Richard N. Pitt, is Assistant Professor of Sociology at Vanderbilt University

Parker J. Palmer, is founder and Senior Partner Emeritus of the Center for Courage & Renewal. He holds a Ph.D. in sociology from the University of California at Berkeley, as well as 13 honorary doctorates, 2 Distinguished Achievement Awards from the National Educational Press Association, and an Award of Excellence from the Associated Church Press.

Michael H. Sands, is an Ordained Baptist Minister of the Gospel of Jesus the Christ. He earned his Master of Divinity and Doctor of Ministry from the Interdenominational Theological Center. Dr. Sands is the 2015 recipient of the Interdenominational Theological Center Martin Luther King Sr. Award for his dedication and contributions to the Black Baptist Church.

For Whom God Calls

III. Inspirational Reading

We begin our journey with an inspirational reading. I believe this reading is apropos since I, too, was introduced to this reading as part of my Doctoral Selection Board interview. After delivering my heartfelt, passionate reason as to why I should be selected to be a part of the doctoral program, one of the Deans suggested I go and read this as soon as I finished the interview. I did, and behold, my life has never been the same.

Before beginning any minister's class I facilitate, students must read and discuss this reading as a class assignment. Dr. Howard Thurman, an inspirational preacher second-to-none, delivered this text at a commencement speech at Spelman College in Atlanta, Georgia. Despite the years that have passed since he first delivered this speech, it remains relevant today. I encourage you to not only read *The Sound of the Genuine* but take the time to digest and reflect on its meaning and how it pertains to your ministry journey. I have yet to find anyone who hasn't been profoundly affected by its message.

"The Sound of the Genuine"[1]
By the
Rev. Dr. Howard Thurman

There is in every person something that waits and listens for the sound of the genuine in herself. . . .

There is in you something that waits and listens for the sound of the genuine in yourself. Nobody like you has ever been born and no one like you will ever be born again—you are the only one. And if you miss the sound of the genuine in you, you will be a cripple all the rest of your life. Because you will never be able to get a scent on who you are.

Do you remember in the Book [Christian Bible] Jesus and his disciples were going through the hills and there appeared in the turn of the road a man who was possessed of devils as they thought. In the full moon when the great tidal waves of energy swept through his organism and he became as ten men . . . screaming through the hills like an animal in pain and then he met Jesus on the road. And Jesus asked him one question: "Who are you; what's your name?" and for a moment his tilted mind righted itself and he said, "That's it, I don't know, there are legions of me. And they riot in my streets. If I only knew, then I would be whole."[2]

So the burden of what I have to say to you is, "What is your name— who are you—and can you find a way to hear the sound of the genuine in yourself?" There are so many noises going on inside of you, so many echoes of all sorts, so many internalizing of the rumble and the traffic, the confusions, the disorders by which your environment is peopled that I wonder if you can get still enough— not quiet enough—still enough to hear rumbling up from your unique and essential idiom the sound of the genuine in you. I don't know if you can. But this is your assignment.

I. Seek Self through 'The Song of the River' There is a children's story written for adults called The Blue Cat of Castleton. You may know it. It is built on a New England legend which says that no cat mother wanted to have a kitten that had all blue hairs and pink ears. Because if she had such a kitten, it would be that kitten's fate to hear the song of the river, and if the kitten heard the song of the river following that melody he or she would have to leave home, learn the song of the river, and go in quest of a home where the song of the river was recognized. So the "kit-hero" of the story was born all blue hairs [and] pink ears except four black hairs in his tail. . . .One by one the black hairs dropped out. This last night the kitten was asleep. He heard rumbling up under his sleeping consciousness the song of the river, and in a kind of drunken stupor he got up, shook himself and wondered down to the river. There the river taught him the song.

For Whom God Calls

Sing your own song, said the river
Sing, sing your own song
Out of yesterday song comes
It goes into tomorrow,
Sing your own song.

With your life fashion beauty,
This too is the song.
Riches will pass and power,
But beauty remains.
Sing your own song.

All that is worth doing,
Do well, the river said.
Sing, sing your own song
Certain and round be the measure
Every line graceful and true

Time is the mold, the weaver, carver,
Time and the workman together,
Sing your own song well,
Sing well, the river said,
Sing your own song well.

So the kitten learned the song and went in quest of a home—and how would he know when he had found a home? He would walk in, stretch out, and begin singing the song and if the person who heard him recognized the song he knew that he had found a home. Without going into all the details one of the first places he went was into a pewter-maker's house. He walked in, stretched out in front of the hearth, and began singing the song. As soon as the pewter-maker heard the first line of the melody, he froze, and a faraway look came in his eyes; then he remembered.

Long, long ago [the pewter-maker] knew the song of the river. During the time that he knew the song of the river, every piece of pewter fashioned was an expression of an inner dream he had about the creative possibilities of pewter. He was so proud of it, until he put his imprint motto on the bottom of it so that everybody would know that he who knew the song of the river had stamped the pewter.

Then he married, babies began coming, tourists began demanding more and more pewter, budgets increased, money was hard, so he began grounding out the pewter cups. He was so embarrassed in his psyche that he didn't want to put his name on it. Then he heard the kitten and he remembered that somewhere along the way he had forgotten that he knew the song of the genuine in himself. A simple story.

II. Follow the Sound of the Genuine. There is something in every one of you that waits, listens for the genuine in yourself—and if you cannot hear it, you will never find whatever it is for which you are searching and if you hear it and then do not follow it, it was better that you had never been born. You are the only you that has ever lived; your idiom is the only idiom of its kind in all the existences, and if you cannot hear the sound of the genuine in you, you will all of your life spend your days on the ends of strings that somebody else pulls.

There is in you something that waits and listens for the sound of the genuine in yourself and sometimes there is so much traffic going on in your minds, so many different kinds of signals, so many vast impulses floating through your organism that go back thousands of generations long before you were even a thought in the mind of creation and you are buffeted by these and in the midst of all of this you have got to find out what your name is. Who are you? How does the sound of the genuine come through to you. . .? The sound of the genuine is flowing through you.

Don't be deceived and thrown off by all the noises that are a part even of your dreams [and] your ambitions that you don't hear the sound of the genuine in you. Because that is the only true guide that you will ever have and if you don't have that you don't have a thing. You may be famous. You may be whatever the other ideals are which are a part of this generation, but you know you don't have the foggiest notion of who you are, where you are going, what you want. Cultivate the discipline of listening to the sound of the genuine in yourself.

Now there is something in everybody that waits and listens for the sound of the genuine in other people. And it is so easy [for you or me] to say, "Anybody who looks like him or her or anybody who acts as this person or the other acts," there simply can't be any sound of the genuine there. I must wait and listen for the sound of the genuine in you.[4] I must wait. For if I cannot hear it, then in my scheme of things, you are not ever present. And everybody wants to feel that everybody else knows that she is there.

    I have a blind friend who just became blind after she was a grown woman. I asked her, "What is the greatest disaster that your blindness has brought you?" She said, "When I go places where there are people, I have a feeling that nobody knows that I'm here. I can't see any recognition; I can't see. . ... and if nobody knows that I'm here, it's hard for me to know where I am."

    There is something that waits and listens for the sound of the genuine in your mother, in your father, in the people you can't stand – and if you had the power you would wipe them out. But instinctively you know that if you wipe them out, you go with them. So you fight for your own life by finding some way to get along with them without killing them. There is something in you that waits and listens for the sound of the genuine in other people. And if you can't hear it, then you are reduced by that much.

    If I were to ask you what is the thing that you desire most in life this afternoon, you would say a lot of things off the top of your head, most of which you wouldn't believe. But you would think that you were saying the things that I thought you ought to think that you should say.[5] But I think that if you were stripped to whatever there is in you that is literal and irreducible and you tried to answer that question, it may be something like this:

- I want to feel that I am thoroughly and completely understood so that now and then I can take my guard down and look out around me and not feel that I will be destroyed with my defenses down.

- I want to feel completely vulnerable, completely naked, completely exposed and absolutely secure. This is what you look for in your children when you have them. This is what you look for in your husband if you get one. That I can run the risk of radical exposure and know that the eye that beholds my vulnerability will not step on me. That I can feel secure in my awareness of the active presence of my own idiom in me.

So as I live my life then, this is what I am trying to fulfill. It doesn't matter whether I become a doctor, lawyer, housewife, that I'm secure because I hear the sound of the genuine in myself, and having learned to listen to that, I can become quiet enough, still enough to hear the sound of the genuine in you. "There is something in you that waits and listens for the sound of the genuine in other people."

Now if I hear the sound of the genuine in me and if you hear the sound of the genuine in you it is possible for me to go down in [my spirit] and come up in [your spirit]. So that when I look at myself through your eyes having made that pilgrimage, I see in me what you see in me. [Then] the wall that separates and divides will disappear, and we will become one because of the sound of the genuine makes the same music.

III. Life's Assignment. Now this is your assignment and you can never say again that nobody told you.

> Go thy way
> All things say
> Thou hast thy way to go
> Thou hast thy day to live
> Thou hast thy need of thee to make in the hearts of others
> Do thy thing and be thou sure of this
> No other can do for thee that appointed thee of God
> Not any light shall fall upon thy road for other eyes
> Thee the angel calls as he calls others
> And the life to thee is precious as the greatest life can be to Him
> So live thy life and go thy way

For Whom God Calls

So that God will not have to forgive Himself for letting you be born.[6]

There is in every person that which waits, waits, waits and listens for the sound of the genuine in herself. There is that in every person that waits—waits and listens—for the sound of the genuine in other people. And when these two sounds come together, this is the music God heard when He said, "Let us make man in our image."[7]

Michael H Sands

IV. Preface

Michael H. Sands

    I surrendered to my call from God while in the military where I attended a small church in a rural community in Mississippi. I remember that with the acceptance of this new direction in my life came a sense of unfulfilled hunger for enlightenment, knowledge, and answers in my rekindled commitment to God. Besides giving me my first bible (I grew up in a conservative, traditional Black Baptist church where personal bibles were not the norm), my pastor gave me many books to read.

    One of my favorite exercises with him during my training was going to the local thrift store and sifting through the surprisingly large selection of religious books displayed on the store's back wall. Though the air back there was musty, there were many treasures to be found. During one such visit, I stumbled across a complete set of The Interpreters Bible (11 volumes) for $11.35! And yes, I still have them! More importantly, his favorite topic of conversation while on these trips was the need for formal religious education. He insisted that I attend the local Bible College to learn more about the mysteries and supernatural powers of the Holy Spirit and how I needed to become more aware of the magnitude of the task of ministry I was undertaking.

    We spent many hours talking about the responsibilities and challenges of ministry and Pastorship and the likely sacrifices necessary to be an influential minister "while serving among the people,"…which was my desire. He frequently spoke of his many encounters with God through his worldwide experiences and his interactions with many religions and belief systems, especially in Asia. What amazed me about this man was even though he was far from financially stable, I watched him faithfully and selflessly

For Whom God Calls

serve the people of this impoverished community with a joy I seldom see.

Because of his mentorship, I decided to dedicate my life to achieve the same level of commitment to serve God's people and connect with God in a way that spiritually matched my physical desire to help others who struggled in this life. Helping people who, despite less than ideal circumstances, managed to maintain their faith in a God that provides for their every need was my passion. During my tenure in this community, I learned how to love, sacrifice, and live authentically among God's people in an authentic way where my own needs and desires became secondary to the needs of the people. For the first time, I allowed myself to become a part of the people, and they became a part of me. I miss them dearly, for they taught me lessons in humility and self-love that continually anchors me.

While there, I did manage to attend a few classes at the local Bible College. Unfortunately, I retired from the military and moved "up North" to continue my professional career. I may have left with a career, but I also left with an unfulfilled desire to serve God's people and the need to learn more about myself and what a relationship with God truly means. During my brief encounter with Bible College, birthed was a hunger for a more intimate understanding and relationship with God. My quest to attain as much knowledge about Christianity and God beyond what was in the bible began.

I could have never imagined that my quest for enlightenment begun in this small community in Mississippi would culminate in earned Master of Divinity and Doctor of Ministry degrees. But like watching world-class athletes on television and marveling at how they've mastered their sport, I can fully appreciate the many sacrifices they made along the way. Few people consider the hours, days, months, and years of hard work and dedication it took for them to reach this level of performance. In other words, they didn't wake up a world-class athlete. Even though many people appreciate their sacrifices, they only see the results of their efforts.

The journey in ministry is comparable to the preparation of a world-class athlete. People observe ministers in pulpits or professors in seminary/bible college and marvel at the depth of their skills and knowledge. But seldom do they appreciate the years of study, prayer, hard-knocks, defeats, and triumphs these highly respected women and men of God experienced to reach this level of their vocation. The fact is, many in ministry that we admire have stories about their journeys that would leave us in wonderment how they endured. The cost of education, the hours of study, and the choice to put God before personal gain is genuinely admirable. The truth is, many of these individuals have gifts that could translate into fame and fortune, yet they chose the path to serve according to God's will regardless of personal gain.

    These observations created within me the need to seek out the "Why." Why would they make such sacrifices? Surely there must be more, some mystical reward for such selfless actions. The pursuit of answers has propelled me through years of study, doubt, and enlightenment that have led me to this moment. What I have discovered more than anything is the need to find oneself among the noise. I discovered that beyond the superfluous accolades and potential for financial rewards is a place where one can serve God in a way that is pleasing in God's sight and not subject to the whims of humankind.

    The reason for this book is to provide a resource of direction for those who may not have the encouragement and guidance of a mentor or someone who can help them reach "self" in a way that serves God and not some worldly stimuli that drive one to pursue ministry. I discovered that ministry is much more than preaching on a Sunday at 11 am and hearing the Amens thrown at you as you triumphantly deliver one inspiring message after another as though you were the second coming of Christ. No, I realize that those who I've encountered that had "it" were those individuals who had been through the fire of not just discovering but confronting physical and psychological barriers found in their journey towards finding their true self.

    Therefore, this book isn't about teaching one to preach. There are many other resources to help one hone that skill set. Instead, this book is about establishing the foundations of a life in ministry and starting on the path of authentic ministry to find out who you are and why God called you if God has called you, to minister to the most blessed miracle of creation, humankind. I encourage you to use this book in a way that helps you reach your

For Whom God Calls

full potential in your chosen ministry, to the glory of God. Reading these pages, you will discover the good, the bad, and the ugly about yourself, as well as challenges to your theology and your motivations for seeking ministry as a primary or secondary vocation. Whatever you do, take this journey seriously. It is God's people who will benefit from your authentic journey. But it is also God's people who will suffer if you succumb to the temptation of taking shortcuts in the pursuit of popularity in the pulpit.

Finally, engage your pastor in this journey if you haven't already done so. If you are blessed to have a pastor who you can trust to take this journey with you, you are fortunate. The reality is that many of you do not have the benefit of serving under a pastor that will unselfishly support your quest. If that is the case, use this book to begin the journey that God has chosen for you and have faith that God will place someone on your path who will help you along the way.

Michael H Sands

V. Introduction

Michael H. Sands

A cry in the darkness, a lone voice in the wilderness, a drop of water in the ocean, a grain of sand in the desert; these are the feelings of many Black Baptist ministers as they seek to fulfill what they believe to be a sincere calling upon their lives, by God, to be ministers the Gospel of Jesus the Christ. These feelings of aloneness, helplessness, and or abandonment are not unusual given that, for the most part, Black Baptist ministers seldom receive any formal religious education, and mentors are hard to find in a denomination that lacks a formal pathway to ministry or Pastorship. Worse yet, one might not receive any mentorship from their pastors, who I feel should have the fulfillment of an associate's journey through ministry as one of the pillars of their pastoral responsibilities. Unfortunately, many associate ministers find themselves on an island of discontent as alone they navigate their way, with varying degrees of success, through their journey in ministry.

I have yet to empirically substantiate the following statement made by my professor of ethics and philosophy at the Interdenominational Theological Center in Atlanta, Georgia. His purpose for making the statement on my first day of seminary, I'm sure, was to reshape our motivations for being there and to establish the relevancy of our matriculation through this school. As students, we were charged with transforming our thinking into the larger context of stopping the deteriorating quality of ministry in the Black Baptist church. For your consideration, his paraphrased statement,

> You all have a responsibility in this seminary. Less than 5% of Black preachers have any type of ministry training,

and even fewer have been or will ever go to seminary or bible college. It is your responsibility as seminarians to determine if you are here for a piece of paper or you want to make a real difference. Making a difference will require you to take what you have learned at this historic institution and share it in the church. You will face resistance; you will be scorned; you will be accused of thinking that you're better than they are because you went to seminary. Nevertheless, you must persevere and share what you have learned. The knowledge you will acquire in seminary will help you determine what and how to share in the local church and what you should leave in the seminary.

Admittedly, such a profound statement was difficult to digest at the time. However, this professor's profound statement affirmed my reasoning for coming to seminary to earn my Masters of Divinity degree. The professor planted the seed to pursue formal religious education in a quest to share what I will learn and experience in seminary. As with other Black Baptist ministers who may find themselves floundering in a sea of conflicting theologies, epistemologies, and distorted inter-church polity, I toss this lifebuoy of hope.

Though already ordained and having had the opportunity to be mentored by pastors who embraced formal religious education, they seemed to have done so knowing my gift and contribution to God's kingdom would be, but not yet revealed to me. I recall the conversational portion of my doctoral interview. After 30 minutes of answering what seemed to be routine questions, one of the Deans on the selection committee asked me what I hoped to accomplish in the Doctor of Ministry program. My honest reply was that I wanted to develop some type of training program for Black ministers, particularly Black Baptist ministers, who would never, for a multitude of reasons, have the opportunity or desire to attend seminary.

Therefore, the context of my doctoral research, A Firm Foundation: Ministry Preparation in the Black Baptist Church, served as an example of the Christian impetus for this book. As with my research project paper, this book must depend on sound Christian doctrine. I selected two periscopes, one primary and the other supplemental, of biblical reflection necessary to undergird this book. The primary periscope describes man's "Human Obedience" as a minister of the Gospel. In 1 Timothy 4:6-16 (NRSV), the scripture reads,

> [6]If you put these instructions before the brothers and sisters, you will be a good servant of Christ Jesus, nourished on the words of the faith and of the sound teaching that you have followed. [7] Have nothing to do with profane myths and old wives' tales. Train yourself in godliness, [8] for, while physical training is of some value, godliness is valuable in every way, holding promise for both the present life and the life to come. [9] The saying is sure and worthy of full acceptance. [10] For to this end we toil and struggle, because we have our hope set on the living God, who is the Savior of all people, especially of those who believe. [11] These are the things you must insist on and teach. [12] Let no one despise your youth, but set the believers an example in speech and conduct, in love, in faith, in purity. [13] Until I arrive, give attention to the public reading of scripture, to exhorting, to teaching. [14] Do not neglect the gift that is in you, which was given to you through prophecy with the laying on of hands by the council of elders. [15] Put these things into practice, devote yourself to them, so that all may see your progress. [16] Pay close attention to yourself and your teaching; continue in these things, for in doing this you will save both yourself and your hearers.

Through the periscope of 1 Timothy 4: 6-16, Paul is encouraging Timothy that adherence to what he is advising him to do will arm him with what he needs to combat this heresy. By first saying to Timothy that placing these teachings before the people will make him a good servant of Jesus Christ because he has been trained daily by the words of faith and good teaching as the first step to success in his ministry and challenges confronting him. (4:6) Paul is careful to warn Timothy that the people have been exposed to "profane and silly myths" and not fall prey to such arguments. Timothy must train himself with the stamina of an athlete, not just for physical strengthening, which does not last, but to train vigorously in godliness, for this is what will endure in this battle. (4:7-9)

Paul reminds Timothy that his sayings are trustworthy because they place their hope in the living God. (4:10) Likewise, Paul affirms his prior instructions as if to forcefully say to Timothy, "Command and teach these things" to the people so they too will not fall prey to the opponent's heresy. (4:11) Paul also recognizes that in doing so, people might dismiss Timothy's teachings because of his youth. Paul is gracious in admonishing Timothy not to let the people (opponents) use that as an excuse to ignore his teachings, and he should lead by example in his conduct, love, faith, and purity. (4:12) Paul in this periscope continuously tells Timothy to once again devote himself to teaching, reading, and exhortation until he comes. (4:13) Not knowing when that will be is, in essence, saying to Timothy to do so permanently. Paul continues to encourage Timothy by telling him not to ignore the "gifts" within him, given that those gifts were confirmed by the "laying on of hands" by the elders. Again, this is another passage where Paul must endorse the genuineness of Timothy's calling. Finally, Paul again warns Timothy to openly practice these things so all may see his maturation through his persistence and example. Doing so will not only save himself but the people adhering to his leadership as well.

In addressing the people of his day, Paul struggled to overcome those against "The Way" who would routinely distort sound doctrine and replace it with some mixture of orthodox Judaism and Jewish traditions and the beliefs and the heathen Gentiles (1 Tim. 4:7 NRSV). In today's context of the 21st century Black Baptist church, there are those within the church who have morphed the authentic Gospel into the same distorted Gospel message that flourished in the antebellum South that prevented the enslaved from attaining spiritual freedom. Today's church faces threats from contemporary interpretations of beliefs and doctrine that fall under self-preservationism, success, and self-promotion, then the communal ideals held by the Black church since its inception.

The Black Baptist minister has historically been one of the stalwarts in the community. Their reputation, wisdom, and leadership played pivotal roles in the survival of the people. We now find ourselves deteriorating into a cadre of women and men who use the ministry to separate themselves from the people to satisfy their spiritual quest for peace, financial gain, or self-affirmation. Suppose Paul were to confront us today? I'm sure he would immediately admonish our behavior as foolish and contrary to the faithful minister's role and an aversion to the community in which we serve (1 Tim. 4:15 and 16 NRSV).

Another point that Paul addresses are threats to Timothy's ministry because of his age (1 Tim 4:12). In Timothy's context, his physical age or seniority in the church may have caused concern and made him an easy target for ridicule by naysayers. I would parallel Timothy's experience with today's ministerial maturity. Paul's lesson of telling Timothy to ignore such fodder is directly applicable to those who spend too much time worrying about prestige and titles and not paying enough attention to the content of their ministerial maturity regardless of time. Many ministers find themselves crippled by these misplaced attacks and must learn to ignore these naysayers as sources of confirmation of their authenticity as ministers.

The supplemental but equally relevant periscope revolves around the "Divine Expectation" of ministry spoken by God directly to the priests of Israel. Using Hosea 4:1-6 (NRSV), the scripture reads,

> [1]Hear the word of the Lord, O people of Israel; for the Lord has an indictment against the inhabitants of the land. There is no faithfulness or loyalty, and no knowledge of God in the land.[2] Swearing, lying, and murder, and stealing and adultery break out; bloodshed follows bloodshed.[3] Therefore the land mourns, and all who live in it languish; together with the wild animals and the birds of the air, even the fish of the sea are perishing.[4] Yet let no one contend, and let none accuse, for with you is my contention, O priest.[5] You shall stumble by day; the prophet also shall stumble with you by night, and I will destroy your mother.[6] My people are destroyed for lack of knowledge; because you have rejected knowledge, I reject you from being a priest to me. And since you have forgotten the law of your God, I also will forget your children.

For Whom God Calls

Here the emphasis switches from a message of human obedience through Paul to the Divine expectations of the Triune God. With chronic calamities ever-present in contemporary ministry, they result in nothing but a clouding of the spiritual growth of church members. The fault lies at the feet of many ministers who are so self-absorbed in their sanctification and holiness that in doing so have ignored the people to the detriment of the church. The people are failing, the church is dying, and the Christian message of salvation fails because many ministers have been unable to teach the people (Hos. 4:6). Ministers have not taught the people because they have not received a comprehensive education and therefore have nothing to teach the people beyond their limited knowledge. If ministers only consume milk, they can only provide the congregation with milk.

This book intends to wean ministers off of milk to, in turn, wean the congregational palette from milk to solid food. Such a transition can facilitate a positive move of spiritual growth in the church. This Pablum diet has resulted in ministers failing God and not living up to the divine calling they have professed. Through the readings and exercises in this book, ministers will gain a revelatory perspective on the expectations of God, so they will dedicate themselves to the pursuit of internal and external knowledge to bolster their ministry and re-charge their resolve to serve God's people.

Given this underlayment of inconsistent ministerial practices among ministers in the Black Baptist church, it comes down to the why. How did this start? Why are so many ministers ill-prepared to preach and teach the Gospel of Jesus Christ? Why has performance and showmanship superseded the substance of the sermon? Why are ministers allowed to continue this cycle of incompetence and blasphemous exercise disguised as ministering and preaching? Why are pastors allowing this in the pulpits of their churches? What is the reason for such resistance to ministerial training and preparation in the Black Baptist Church?

Addressing these and other questions is the motivation for this book. It is time that we begin to deal with this trend of ministry training shortfalls and approach this problem head-on. I will attempt to address these questions constructively and beneficially rather than produce a destructive critique of the state of the Black Baptist church.

This book is organized to guide one systematically through the process of examining yourself and your call. The three parts of the book, The Why, The What, and The How should take you to a heightened level of discovery as you learn to appreciate not only the history of the church and your predecessors but begin a symbiotic relationship with the people to whom you'll be ministering. Most importantly, you're going to learn about yourself.

Each chapter will introduce the topic, followed by a reading that I found to be particularly pertinent to understanding said subject matter. At the end of each chapter will be deliverables that readers are encouraged to complete. The reflection paper is a document that concisely describes how the reading has affected you and what influence, if any, it has in your present ministry context. It is not a direct critique of the reading or a book report. You are documenting, in writing, what the reading means to you.

Separate from the reflection paper are questions to explore specific questions brought out by the readings. Feel free to challenge what you have read, but do so not from an emotional reaction but rather from a well-thought-out response to what you have read. Even if you agree, then state why? After finishing these exercises, take the time to share your thoughts with your pastor or mentor, if applicable, about what you engaged. They may help you through this process. This work is not easy and isn't meant to be. It will require you to dig deep into your very being to extract truth in ways you may not feel comfortable.

Part One, The Why, focuses on the truths of the Black church. Chapter 1, Origins, starts our journey with a brief overview of the beginnings of the Black church and the influence of the Black pastor. Anchored by the reading from professor Love Henry Whelchel from his book, The History and Heritage of African-American Churches: A Way Out of No Way: The Black Church and Black Reconstruction The Emergence of Independent Black Churches and Preachers, this reading, as well as his entire book, serves as an excellent backdrop to forming an appreciation for the sacrifices our forefathers in ministry made and their contributions to American history that have brought us to where we are today.

For Whom God Calls

Chapter 2, Contemporary Black Preaching: What Cost the Amen will focus on a critique of Black Baptist Pastors/Preachers from a lecture by Isaac Rufus Clark from the book, Teaching Preaching A Critique of Contemporary Preaching by Katie Geneva Cannon. Though taught initially to his preaching class at the Interdenominational Theological Center more than 30 years ago, Dr. Clark presents an unabashed assessment of the state of Black preaching that is still relevant to this day. Every contemporary minister should take Dr. Clark's viewpoints under advisement if they are to be a more authentic messenger of the Gospel.

Chapter 3, The Back Congregation and the People Within, will discuss the souls whose presence makes up the Black Congregation and the psychological environment amongst the pews as seen through the eyes of the renowned black psychologist, Na'im Akbar, Ph.D. This reading taken from Akbar's book, Breaking the Chains of Psychological Slavery: Liberation From Mental Slavery, focuses on the crucial aspect of ministry preparation that helps one appreciate who ministers are preaching to and teaching, a consideration often overlooked by many ministers.

Part Two, The What, focuses attention on the many possible motivations behind accepting the call to be a minister of the Gospel of Jesus the Christ and the many attitudes towards the need for Christian education in ministry. Chapter 4, Expectations and Misconceptions of Ministry and The Call, is an essential introduction to the realities that undergird the call to being a minister as expressed through the experiences of the esteemed retired Methodist pastor and scholar Rev. Dr. Virginia Samuel Cetuk. The reading from her book, What To Expect In Seminary: Theological Education as Spiritual Formation: The Call To Ministry, is a standard read for beginning seminarians. It delves into the many underlying reasons that one chooses the vocation of ministry. Here we begin to move away from external motivations to internal stimuli that result in surrendering to the ministry call.

Chapter 5, The Need for an Edified Ministry, presents various arguments for and against education as a prerequisite for effective ministry in the contemporary Black church. The reading, "A Stutter and a Stick" The (Non-)Value of Educational Credentialing, by Richard N. Pitt. Seeking not to hide behind traditional viewpoints that have kindled the flame of contention between the two camps, you, as a potential or established minister, must decide which side of the pendulum you support. It should be evident from the mere existence of this book which side I support. However, this does not mean that I have not taken into consideration the validity of both arguments. I challenge you to appreciate the rationale behind both factions and decide how it will affect your ministerial path.

Part Three, The How: The Ministry Declaration – "The Call" Paper, marks the beginning of the personal journey to self-discovery and how to formulate, discern, and articulate the call to ministry. In this section, you will begin the process of self-reflection that is so often overlooked by those entering the ministry. I fully support the stance that the pulpit should not be the place to work out one's demons, nor should the congregation be one's therapist. It is the task of ministry to be a messenger of God's word, and given that God has no hang-ups or issues, you as a minister should avoid exposing such personal vulnerabilities to the congregation outside of an encouraging testimony that glorifies the powerful movement of God.

Therefore, beginning with Chapter 6, Reflection of the Self, the journey starts with a profound reading from the book, Recalling Our Own Stories (Spiritual Renewal for Religious Caregivers) Suzanne Allowing the True Self to Surface, by Edward P. Wimberly, Ph.D. Dr. Wimberly's gift of storytelling steeped in the tradition of Sankofa uses the narrative of Suzanne, a minister, as an example of a person whose life is full of contradictions in need of healing. You will discover through this reading that you will most likely be able to supplant portions of Suzanne's journey into your own, for we all have similar stories to tell. Such narratives, which have influenced our socialization in this world, can adversely affect our ability to minister authentically to God's people if left unresolved.

Continuing along the path of self-discovery and heightened self-awareness, Chapter 7, Let Your Life Speak: Listening for the Voice of Vocation: Now I Become Myself, by Parker J. Palmer, cuts to the heart of the matter of vocational choices. Using his experiences, Palmer helps us deal transparently with the decision to begin this vocation of ministry and the expectations and vulnerabilities associated with that decision. You must confront your decision. Failure to do so will affect how you see the call to ministry and whether that call is authentic.

Chapter 8, An Exercise in Self, is a precursor to the Call paper. You will practice the authenticity, transparency, and raw emotions you must pull from to reflect upon and reveal your call to ministry through the provided example and exercise. Writing about one's fears is a delicate matter, and it would surprise you how many people avoid dealing with their fears, especially writing them down. Once you write it down, share it with someone.

Chapter 9, The Call Paper, will be the culmination of what you have read. Since I'm accustomed to teaching ministers in a classroom setting as part of the process of preparing for ordination, this "Call Paper" is a requirement, if not their capstone, before them being "Turned Over" to the pastor for final ordination reconciliation. I critique call papers not for content so much as listening for the voice of authenticity. As you begin to write your call paper, it will be easy for you to editorialize your call to ministry rather than get to the essence of your call.

Hinting about issues rather than confronting them is very common. I also read call papers fraught with rationalizations and generalizations when dealing with the call. One unwavering rule and an expectation in the call paper is specifying the ministry in which you're called. Stating that you are called to be a minister is insufficient. Like Jonah, God calls ministers for a specific task. So generalizations are highly discouraged. The outline provided for your call paper will help keep you on topic with organizing your thoughts. Not only will the outline keep you focused, but it will also help your pastor/mentor discern what you are called to do in ministry and how they can help your reach your objectives.

Chapter 10 walks you through Building Your Library, a necessary resource for any minister. You should always be reading and studying something. Even a doctor continues to learn from outside resources. As a minister charged with the care of souls, keeping abreast of current events and the many aspects of theological reasoning should be high on your priority list.

Finally, I conclude with Chapter 11, Next Steps. Here I summarize this beginning journey into ministry with closing thoughts that I hope will inspire you to keep moving forward on this journey.

Ultimately, this book fulfills that portion of my calling to help ministers achieve their God-given call to minister to the people of God in a way that is biblically sound and free from embellishments inconsistent with the Holy Scriptures or sound theology. You will find that this book, though offering an unfettered critique of preaching, is not about preaching! Nor is this book a substitute for mentorship by your pastor. Ideally, your pastor should walk with you as your progress through this book. Many ministers focus on preaching and neglect the other 95% of the demands, expectations, and servanthood required of a minister of the Gospel. Use this book as an aide to discovering how to model "Human Obedience" and fulfill God's "Devine Expectation" in service to the church and God's people. I pray that anyone who has the courage and faith to begin their ministerial journey be set free to walk on the path of an authentic ministry.

Getting the most out of this book and its intended use requires commitment on your part. First, as I discovered in my research project, students found it highly beneficial to write a reflection paper about each reading. It is critically important to understand that this reflection paper is not a review of what you've read. Instead, it should focus on what the reading meant to you, how it affects your current thinking, and whether or not it has the potential to influence your understanding of ministry in your ministry context. I encourage you to review your reflection paper with your mentor. Doing so will allow them to challenge your ideas and feelings to get to an authentic response to what you've read. There is no good hiding behind glib answers that are politically correct to prevent upsetting traditional thought or distorted epistemological frameworks. With this book, you have the freedom to express yourself in such a way that you can "work things out here and not in the pulpit or classroom!"

Second, complete the exercises and questions by writing them out. Don't just give them a mental perusal, but put your ideas and opinions to paper. Read it back to yourself and challenge yourself to dig deeper into what you feel. Again, find someone to share your responses with that you trust so they may provide you with non-opinionated feedback.

For Whom God Calls

    Finally, share your journey through this book as well as your call paper with your pastor. Hopefully, they will help you with the practical application of what your spirit is processing to help with your ministry and guide you to fulfilling your ministry objectives.

    Now, if you're ready to "Do The Work," praise God, and read on…!

Michael H Sands

Part One – The Why
The Black Church and the People Within

For Whom God Calls

Michael H Sands

CHAPTER 1
ORIGINS

My alma mater, The Interdenominational Theological Center in Atlanta, Georgia, is undergirded by the principle of Sankofa, which states:

Sankofa recognizes the significance of weighing that the utility of our past relies upon how we carefully and cautiously position our future (the egg) in balance with our present realities. We cannot use our past to imagine our future without engaging our present context.

This powerful foundational principle understands the relevancy of looking back to our African ancestors so that we in the present might gain an appreciation of our rich philosophical and anthropological history and use that precious history to inform our present circumstances. Therefore, the influence of the Sankofa experience offering an enlightened approach to our contemporary relevancy couldn't be more apropos to the subject of the need for Black ministers of this age to familiarize themselves with the more significant moments in the history of the Black Church in America.

I contend that any minister whose calling is to minister in the context of the Black Baptist Church tradition, new or old, must have a continual connection with the people they serve. Part of this effort to understand African American people is to appreciate the oldest and most influential organized entity within the African American community, the Black Church. In essence, the Black church is the messenger of the social teachings of the black community and is thus the best conduit for a moral compass that exists. Even though many may argue, me among them, that the influence of the Black church has waned in recent years, the *institution* of the Black church remains the most effective conduit of communication to the heart of the African American community.

Many scoff at this notion and believe that the history of African American peoples and the diaspora experiences are irrelevant in today's society, and recollections of the painful history of this much-maligned population in the Americas are neither necessary nor applicable. I would argue that the opposite is true. It is more critical than ever in these times. The legitimacy of an entire race and culture of a people continue to be marginalized by a systemically oppressive society. Economic and moral standards are set not by cultural-religious norms but by those who monopolize money and power.

As a Black minister, it is an essential need for one to develop an appreciation for the contributions of the postbellum civil war Black minister and their attempts to assimilate the newly freed African American people into mainstream American society. Their forgotten contributions are one reason I feel that the contemporary Black minister has the duty and responsibility to build a bridge to the past to shape the present and future; *Sankofa*.

Likewise, congregations can also benefit from learning about social awareness and the relevancy of Black people in America. It is painful to admit that most African Americans only show any appreciation for Black culture during Black History Month. Even that re-education period has lost its appeal. Unfortunately, many churches reserve only one Sunday in the month for a brief recognition, wearing costumes (African garb) and recitations of famous African Americans. Shamefully, it took a movie, Black Panther[TM,] to rekindle the remembrance of years of struggle and protest in this nation and the advances African Americans have made since being enslaved.

The following reading by Dr. Love Henry Whelchel, who many consider the foremost authority on African American Church history living today, provides a concise yet comprehensive overview of the origins and evolution of the African American church and people during reconstruction. You will be exposed particularly to the significant contributions of Black preachers of that day and their involvement in the politics of that time and how political activism by the Back preacher is not a recent phenomenon, but rather an essential component and responsibility of the Black preacher who spoke for those who lacked a voice.

The Black Church and Black Reconstruction
The Emergence of Independent Black Churches and Preachers

Henry Love Whelchel

General William Tecumseh Sherman launched a massive Union invasion of the Confederacy early in 1864. In July and August of 1864 he engaged in one of the most noted campaigns in military history through north Georgia's Kennesaw Mountains as his troops crushed the forces of the Confederacy. This campaign was a prelude to his famous march "from Atlanta to the sea." Atlanta was a major supply and distribution center for the Confederacy. It was widely believed by Union generals that the fall of "the gateway of the South" would ensure a victorious outcome for the Civil War. On the eve of Sherman's attack on Atlanta, he telegraphed General Bullock, describing the importance of the Union's campaign against the hub of the South. He relayed that in addition to having a military success, the capture of Atlanta by the Union Army would ensure the reelection of Abraham Lincoln in the November election. Also, although mostly overlooked, *Sherman's march to the sea initiated a process in which Black churches would begin to play the role of the central organizing institutions in their respective communities during the Reconstruction period and thereafter.* Until that time Black churches in the South were almost all directly under the supervision and control of their White counterparts.[1]

While north of Atlanta, General Sherman captured the town of Marietta, and in the process Zion Baptist Church was freed from the control of that city's First Baptist Church. The relationship between the two churches began when an enslaved woman named

For Whom God Calls

Dicey was permitted to join the First Baptist Church in 1836. Other slaves soon followed her lead, including Ephraim Rucker, who aspired to preach and pastor his own people. While the Blacks were members of the White church, Rucker emerged as their spiritual leader. His influence with the Blacks aroused the suspicion of some of the White members. On a number of occasions Rucker was severely whipped for leading slaves in unauthorized prayer meetings. Like many Black men who aspired to preach, Rucker was accused of being a troublemaker.[2]

During the years when the Zion Baptist Church was an appendage to First Baptist Church, the members longed for an independent church and a pastor of their own. Each time the Blacks petitioned for autonomy and independence they were met with strong opposition. After the first two years of the Civil War, most of the able-bodied White men of the First Baptist Church had enlisted in the Confederate Army. With the White membership depleted, the congregants were soon outnumbered by the Black membership. A White woman, who only supported Blacks worshipping from the church balcony, adamantly objected to any notion of religious independence for the slaves because they would be "just getting" carried away. Why, you people can't be quiet in church."[3]

The Blacks' quest for a church of their own came to fruition when General Sherman captured Marietta in June of 1864. The general turned First Baptist Church into a hospital to care for his wounded soldiers, effectively releasing Zion Baptist Church from White control. Rucker realized the significance of the moment and began to organize his congregation. The First Baptist Church granted letters of demission to the Blacks, including 66 females and 23 males, so that they could start their own church. The historic Zion Baptist Church was officially organized on April 8, 1866.[4]

In the aftermath of Sherman's devastating destruction of businesses, homes, schools, and churches throughout Atlanta, Black churches emerged as beacons of hope and bases for community organization. During the burning of Atlanta, Sherman intentionally preserved the Big Bethel A.M. E. Church whose members originally started out in the Union Church, Atlanta's first White congregation. Blacks who had been members of the White church became the charter members of Big Bethel. They struggled for their religious freedom and worked ardently to build their own church in downtown Atlanta on Auburn Avenue. Big Bethel went on to become the cultural womb of significant institutions in the Black community of Atlanta. The first African-American public school, the Gate City Colored School was born and housed in Big Bethel. Also, Morris Brown College was conceived and delivered within the hallowed halls of Big Bethel.[5]

Fueled by the decisive defeat of the Confederates in Atlanta, Sherman moved east of the city to Stone Mountain, Georgia. There he liberated the Blacks and their Bethesda Baptist Church from control of the First Baptist Church. The Blacks honored Sherman by naming their neighborhood Shermantown.[6] From Stone Mountain it was on to the handsome hamlet of Covington. Here Sherman continued his campaign of delivering Blacks from the tyranny of slaveholders and their churches from the control of White churches. The Bethlehem Baptist Church (originally known as Bethlehem Baptist) was an appendage of First Baptist Church.[7] The Black membership in the church more often than not exceeded the White membership.[8]

When the White Methodists erected a new church in Stone Mountain, they donated their wooden building to the Blacks of the Bethlehem Baptist Church, and it was moved to the east side of Dried Indian Creek. After the pastorate of the Reverend T. Baker, the Reverend A. D. Williams, the maternal grandfather of Martin Luther King, Jr., became pastor. This began a long and storied legacy of Baptist preachers in the King family. The Bethlehem Church was also served by the Reverend Joel King, the brother of Martin Luther King, Jr.'s father, from 1935 to 1941.[9]

Owing to the large number of Black members, the church held a special Sunday afternoon service for them, conducted by the White minister. The Blacks desired to have their own preachers; they wanted to worship in their own way, and occasionally they found ways of expressing their dissatisfaction with White control of their religious services. For more than thirty years the Black members applied for licenses to preach and to form a church of their own, but the Whites steadfastly refused. During slavery, Whites were often suspicious and even paranoid when it came to the congregation of Blacks outside of their supervision.

For Whom God Calls

The arrival of General Sherman was welcomed by the Blacks, not only because it delivered them from physical bondage but also because it meant their spiritual deliverance as well. After Sherman freed their church, they held their first service in a small house near the central depot, with the Reverend Henry Fresh conducting services. Soon the crowds became so large that a log hut was built where Bethlehem Baptist now stands and it was designated years ago as the "Colored Baptist Church." A formerly enslaved man, Toney Baker, who had been ordained by the White pastor of the First Baptist Church, became the first pastor of the "Colored Baptist Church," where he served for 46 years.[10]

Sherman's encounter with the Black congregations along the way from the north Georgia mountains to the port city of Savannah left him with a favorable impression of the Blacks. Also, he was impressed with the formerly enslaved people's insatiable desire for freedom as they abandoned plantations in large numbers following the march of the Union Army. While in Covington, Georgia, Sherman greeted an elderly gray-bearded Black man and asked him if he understood the progress of the war. The elderly gentleman replied that he had been looking for an angel of the Lord ever since he was knee high. He told the general that slavery was the cause of the war and that the Union's success would free the slaves. The freedmen were eager to abandon the plantations and follow Sherman and the Union Army. Follow to what they knew not, but they saw the defeat of their former slave masters and they were ready to become a part of this new reality which would surely be more positive than the old one. Sherman discouraged the former slaves from following. His army survived by foraging off of the land, taking food and supplies wherever they could be found. He did not want to be responsible for the care of thousands of ex-slaves, as they would eat food and consume supplies needed by his men.[11]

By the time the Union troops reached the outskirts of Savannah, the news of Sherman's torching of Atlanta had already reached the city. The business and civic leaders of Savannah came together in hopes of saving their city. The city leaders greeted Sherman just outside of Savannah to offer their surrender in hopes of averting the fate that befell Atlanta. Without firing a shot, the Union gained control of Savannah on December 21, 1864. A wealthy merchant, Charles Green, offered Sherman the use of his mansion.[12]

It appears to be both providential and poetic that Savannah was the place to formally initiate the emancipation of the enslaved. Savannah was on the Atlantic Ocean, and it was one of the ports at which enslaved Africans were first brought into America. Also, the Savannah area was the region of the birthplace of the independent Black church movement and the institutional life of the Black community. The people of that region had benefited from the pioneering influences of George Liele, Andrew Bryan, and Andrew Marshall, whose sacrifices laid the foundations for Black religious institutions. Immediately after Sherman's arrival in Savannah, William Campbell, pastor of the First African Baptist Church, organized a small cadre of religious leaders and requested an appointment to meet with General Sherman in order to discuss the implementation of the Emancipation. General Sherman and Edwin Stanton, the Secretary of War, arranged to meet with 20 Black ministers and religious leaders at Sherman's mansion headquarters on January 12, 1865. Less than a week out of slavery, these twenty religious leaders provided a notable road map for the development of African-American communities going forward.[13]

Secretary of War, Stanton was sent to Savannah by Abraham Lincoln to find out from the former slaves how best to proceed. The meeting would allow Stanton to gain some insight into the caliber of character and temperament of these people who figured prominently in the postwar plans. Although all the 20 leaders had been enslaved, they were by no means ill-prepared for the opportunity that history had provided. They were all literate and they had all played leadership roles in the Black churches. On average they could boast of more than 14 years' experience in ministry, and four of them had ministered for 20 or more years. This was indeed a remarkable profile of leadership experience for a group of people who were generally denied access to education and who had been unable to openly develop the cultural practices of their African ancestors which were subject to systematic suppression. Their drive, determination, creativity, and innate ability compensated for their lack of formal education. The majority of this cadre of Black leaders received training and leadership experience from the First, Second, and Third African Baptist Churches.[14]

Among the Black religious leaders was William Bentley who was the senior pastor of Andrew's Chapel, which had a congregation of 360 members and church property worth about $20,000. He had 20 years 'experience in ministry and was widely respected in the community. Also, there was James Lynch who had been born in Baltimore, Maryland; he represented the A.M.E. Church and was assigned to evangelize the South. Before the leaders arrived at Sherman's headquarters, they had met and organized themselves in order to maximize the chances for a positive outcome. They designated the 67-year-old Reverend Garrison Frazier, a minister of 35 years, as their spokesperson. He was a native of North Carolina, where he worked until he saved enough money to purchase the freedom of his wife and himself. As free persons, he and his wife moved to Georgia where he was ordained to preach, but his poor health prevented him from pastoring a congregation.

After the twenty leaders had assembled, Stanton proceeded with a question-and-answer session. The Secretary of War asked them to state their understanding in regard to acts of Congress and President Lincoln's Emancipation Proclamation concerning the condition of colored people in the rebel states. Reverend Frazier responded thusly:

> So far as I understand President Lincoln's proclamation to the Rebellious States, it is, that if they would lay down their arms and submit to the laws of the United States before the first of January, 1863, all should be well; but if they did not, then all the slaves in the Rebel States should be free henceforth and forever. That is what I understand.[15]

When Stanton asked the group of Black religious leaders how they thought their people could best take care of themselves and how the government could assist in maintaining their freedom, the spokesperson gave the following answer:

> The way we can best take care of ourselves is to have land, and turn it and till it by our own labor that is, by the labor

of the women and children and old men; and we can maintain ourselves and have something to spare. And to assist the government, the young men should enlist in the service of the Government, and serve in such manner as they may be wanted. The Rebels told us that they piled them up and made batteries of them and sold them to Cuba; but we don't believe that.[16]

After Pharaoh's Emancipation of the Hebrews, those former slaves immediately separated themselves from their former slave masters and oppressors. However, unlike the Hebrews in Exodus, the emancipated African Americans would remain bound to the same land and in the presence of their agitated former slave masters. The Secretary of War addressed this issue by asking the group whether they would rather live scattered [integrated] among Whites or in colonies by themselves. Reverend Frazier replied:

I would prefer to live by ourselves, for there is a prejudice against us in the South that will take years to get over; but I do not know that I can answer for my brethren. [Mr. Lynch was the only dissenter from Frazier's proposal. All of the other Black religious leaders present being questioned one by one answered that they agreed with Brother Frazier. The divergent view of Lynch likely reflects his roots in Baltimore on the Mason-Dixon Line while all of the others were native to the Deep South.[17]

The charge of the inherent inferiority of the Negro was the most potent accusation leveled by those who opposed the emancipation of the slaves. Also, *the pro-slavery argument questioned whether or not the Blacks had the intelligence or the character needed for full citizenship in America.* In response to these rationales, Secretary Stanton wanted to know whether the Blacks had the cognitive ability to understand the cause of the Civil War and its outcome and their new responsibilities as citizens. He asked whether Blacks had sufficient intelligence and feelings of loyalty to the United States and the ability to understand their responsibility to support and respect the side of the federal government. Reverend Frazier gave a terse affirmation to the intellectual capacity of Blacks. He then gave an insightful response that both demonstrated that capacity and further revealed that the Blacks had a keen awareness of their conditions and those forces operating for and against their interests:

> I think you will find there are thousands that are willing to make any sacrifice to assist the Government of the United States while there are also many that are willing to take up arms. I do not suppose there are a dozen men that are opposed to the Government. I understand as the war, that the South is the aggressor.

President Lincoln was elected President by a majority of the United States, which guaranteed him the right of holding the office and exercising that right over the whole United States. The South without knowing what he would do rebelled. The war was commenced by the Rebels before he came into office. *The object of the war was not at first to give the slaves their freedom, but the sole object of the war was first to bring the rebellious states back into the Union and their loyalty to the laws of the United States.* Afterward, knowing the value set on the slaves by the Rebels, the President thought that his proclamation would stimulate them to lay down their arms, reduce them to obedience and help to bring back the Rebel States; and they're not doing so has now made the freedom of the slaves a part of the war. It is my opinion that there is not a man in the city that could be started to help the Rebels one inch for that would be suicide. There were two Black men who left with the Rebels because they had taken an active part for the Rebels, and thought something might befall them if they stayed behind; but there is not another man. If the prayers that have gone up for the Union Army could be read out, you would not get through them for two weeks.[18]

The Secretary asked the Black leaders a battery of other questions focusing on the sentiment and feeling of Blacks in general about the Union, the willingness of young Black men to enlist in the Union Army, and the most effective way for them to recruit Black soldiers. These religious leaders responded to Stanton's questions in such a way as to unequivocally assure the Secretary that the Blacks were prepared to move forward. *The leaders further assured Stanton that the nature of their ministries in serving the people put them in position of knowing the pulse of the community.* The leaders reminded Stanton and Sherman of the thousands of slaves who abandoned the plantations to follow the Union Army as indicative of their understanding of the war and its consequences. The Black religious leaders offered to take the initiative in recruiting young Black men for the Union Army. Reverend Frazier recommended that the U.S. Congress suspend compulsory recruitment of Black soldiers and empower the Black religious leaders with the responsibility of enlisting young Black men.

    This meeting was historic for a number of reasons, the most important of which is that it represented the egression of leadership of the Black church and Black preachers. Such leadership had already begun to emerge, as *it was Black churches and Black preachers who first organized and stood up for the interests of African Americans.* Four days after the historic meeting, General Sherman issued Special Field Orders, No. 15, which set aside a large region of coastal land, stretching from Charleston, S.C., to northern Florida, "for the settlement of Negroes now made free by the acts of war and the proclamation of the President of the United States." Each family would be allotted "forty acres of tillable ground ... in the possession of which land the military authorities will afford them protection, until such time as they can protect themselves, or until the Congress shall regulate their title."[19]

    Thus, *the Black church and the Black preachers began a long and historic legacy of working with government officials and sometimes against them on behalf of the Black community. Long before Black politicians, political scientists, and pundits, Black preachers were policy makers, organizers and advisors.* Sherman and Stanton were surprised at the sophistication and intelligence exhibited by these religious leaders, who were only a few days removed from slavery. Certainly, their presentation disabused Sherman and Stanton of any notions that Blacks were inherently inferior or incapable of citizenship. *In Stanton's evaluation of the meeting, he reported that the response was so profound that he could not have received a better response if he had been speaking with the President's cabinet.*

For Whom God Calls

These Black religious leaders vindicated the character and intelligence of the freedmen. Their responses to Stanton's questions were proof enough that African Americans had the capacity, if given the chance, to become productive and responsible citizens. The leaders also encouraged Sherman to provide the Black community with some reassurance and a clear explanation of the emancipation by addressing the Black community on the steps of the Second African Baptist Church.

Special Field Order 15 set aside the cities of Beaufort, Hilton Head, Savannah, Fernandina, St. Augustine, and Jacksonville, along with surrounding areas, as land that was to be exclusively for the settlement of Blacks. The order provided for each Black family to be allotted land and protection. The importance of this event, although mostly overlooked by current historians, cannot be overstated. *The Black leaders and the White governmental officials of that time clearly intended for Blacks to develop themselves economically and socially, and they further understood that material resources were required for such an undertaking.*[20]

General Rufus Saxton was in charge of supervising the resettlement of Negroes on the land and by the end of June 1865 more than 40,000 freedmen had moved onto their new farms. There was great enthusiasm among the Blacks as they looked forward to freedom and an improved quality of life. *But, this movement toward independence and social uplift for Blacks would be aborted before it could be firmly established. Abraham Lincoln was assassinated and his successor, Andrew Johnson, in August of 1865 issued orders of pardon and restoration for the slaveholders and property owners of those lands. Thus, the freedmen were turned off of the land, some at the point of a bayonet. Although Congress passed legislation granting the evicted Blacks an option to purchase other government-owned land in the South, most of these recently freed slaves were instead compelled by pressing economic circumstances to go back to work for their former slave masters.* The Reconstruction period would come to a tragic conclusion after beginning with great hopes for real democracy in America.[21] *The failure of the government to fully implement Special Field Orders, No.15 and to provide Black people with the means to develop their own communities left the United States with a legacy of racial injustice that it has yet to fully resolve.* Returning the ex-slaves to conditions near what they had experienced in servitude and under the oppressive regime of the very same people who had just been defeated in war was yet another monstrous injustice done to Black people. *The reversal of Special Field Orders, No.15 was the first in a long string of broken promises made to Blacks. The Emancipation Proclamation freed the slaves but ignored the Blacks.*

The period following emancipation from 1865 to 1877 is called Reconstruction. Reconstruction originally referred to a political process by which the defeated southern states, which had rebelled and seceded from the Union would be reinstated as part of the United States of America. But, beyond the political process, there were important social and religious implications to the Reconstruction period. The Southerners had been thoroughly routed, and any hopes for a Confederacy were completely smashed. *Yet the racist attitudes and prejudice of most White Southerners were unabated. They continued to treat Blacks with wanton disrespect as they viewed them as subordinate, regardless of age or educational status, and they considered Blacks in general as resources available for exploitation.*

THE SOUTH AS A FIELD OF MISSION

During Reconstruction, various political, commercial, and religious institutions sought to influence, manipulate, and exploit the conditions in the South. Politically, at least on paper, *Black men in the South had acquired the right to vote. But such rights would later be curtailed with poll taxes, literacy tests, and intimidation.* Thus, White men were able to perpetuate their control and domination of the political process and economic resources in the South. Some Whites pretended to befriend Blacks in hopes of garnering their votes and manipulating the political process. These people became known as scalawags. As Blacks learned of the treachery and duplicity of the scalawags, they turned to White northerners. Some of these White northerners had descended upon the South in order to take advantage of the disorder in the aftermath of the Civil War for economic gain, and they were known as carpetbaggers. The Blacks also gained the attention of White churches based both in the North and the South as the churches competed for Black converts.[22]

All the mainline denominations in the United States divided over the contentious issue of slavery in the years prior to the Civil War. After the schisms over slavery, the religious conversion and training of slaves was left to the southern branch of the various denominations, as northern missionaries and abolitionists were generally not welcome in the South. But during the Reconstruction era, northerners interpreted the outcome of the Civil War as a divine dispensation opening the gates of the South to northern evangelists, preachers, and teachers in order to educate, convert, and save the downtrodden former slaves.

The southern Methodists, Baptists, and Presbyterians were the most committed and most successful in evangelizing among the slaves. Prior to the war, the denomination with the largest slave membership was the Methodist Episcopal Church, South, which had separated from the northern Methodists over the issue of slavery in 1844. After the Civil War and the defeat of the South, the northern Methodists sent missionaries to the South to convert and reclaim both Whites and Blacks. All the Methodists, including the Methodist Episcopal Church, the African Methodist Episcopal Church, and the African Methodist Episcopal Zion Church viewed the South as a mission field where they had an opportunity to add to their existing membership rolls.[24]

Blacks took full advantage of the occasion of freedom as they sought to build and maintain their own religious and educational institutions. *After the Civil War, there was a massive withdrawal from White churches and White denominations. Throughout the South, during Reconstruction, Blacks pooled their resources to purchase land and to erect churches. The mass defection of Blacks from White churches redrew the religious map.* On the eve of the Civil War, 42,000 Blacks worshipped in South Carolina's White Methodist churches. By 1870, only 600 remained. In Cleveland County, North Carolina, there were 200 Blacks reported as members of White churches in 1860, but only 10 in 1867 and not a single one five years later. Overall, two-thirds of the Black members of the Methodist churches in the South exercised their newfound freedom by leaving the White denomination. The mass defections did not cease until the Black members of Methodist Episcopal Church, South, were assured of the transfer of property to an independent Colored Methodist Episcopal (C.M.E.) Church.[25]

Both northern White and Black missionaries from the various denominations made efforts to convert the freedmen. However, in some ways they proved no more successful than the White Southerners in making converts. Social, cultural, and regional differences proved to be a barrier for many of the northerners. *There was also a general condescension toward the unlettered southern Blacks. Many northern missionaries denounced the tradition of slave preaching and worship, which emphasized shouting, dancing and demonstrative expression. They advocated a religion of the head rather than the heart, and they intended to suppress religious dancing, shouting, foot stomping and hand clapping. Most northerners came with cultural biases, and only a few listened long enough to appreciate the grammatically imprecise yet profound words of wisdom from southern Blacks and the remarkable effectiveness of the story-telling sermonizing of Black preachers.*[26]

The Black denomination that wielded the most influence both before and after the war was the A.M.E. Church. *The size of the overall membership in the A.M.E. Church was less than that of the Baptists, but the episcopal structure of the A.M.E. denomination facilitated better organization, more effective use of resources, and the capacity to speak with a unified voice on various issues.* The A.M.E. Church helped to initiate the independent Black church movement, and it grew rapidly over the years. During the final days of the Civil War, the Reverend James Lynch "crossed the Rubicon" as he referred to the Potomac River in 1861, and followed Black troops and civilians preaching everywhere he went. The day after Sherman took Savannah, Lynch converted the Andrews Methodist Chapel over to the African Methodist Episcopal Church as the White minister had fled the city. This began the competition for converts that would continue throughout the Reconstruction period.[27]

Southern Blacks overwhelmingly preferred to worship among other Blacks and under the ministerial leadership supplied by those of their own race. The African Methodist Episcopal Church and the Black Baptist churches gained the advantage over the White denominations in winning Black converts. The A.M.E. Church had originated in the North more than 50 years prior to Reconstruction. The A.M.E.s were also better organized and more successful than the A.M.E. Zion Church. About a third of Black Methodists retained a relationship with the White Methodists until they organized their own independent denomination. It was originally known as the Colored Methodist Episcopal Church and became the Christian Methodist Episcopal Church in 1954.[28]

Besides gaining control of their churches and establishing historically Black colleges and universities, Blacks were often able to reconstitute their families. They established the tradition of family reunions as they literally reunified their families by seeking out and finding those family members who had been sold off into slavery. Also, it was during this time that Black state legislators in North Carolina established the first free and open to all public schools.[29]

Black Preachers as Political Leaders During Reconstruction

The Black church was the first social institution owned and administered by African Americans. In many *ways the Black church has been the cultural womb of the Black community, giving birth to schools, hospitals, and banks and providing a forum for social and political issues. The churches also served as ecclesiastical courthouses adjudicating family disputes, promoting moral values, and monitoring the community for illicit behavior.*[30]

Given the central role of the Black church in Black communities, it was inevitable that Black preachers would play a prominent role in the political arena during Reconstruction. Charles H. Pearce, who was an office holder during Reconstruction in Florida as well as an A.M.E. minister, commented that it was "impossible" to separate religion from politics. *Black ministers quickly grasped that the interests of the ministry and politics coincided when it came to the well-being of their communities. The Black ministers were often the best-prepared and most-respected members of their communities, and they often played the roles of mayor, state representative, senator, and even governor during the "mystic years" of the Reconstruction period. In all, more than one hundred Black preachers served as elected officials during Reconstruction.*[31]

Henry McNeal Turner was born in South Carolina on May 1, 1834. He went on to become one of the most influential ministers of the period and one of the most courageous to embrace political involvement. Unlike most of the Black ministers of his generation in the South, he was never a slave. His mother was an African princess, and according to custom, the British refrained from enslaving African royalty. *The British policy of not enslaving African royalty was not so much due to respect for the Africans. It was yet another scheme to corrupt and disarm the leaders by giving them a false sense of entitlement and privilege, making them less likely to oppose the wholesale exploitation of the masses of people they were supposed to be leading.* Nevertheless, while growing up in Abbeville, South Carolina, Turner worked in a cotton field. After his father's death, to help support his family, he became an apprentice to a blacksmith. He was also employed for a time as an errand boy for a lawyer. While employed by the lawyer, Turner learned to read and write. He was licensed to preach in the Methodist Episcopal Church, South, in 1853 in Georgia. One of his most notable converts was Lucius H. Holsey, an early bishop of the C.M.E. Church and one of the founders of Paine College. In 1858 Turner joined the A.M.E. Church. He was appointed to the Baltimore-Washington area, and outside of the restrictive environs of the Deep South, he seized the opportunity to study Latin, Greek, and Hebrew at Trinity College in Baltimore. In 1862 at the height of the Civil War, he was assigned to the Israel A.M.E. Church in Washington, D.C. He immediately involved himself in the politics of the war. He publicly called for President Lincoln to free the slaves, and he predicted that the Union would lose the war without Black soldiers. As a consequence of his outspoken stance, his church was threatened with being burned to the ground. Nevertheless, he remained steadfast in his position and his determination and tenacity soon bore fruit. The war indeed turned badly for the North, and Lincoln and his advisors soon realized that the inclusion of Black troops would give a much needed boost to their war effort. Turner organized a regiment of Black soldiers and Lincoln commissioned him to be their chaplain with a rank of major. After the Civil War, President Andrew Johnson renewed

For Whom God Calls

Turner's appointment in the Regular Army, and he assigned the nation's first African-American chaplain to work with the Freedmen's Bureau in Macon, Georgia.[32]

Georgia was familiar ground for Turner and he got off to a quick start in his new assignment. Turner preached a message of liberation and resistance to oppressed Blacks, and this greatly disturbed many Whites. He was threatened and driven out of Macon in 1865, but he returned in 1866 with the same zeal and passion for freedom and the uplift of his people. He chided the freedmen for their attachment to a subservient status as he promoted racial pride and unity. He even called on Blacks to worship God in their own image, as to do otherwise, he relayed, would be unworthy of real men:

> *We have as much right biblically and otherwise to believe that God is a Negro, as you buckra or white people have to believe that God is a fine looking, symmetrical and ornamented white man. For the bulk of you and all the fool Negroes of the country believe that God is a white-skinned, blue-eyed, straight-haired projected nose, compressed lipped, finely robed white gentleman sitting upon a throne somewhere in heaven. Every race of people since time began who have attempted to describe their God by words or by painting or carving or by any form or figure have conveyed the idea that the God who made them and shaped their destinies was symbolized in themselves, and why should not the Negro believe that he resembles God as much as other people? This is one of the reasons we favor African emigration, or Negro naturalization, wherever we can find a domain, for, as long as we remain among the whites the Negro will believe that the devil is Black and that he (the Negro) favors the devil, and that God is white and that he (the Negro) bears no resemblance to him, and the effect of such sentiment is contemptuous and degrading and one half of the Negro will be trying to get white and the other half will spend their days in trying to be white men's scullions in order to please the whites.*[33]

Turner was an outspoken cultural critic who admonished both Blacks and Whites to improve their social conditions. Once while speaking to an integrated audience in Greensboro, Georgia, he urged Black men to keep their women away from White men. Some of the White men in the audience drew their guns, but because the Black men were also armed, the Whites backed down without a fight. Turner did not believe that Blacks should remain defenseless in the face of brutal oppression. After he became a bishop in the A.M.E. Church, he continued his staunch advocacy of community development and self-defense for Blacks. At one church meeting he laid two revolvers atop his Bible and declared, "My life depends on the word of God and these guns."[34]

Turner was one of the most prominent African Americans of his era. His keen intellect and incisive oratory helped to inspire the Black community during a period of great transition and upheaval. He was also the consummate preacher/politician. He was elected to the Georgia Constitutional Convention, which convened in 1867 and 1868. The Black representatives were major contributors to writing the new state constitution, and it was Black votes that enacted it, as 80 percent of Blacks voted for the new constitution but only 12 percent of the Whites did so. He was then elected to the Georgia House of Representatives, where he introduced bills to establish eight-hour work days and prohibiting Jim Crow seating on public carriers. Also, he supported universal public education. Surprisingly, while in the legislature he pushed for the pardon of Jefferson Davis, the former President of the Confederacy. The Black legislators did much to strike political compromises with their White counterparts, but their hopes for an era of racial reconciliation would not be realized. Before long, the White legislators turned on the Blacks and had them expelled from the Georgia House of Representatives. This incensed Turner and his views turned to more radical approaches to resolving racial conflicts for Blacks.

In the 1870s, many White and Black churches were swept up by a zeal and enthusiasm to send missionaries to Africa. John Wesley Gilbert (1865-1923) was an African-American missionary who graduated from Paine College and later from Brown University as a classical scholar. He pioneered in archeological work in Greece, and he became Paine College's first Black faculty member. In 1911, Gilbert traveled as a C.M.E. missionary to the Belgian Congo (now the Democratic Republic of the Congo) in Central Africa. Also, Henry McNeal Turner embraced missionary efforts to Africa and even supported efforts toward the resettlement of Blacks to Africa. William H. Heard, an A.M.E. minister born in Elbert County in 1850, raised funds for the back-to-Africa initiative before he was elected bishop.[35]

Richard Harvey Cain (1825-1887) continued the precedent set by the 20 religious leaders in 1865 as he engaged in Reconstruction politics. Cain was a native of Ohio, and he was nurtured in the Methodist Episcopal Church. He became disenchanted with that church and later joined the A. M. E. Church, attending its denominational school at Wilberforce University. In 1862, he was transferred to the New York Conference, where he was ordained deacon by Bishop Daniel Payne. Cain was sent by his denomination to South Carolina at the close of the Civil War to seek new converts among the freedmen. He was appointed to "revitalize" and reorganize Emmanuel Church, which had been closed by Whites since 1822, after the Denmark Vesey slave revolt. At the time it was closed, the church had 3,000 members, but their pastor, Morris Brown, was run out of town by a White mob that accused him of being an accomplice to Vesey.[36]

In keeping with expectations of Black ministers during Reconstruction, Cain was drawn into the vortex of politics. In June of 1865, Blacks from South Carolina were represented at the National Union convention in Baltimore. After this convention refused to address issues of importance to the Black community, the Blacks met at the Zion Church in Charleston and denounced the mistreatment they received at the National Union Convention. The church gave Cain immediate visibility, and he was chosen to give an important speech at the Colored People's Convention held at the Zion Church. Cain's brilliant presentation at the convention earned him leadership recognition beyond the walls of the church. In 1866, he was elected as the editor of the South Carolina Leader, the first Black newspaper in that state. He served in a similar capacity for the Missionary Recorder.[37]

Similar to many Black ministers across the South, Cain's connection with the church provided a political base for launching a career in politics. In 1868, Cain was the leading delegate to the Constitutional Convention for the State of South Carolina, at which he initiated a drive to institute universal male suffrage for the first time in that state. Also, recognizing that freedom without land and resources was a delusion, he championed the campaign to obtain land for the freed men. He reminded the convention of the popular slogan "forty acres and a mule" for every Black man, symbolizing the passionate desire to own the very land they and their forbears had worked so hard on for the benefit of others.[38]

Both Turner and Cain effectively used their churches to expand their ministries so that they could not only address the needs of their congregations but could also address needs of the community at large. Cain's political influence and success eventually extended to the state and national levels. He was elected to represent Charleston in the state Senate, and in 1872 he was elected to the U.S. House of Representatives. He did not stand for reelection in 1874, but he was reelected in 1876. At this session of Congress, he introduced bills calling for money from the sale of land to be set aside for education. He also supported women's suffrage and advocated for trade and a steamship line between the United States and Liberia.

At the end of Reconstruction, when Blacks were expelled from political offices, Cain left South Carolina. He was elected as the fourteenth bishop of the A.M.E. Church and assigned to their districts in Louisiana and Texas. He was one of the founders of Paul Quinn College in Waco, Texas, and took a leave from his episcopal duties to serve as that college's second president. In 1880, he returned to his Episcopal duties and presided over conferences in New York, New Jersey, New England, and Philadelphia. When we consider the achievements of Cain and Turner, we observe two of the brightest lights among the many Black preachers who helped to lead their communities out of slavery.[39]

Ending slavery was the highest priority for northern Blacks. They were deeply concerned about the plight of their brothers and sisters in the South, not least of all because almost all of them had relatives south of the Mason-Dixon Line. Jonathan C. Gibbs (1827? -1874), a clergyman born in Philadelphia, was one of the strongest advocates for Blacks in the South. He turned from

Methodism to Presbyterianism while attending Dartmouth College. After only two years of studying at Princeton, he was called to a Black Presbyterian congregation in Troy, New York, where Nathan Ford, the president of Dartmouth, preached his installation sermon. In the 1850s, Gibbs moved to Philadelphia, where he became active in the Negro Convention Movement, which provided a national platform for Black leadership to advocate for their communities, protest slavery and eventually support the Union Army.[40]

The missionary fever that had swept the leadership of the northern White Methodists and the A.M.E.s after the war, also affected Presbyterians. Gibbs was sent south to open schools and win converts for the Presbyterian Church. He began his work in South Carolina. He was introduced to politics by attending the Colored People's Convention which convened in Charleston in 1865. He moved back and forth between North Carolina and South Carolina working with the Freedmen's Bureau before settling in Florida in 1868. Ln Florida, Gibbs was elected to the 1868 Constitutional Convention, and he served as Secretary of State from 1868 to 1873 and as the Superintendent of Public Instruction from 1873 to 1874.[41]

Gibbs's achievements in the area of education caused the scholar W. E. B. DuBois to give him his highest marks. DuBois credited him for establishing the Florida Public School System. Gibbs authored and helped to pass the bill that made educational opportunities available for the first time to all classes of people in the state of Florida. His keen intellect and stately demeanor made him one of the most respected leaders in the state of Florida during Reconstruction. In 1874, Gibbs was attracting a great deal of public support in a bid to represent Florida in the United States Congress when he mysteriously died. It was believed by many Blacks that he had been poisoned, as many Whites resented the level of authority and respect that he had achieved.[42]

The church, education, and politics were closely related throughout the Reconstruction period for Blacks. Achievements in the fields of education and politics would not have been possible without the leadership of Black ministers. And many Black ministers were keen on developing the capacity of their communities through education and politics. Francis Louis

Cardozo (1837-1903) was a successful minister, educator, and politician during the Reconstruction Era. He was born to free parents on February 1, 1837, in South Carolina. He studied at the University of Glasgow in Scotland and later entered the ministry. He served as the Secretary of State for the state of South Carolina in 1870 and planned a statewide public school system. Also, he served as the principal of Avery Normal Institute and eventually as professor of Latin at Howard University.[43]

Black preachers across the country led the first great mass movement for free and open-to-all public education, north and south. *The genesis of the modern concept of public education originated with Black ministers, who saw education as the chief means of uplift and development for their people. Beyond public schools many Black ministers were also interested in building private church-related educational institutions. The impetus toward educational development for Blacks came out of the Black church, which served as the platform, funding source, and support mechanism for many Black colleges and universities.* The uniqueness of the African-American community in Atlanta, Georgia, is largely due to the presence of the Atlanta University Center, a group of religiously affiliated schools that were begun by Blacks after the Civil War.[44]

The northern-based American Missionary Association (A.M.A.) sent White missionaries to introduce New England educational ideals into the southern Black schools and churches. The A.M.A was one of the first organizations to respond when Sherman called for relief supplies to assist the Freedmen following his capture of Savannah. The goal of the A.M.A. was to come south and build Congregational churches and a school by every church to thus provide Blacks with a classical New England brand of education. Their strong denominational stand, however, insisting on a cold, unresponsive, and unemotional worship service, did not appeal to many Blacks. The First Congregational and the Friendship Baptist Churches were competing to win the souls of Atlanta's Black elite. The First Congregational Church of Atlanta was organized in 1867. It was the most integrated church in Georgia. By 1891, the congregation consisted of 351 members, mostly teachers and students from Atlanta University and the city's growing Black elite. About the same time of the founding of the

Congregational Church in Atlanta, the A.M.A. planted the First Congregational Church of Savannah.[45]

The Determination and Drive to Establish Independent Black Churches

The importance of the independent Black church movement with its genesis in Silver Bluff can hardly be overstated. The Silver Bluff Church initiated the independent Black church movement, which then contributed greatly to helping African Americans establish some sense of identity, raise their collective self-esteem and develop the organizational mechanisms necessary to survive the often harsh realities of being Black in America. The churches saved African Americans from the demoralizing prospects of having to completely rely on Whites for resources, financing, organizational structure, discipline, and leadership. In short, *the independent Black church movement emerged as a result of the struggle to hold on to a sense of dignity and self-worth in the face of enslavement, degradation, and humiliation. The churches thus became the first (and continue to be the most important) institutions owned and controlled by Black people. The Black church has long been the pivotal training ground for developing political leadership, musical talent, rhetorical skills, and business acumen in the African-American community.*[46]

The independent Black church movement, which manifested itself on the Bryan Plantation, had previously come forth as the Invisible Institution, hidden in the bush harbors and thickets beyond the prying eyes and ears of the slaveholders. But the origins of the Invisible Institution lay beyond the shores of America. The Black church and the Black Preacher became the transformed vehicles of the various traditional African spiritual systems that helped African Americans survive the horror of the Middle Passage, the process of natal separation, slavery, and the spiritual and cultural holocaust inflicted on them. Consequently, *the Black preacher has the longest and most storied tenure of leadership in the African-American community. No other profession can claim the level of influence or a heritage that stretches back to the very beginning of the African-American experience.*[47]

The Black church became the cultural womb of the African-American community and the center of all institutional activities for Black people until the end of segregation. Near the end of the nineteenth century, W.E.B. DuBois recognized the Black church "as the only social institution of Negroes which started in the African forest and survived slavery under the leadership of the priests and after emancipation became the center of Negroes' social life."[48]

After slavery, southern White churches sought to maintain control over the religious affairs of their former slaves and to prevent the influence of the northerners, thus ensuring their political and economic domination in the South. However, they would soon discover that direct control of Black religious expression would not be possible. *The Freedmen's determination and drive to build their own independent churches illustrate two key points about African Americans of that era: (1) contrary to the view of some historians, Black people were not enamored of their former slave masters and they sought to establish their independence from them as soon as it became clear that there was an opening to do so and (2) overwhelmingly, the formerly enslaved Africans had more confidence and faith in their own ministers, religious expressions and their traditional view of the divinity than they did in White churches.* The Freedmen were frequently adamant and insistent about having their own ministers and churches. The Protestant Episcopal Church of Alabama gave up trying to evangelize Blacks because "the ex-slaves would take neither their politics nor their religion from their former owners."[49] Also, the development a growth of independent Black churches was a potent testimony against the argument that African Americans were inherently inferior and incapable of governing themselves. The proliferation of Black independent churches showed a willingness of the freedmen to make sacrifices to achieve collective goals. With limited resources, African Americans pooled their finances and improvised until they could construct a House of the Lord. The humble beginnings of many Black churches were in such places as the basement of White churches, boxcars, tobacco warehouses, carpenter and blacksmiths' shops, and individual homes. For example, in Richmond, Virginia, the Rising Mount

For Whom God Calls

Zion Baptist Church began with a prayer meeting held in a woman's home.[50]

The spontaneity and resourcefulness of the freedmen was matched only by their determination to establish independent churches. In Thomasville, Georgia, in 1865, the Black members of the Methodist Church decided to withdraw from the White church, and they petitioned the White church in order to purchase the praise house in which they had been worshipping with them. The White church offered to sell the property at an exorbitant price which the Black members rejected, and the Blacks further insisted that as they were two-thirds of the church membership they were therefore entitled to two-thirds of the church building.[51]

Most of the Black preachers who inspired the independent Black church movement were unlettered with no formal educational background. They derived their confidence and leadership ability from the "power and irresistible call to preach" and desire to minister to the people. The first A.M.E. Church conference in Savannah was in 1866, when Blacks were only one year removed from slavery and almost none of them knew how to read or write. They had to get young White boys and poor White men to act as secretaries for their Quarterly Conference. They struggled to achieve literacy and to build great churches and to organize their communities around their churches. And their efforts quickly paid off as they found ways to expand and develop their churches and communities.[52]

Finally, *Black preachers sometimes paid the price in blood for their efforts to organize and uplift their people. Many politically active Black preachers were persecuted and a few were killed for their efforts. Politically active Black preachers did not confine their ministries to the four walls of the churches and the members of their own congregations. The entire community was their parish. They were in a real sense the whole community's preacher or "community preachers." Black communities looked to Black preachers for leadership.* The local Black churches were meeting places for political rallies, social justice campaigns, and economic development initiatives. Racial justice was often high on the agendas of these churches during and immediately following Reconstruction. Of course such courageous efforts were bound to lead to confrontation with racist Whites.

Michael H Sands

A formerly enslaved Black man from Gainesville, Alabama, Richard Burke, was called to preach in 1870. He expanded his ministry and served in the State Legislature as a Representative of Sumter County. He was noted for his peaceful and conciliatory demeanor. Yet he was shot to death by a White mob when they attempted to break up a political rally he was attending. As the vicious mob approached, Burke stood up and denounced them. He addressed them as, "cowardly sons-of-bitches; you go back" and he exhorted the Black men to load their guns and fight to the last man.[53]

The Black church was also the place where the Emancipation Proclamation was commemorated, a tradition that has continued in some churches until the present era. At one of the first such services, the Reverend William Thornton of Hampton Virginia was speaking in his hometown on January 1, 1866, when he was murdered by a White man. The perpetrator declared, "We hope the time will come that these Yankees will be away from here, and then we will settle with you preachers."[54]

Community involvement and social development have characterized the evolution of Black preachers and their ministries from the time of the historic meeting of the 20 Black religious leaders with Stanton and Sherman. In the Old Testament, prophets are often identified with the reigning monarch at the time of their prophesying. Isaiah is associated with King Uzziah and King Hezekiah, Moses with Pharaoh, and Amos with Jeroboam II. The careers of the kings and the prophets paralleled each other. The relationships between the kings and the prophets defined their respective legacies. During Reconstruction, the Black church and many Black preachers arose to recapture the Old Testament model and, as with the ancient prophets, they felt called to speak truth to power on behalf of God's people.

DELIVERABLES

REFLECTION PAPER & Questions

1. Given the "examination questions" from Secretary Stanton the black leaders had to respond to, do you feel that in our present day,

For Whom God Calls

African Americans still have to answer such questions. If yes, and you are a representative of the African American people which as a black preacher you are, what would your responses be to such questions if presented to you in your present location?

2. Are you an advocate of assimilation or separation for the African American community, and why?

3. What similarities, if any, do you see in the practices of reconstruction designed to stifle the rights of Black people yesterday, today? Things such poll taxes, literacy tests, and intimidation.

4. In the reading Dr. Whelchel mentions the condescending attitude toward southern blacks by northern missionaries, black and white. Does this schism still exist today? If so, how and why?

5. Henry Turner critiques the notion of an Anglo-Jesus and negro assimilation. What is your view of this critique in your contemporary context?

Michael H Sands

Chapter 2
The Black Preacher and Contemporary Preaching: What Cost the Amen?

    As I sat in disbelief, listening to what up to this time had been the worst sermon I've ever heard, the seed was planted in me to create some type of ministry to provide comprehensive training for associate ministers in the Black Baptist church setting. Listening to this biblical heresy, a shock went through my body as I, for the first time, got up during the sermon and left the church. The sermon for me is the highlight of the worship experience, and witnessing a so-called minister of the Gospel fumble their way through a diatribe of meaningless banter that had nothing to do with salvation was to me meant more for entertainment than enlightenment was painful as well as sad.

    The setting was a rather large suburban Black Baptist church whose pastor was out of town and had left the pulpit in the hands of a new associate minister. He began the sermon experience without issue, given that he started with prayer. But everything went downhill from there. Failing to cite scripture was the first warning sign, and basing the subject on the lyrics of an R&B song was the second. As I squirmed in the pew while they attempted to use humor as a means to connect with the congregation, I quickly realized that they didn't have a scriptural foundation for the message. The sermon also showed apparent signs of a lack of spiritual preparation nor the inclusion of any standard components that make up a comprehensive sermonic experience.

    The sermon that this young man presented, and what I hear all too often from ministers who lack adequate training/preparation, was not constructed to enrich the congregation's lives. What I heard was an aimless religious rambling seasoned with a couple of tradition-based sermonic clichés in an attempt to get that much sought after affirmation from the congregation, the almighty, *"Amen."*

After ten minutes of this, I began to feel the patience of the congregation waning. The atmosphere changed from eager anticipation of an excellent sermon to sheer disbelief as this minister tried to salvage what even they must have known was a colossal failure on their part. After being among the first group of people to leave the church, which took everything inside of me to do since everyone who has preached the Gospel of Jesus Christ has at one time or another fallen short of expectations in delivery, preparation, or contact with a congregation. But this situation was different. I wasn't judging this preacher from the viewpoint of a message lacking content per se but felt more embarrassed for this preacher who had no idea what they were doing.

The following week, after what I'm sure was a scathing report to the pastor about how disastrous the Sunday message was, we received a letter from the church. The pastor apologized for his failure to ensure that a qualified minister preached to the souls of his flock. I understand the apology, but what if there was a lost soul in the congregation (we are all lost to some degree or another) who desperately needed a message from the Lord. God placed them in this space and time to get salve for their wounded soul, and to hear something so superficial and blasphemous was a lost opportunity that may not present itself again and maybe have fatal consequences.

The pastor admitted that he was in error for putting someone he thought would represent him in his absence would stray so far from that objective. He also admitted that he should have insisted on reading the associate's sermon before letting him preach. If he had, he would have never allowed his flock to hear this sermon. What we'll never know, and the pastor did not reveal, was actually how much and what type of training did this associate receive. The apology might have been a circumstance where the pastor made a conscious effort not to sacrifice the associate and take all responsibility for the failure. The pastor may have provided what in his mind was adequate preparation for his associate. Maybe that training was similar to the type of training he received, and he believed that the Holy Spirit would lead his associate to preach the sacred Gospel with the passion of a Holy

Spirit-filled sermon. If this was the case, I commend the pastor for protecting his associate from the scathing recourse that can happen in the Black Baptist church, but it is not a pass for this failure in oversight.

To be fair, and if anyone reading this book is of the Black Baptist tradition, I'm sure you'll agree that associate ministers failing to competently preach the Gospel of Jesus the Christ is an all too frequent occurrence in our pulpits. So frequently does this happen that pastors make a concerted effort not to divulge who is preaching in fear that the congregation will not come to church that Sunday. I've witnessed members come to church, and once they realize that the pastor is not preaching and minister "so and so" is preaching, turn around and leave.

However, I don't want to confuse substance with delivery. I have come across many associate ministers who metaphorically preach the paint off the walls! Phrasing, timing, whooping, dynamics, and connection to the congregation are all mesmerizing. The congregation is taken to many levels of spiritual ecstasy as they hurl "Amens" to the pulpit and demonstrate all sorts of physical connotations of sermonic affirmations. However, this phenomenon of the *empty* powerful sermon experience amounts to nothing more than Sunday entertainment whose theme few can remember just minutes after the sermonic moment. Congregants leave the sanctuary superficially fulfilled and spiritually empty, as they exclaim, "what a message."

When associate ministers see this enthusiastic reaction to a spiritually weak message, their focus shifts from preaching what they feel to be an authentic Gospel message and shift to a message geared at instigating an ecstatic reaction from the congregation. In other words, they need and seek the affirmation of the people, not God.

Enduring *"Gospel Message Failures"* where the almighty *"Whoop"* is the saving grace of a bad sermon, or *"Taking Them To The Cross"* becomes the lifebuoy for a message that lacks structure, objective, or credibility. The Sunday sermon then turns into a performance to gain popularity among the congregants. Pursuing the almighty *"Amen"* turns into a game of one-upmanship as associates strive to outdo one another, or worse yet, try to preach like the pastor.

For Whom God Calls

    Conversely, when a preacher is preaching a pertinent, spirit-filled sermon, the congregation often appears non-moved, for they too are stimulated by an excellent performance more than a great message. Many churches pursue that fabulous, rockin' choir with professional-caliber musicians and singers to get the service moving and to attract newcomers to the church. The performance aspect of contemporary church services has created an environment where entertainment, and thus motivated giving, are the objective and tithing falls into the category of the cost of admission, and not the sacred part of worship to ensure the survival of the church and its mission.

    So as not to think that my viewpoint is in the minority among observers of the Black church and Black church worship experiences, what I have described is noticeable and no less controversial in seminary. The following reading is an honest critique of today's sermon experiences in our churches. Put plainly, and this reading begs the question, where are you in your preaching. How much time do you spend putting together a sermon message? How deep is your subject matter, and do you even know what liberation preaching is, and ultimately, what price are you willing to pay for the almighty, "Amen"? If, like mentioned in the reading, you give excuses and rationalizations for your shortcomings, then the author will have proved their case.

The Black Preacher and Contemporary Preaching
A Critique of Contemporary Preaching

Katie Geneva Cannon

    Clark's critique of contemporary preaching is a ministerial indictment that much of our preaching has been either light or lying or both, wherein far too many of us have slung together some spiritual slop callously or carelessly, late on Saturday night or early on Sunday morning, with the inevitable consequence of parishioners running from church to church, hollering and knocking over benches in search of genuine food for their souls.

With our practical definition in mind – preaching is a divine activity, wherein the Word of God is proclaimed or announced on a contemporary issue with an ultimate response to our God – and with you looking like and acting like you know that you ain't through with the definition of preaching yet, we are now in position to give our attention to a new issue that we will be wrestling with in this lecture, "a critique of contemporary preaching." We will endeavor to use our working theological definition of preaching as a background for making a contemporary critique. We will use what we now understand about preaching to make a critical judgment on preaching today. You do indeed need to have some idea of where you now stand in relation to this preaching business, so that you can have some idea of what you must be doing in the future as aspiring preachers. You must assess the preaching situation in the present, so that you can know what the future preaching situation calls forth from you. Ain't no sense in trying to carve out a preaching future unless you know what the preaching score is now on the contemporary scene, because your preaching future is based on the preaching situation existing now in the contemporary context.

For instance, if you find the existing preaching situation today to be sound then you merely need to build upon that sound foundation in your future endeavors. If there is a sound foundation, then just build on it. But, if you find that the existing preaching situation is full of honky-donk in the present, then you need to recognize that you will have to clean up that bad situation at the very beginning of your future endeavors. If you got honky-donk on the scene, then you got to clean it away. Every act in the future is based on the present reality. Thus, we need to make an honest critique of the present preaching situation so that you can know how to get started in the future endeavors of your preaching ministry.

And we especially want to make an honest critique of the black preaching situation, since we are definitely interested in the meaning and implications of preaching for future black liberation. You got to know what you got to do if you are about liberation.

For Whom God Calls

We definitely want to see what and how and why preaching can help black folks to really overcome in this land of ours through our preaching.

Without prejudicing the case completely beforehand, let me say that you will definitely need some hip boots and dungarees in your future ministry. You ain't going to need no suit and no tie, no robe and no high heels, to do a relevant job in your future preaching ministry. Because any time you are working in an outhouse, any time you are wading in piles and piles of do-do, you definitely need hip boots and dungarees rather than a suit and a tie or robes and high heels to do that kind of work. Don't think that your main job is with a suit and tie, or robes and high heels, when you get started. It ain't. I don't want to prejudice the case, but I need to alert you to the kind of clothes you will need to wear. If you are really interested in helping black folks to overcome through some powerful preaching, then let us make a threefold critique of the contemporary situation of preaching.

First of all, we will make a general assessment of the preaching situation in mainline Protestantism in America. Second, we will endeavor to prove that our general assessment is accurate by calling in some unimpeachable witnesses to testify before the judge and the jury. And third, we will give some didactic causes for the bad situation on the present preaching scene. Three things we got to do. We are going to give you an assessment of how things are. We are going to prove it. And then we are going to tell you why it is like it is. So, let us begin with this necessary critique, for liberation purposes, by making this general assessment in the light of our working definition of preaching.

If our definition of preaching has any theological validity at all – and it does – and if there is any virtue in it for your usage – and I believe that it has that – then our definition should make us acutely aware of a serious indictment against much that parades around under the disguise of preaching in our midst today. For many of those preaching impostors need to be arrested for impersonating genuine proclaimers of the Most High. Much of contemporary preaching is like what Albert Knudson said about contemporary theology in his time. For the most part, not every part, but for the most part, for the predominant part, preaching is shallow and in the shadows."

Now, by assessing much of contemporary preaching as being shallow, we mean that much of so-called preaching today is not getting at the deep, fundamental, serious questions of life that people are concerned about. Much contemporary preaching is often lacking divine depth and human depth. No sound theology is in it and no understanding of sound psychology or sociology is under it. There is often no great import, divine or human, in much of today's crap-trap. There is often no profound impact on the thinking and behavior of people in their living today. In that sense, much of today's preaching is about as deep as a single dewdrop on the desert sand at high noon, shallow. Pish! There is a drop of dew out there, but you don't even know that it is out there.

Now, by assessing much of contemporary preaching as being in the shadows, we mean that most people today don't normally take preaching seriously. Thus, preaching today is no longer in the limelight as it once was, but it is often more or less a sidelight in church. Like the monkey that ask me, "Do you think that we ought to have some drama?" Yes, I think we ought to have it on Sunday evening, when you are going to have some kind of program, but not in the place of preaching. "do you think that we ought to have a cantata at 11:30 on Sunday morning?" Hell no! Hell no! If it were not for preaching, you wouldn't have a church. I am talking about the things that brought the church into existence. Some people are now putting preaching aside so that we can have a songfest. Yes, there is gospel in music. And there is gospel in drama, nobody is denying that. All we are saying is that music and drama did not bring the church into existence, and it ain't going to keep it in existence.

Don't let no devil fool you out of your place in the pulpit. There is only one time when the devil ought to fool you out of the pulpit, and that is when you ain't got no message. Sit down and let the choir take over, for maybe they can sing some gospel. If you got your message ready, like you ought to have it ready, then you tell the choir that they have their part. Let the choir sing, and you

For Whom God Calls

don't want no whole lot of humming and no organ playing while you are trying to preach the gospel, talking about needing some help. If you ain't got your sermon ready, then let the organ drown you out.

Let's be sure, what I am saying is that preaching is more on the sidelines today. People are asking questions about whether they even need a preacher. And even preachers talking about, you think that we ought to have drama instead of a sermon. You need to be sure that preaching is still a part of our cultural heritage. No one denies that. And most people today would be upset with a drama or cantata if we did do it every Lord's day.

For the most part, contemporary preaching is something being done for the record only. It is something for the sake of religious appearances. We can't have a service without preaching. What would the folk outside say? So much of today's preaching is about keeping up our religious image, but it is actually nothing to get serious about for most people today, including jacklegs with nasty collars on backwards.

Preaching is often shallow and in the shadows, often some kind of shady affair in the shadows even for many with nasty collars on backwards. You can tell that by the time preachers give to preparing to preach. Some fools think that they can get a sermon together in two or three hours. They are crazy. It will take the average one of you, if you really do it right, it will take you about forty to sixty hours. It takes me twenty hours to get all these lectures together. It takes me twenty hours to get a decent sermon out. Did you know that? Yes, it does. Every lecture that you receive means that you got twenty hours of me, every time I come before you up here. And, if I got these ideas and concepts internalized, and I got to put my sentences together automatically, then I know what kind of time it is going to take you. Night and day, wrestling with an angel until day breaks and the Lord blesses you.

So that is my general assessment of the preaching situation in mainline Protestantism in contemporary America. Generally speaking, it is most definitely shallow and in the shadows. It is shallow in content as it relates to the deep issues in contemporary life. And it is definitely in the shadows in interest as it relates to being significant to most people trying to find answers to problems of life here and now. Most people, when they got problems, they don't even think about the preacher any more. The preacher is that fellow who gets up there and talks real light and doesn't know anything.

Well now, why Doc talking about preaching that-a way! Doc must be mad at the world talking like that. How can Doc say a nasty thing like that about his brethren of the cloth! Something definitely must be wrong with Doc talking about preaching being shallow and in the shadows. Listen brothers and sisters let me I tell you about it. I know what Doc's problem is, so let me tell you all about Doc. [Now, when you run into a fool talking like that, then you know that he ain't got no damn sense. It is not that he is thinking wrong, it is that he ain't got no thought and trying to get one.] See, Doc is upset about one of two things. See I know what makes a man talk like that, talking the way that Doc is talking. It is either one of two problems that he got. So let me tell you all about Doc's problem.

On one hand, a man talks like that because of his frustrated vocational ambitions, talks like that when he did not get what he wanted in life. And you see Doc always wanted to be a bishop in his church. You know, all AME preachers want to be bishops and Doc ain't never been elected as a delegate to General Conference. Doc can't even make it as a delegate. He has been ordained twenty-five years and he can't even make delegate.

So on one hand [You know these are fool lies. I ain't never been a delegate because I never ran. I have always been on my own turf trying to teach fools like you. This fool acts like this is the truth coming out. All of this is a lie.], it could be Doc's frustration with AME politics that causes Doc to talk that way about preaching being shallow and in the shadows.

On the other hand, a man talks like that also because of sexual frustration. A man talks like that also when he needs some good loving in his life. Good loving changes things and makes a man see things differently. Some good loving would straighten Doc out. It would make Doc see things differently about the preaching situation. Cause I know. I know that good loving changes things, makes a man see things differently.

You see brothers and sisters, I knows all about sexual frustration, because I use to go around sexually frustrated myself. I

For Whom God Calls

used to go around mad at the world until I see the light. Because one day, one day the heavens opened to me. And one day, one day it all became clear to me. One day the heavens opened and I seed things clearly for the first time in my life. So let me tell you about what happened to me. One day, things changed for me, heaven opened up, and I remember that blessed day. It was like it was just yesterday.

I left home early one morning on my way to work. I was sad in my heart and I was mad at the world. And then on my way to work, the lightning flashed and the thunder rolled and I heard a voice saying something to me on my way to work. It said, Son, Son, I know that your heart is heavy, and there is sadness in your heart on your way to work. Son, Son, I got a blessing for you that is going to make everything alright. Son, Son let me tell you what I want you to do. Son, I want you to go down to big-leg Susie's house because I got something down there to put joy in your heart.

Maybe this seminarian does have a point. Maybe I do need to be taken to big-leg Susie's house to get a good piece of loving. I ain't going to argue against that. Nobody knows all about himself. It takes someone else, as I have said before, to see some things that we can't see about ourselves. Maybe my meanness and all my nasty talk are based on the fact that I need a good piece of loving. I will take the recommendation under serious advisement. But now that I have heard your story, let me tell you something. Even after, even after I get that good loving from big-leg Susie, I will still be saying that much of contemporary preaching is shallow. Even after I get some good loving, I will still be saying that much of today's preaching is shallow and in the shadows, fool.

And I will tell you something else, fool. Big-leg Susie would have to have some mighty good loving to convert all these witnesses I got lined up. We have a whole gang of witnesses lined up all of whom have come forward gladly to testify in court that much of today's preaching is shallow and in the shadows, even so-called powerful black preaching, even in my own denomination.

So big-leg Susie would have to roll a whole lot of folks in her nasty brass bed to get all of these witnesses to see things differently, fool. And I don't believe that nobody's stuff is that good, at least not good enough to convert all of these witnesses on my side. So let's forget about good loving for the moment. Good loving ain't got a thing to do with what we are talking about at this time. Can't no sexual act perform the miracle of changing all this preaching do-do on the contemporary scene into no ice cream soda. So even after we all get that good loving, I will still say that much of contemporary preaching is shallow and in the shadows, if we assess it objectively. So it must have been a devil who was talking with you on your way to work, fool, because it sure wasn't the Lord. The Lord tells us that preaching today is shallow and in the shadows.

Well now, since I have set forth a serious indictment against so many preachers on the contemporary scene, I am under divine obligation to prove the charges or be liable for slander and defamation of preaching character. So I want to prove these charges in court by calling upon some unimpeachable witnesses. Now, this set of witnesses that we need to call will verify my indictment of today's preaching. And because time is of the essence, permit me to call upon my main witness at this time. We might call upon other witnesses, later if needed.

Now, our main witness, Billy Grahamism, came to my attention several years ago when he conducted a two-week revival crusade in Los Angeles. The thing that struck me was that at the particular crusade, there was an exceptionally large crowd participating. Graham always gathered a great big crowd, but that Los Angeles crowd was exceptionally large. Listen to these statistics. That crusade in Los Angeles involved some 930,344 persons. Not nine thousand, but nine hundred and thirty thousand, three hundred and forty-four, almost a million folk involved in that crusade in Los Angeles during those two weeks. And listen to this, ladies and gentlemen of this jury, more than forty thousand souls, not four thousand souls, but more than forty thousand souls came running down that aisle in that crusade to accept Christ for the first time. Thousands streaming down those aisles coming to Accept Christ with tears in their eyes.

Now hear this, most of those forty thousand converts, not just half of them, but most of those forty thousand converts, were already members of local churches, Your Honor. Most of those converts had sat listening to local pastors and felt absolutely nothing, unmoved, Sunday after Sunday. But now in that crusade, those same members did feel something and were moving down

For Whom God Calls

those aisles by the thousands. Why, Your Honor? Why Graham and not those local pastors, Your Honor?

Your Honor, and ladies and gentlemen of this jury, maybe lying pastors and those future lying pastors in the seminary will conjure up all kinds of lies to account for Billy Graham's apparent success as over against the obvious failures of pastors on the local level. They make up all kinds of great, big lies trying to make Graham's success look bad and their own failures look good, Your Honor.

So you will hear these kinds of lies being bellowed from local pastoral liars and their disciples in the seminary about Billy Graham's apparent success. Some will say, for instance, that it must be that many of those folks love to put on a great big show and get converted in a large setting, trying to make a big deal about their conversion on television. They wouldn't be streaming down there except for the fact that the television cameras are on the scene. That is why he got so many and we don't get none.

Some others will say that it must be that Graham has some penny actors to start that flow down those aisles, and those forty thousand people were merely playing follow-the-leader unknowingly. He had some actors back there to start with the tears rolling down their cheeks, and the power of suggestion influenced others to follow their behinds. "If you get things started and end up having a whole lot of folks streaming down those isles, here is fifty dollars for you. And as you come down the aisle it will throw a suggestion to the crowd and more people will follow." It must be that.

And still others might say that it must be Graham's brand of fundamentalism, always talking about the Bible and what the Bible says. He has a Bible in his hand that is capturing the religious right, the same way that the box brand of conservatism captured the segregationist right in 1966 and in 1970 in Georgia. The conservatives got the majority vote in 1970 because they appealed to the segregationists. I think that is what is happening with Graham holding the Bible up there. It is impressive and folks come.

And still others might come up with this great big lie, and this lie might have some disciples in this room. It must be, it has got to be the persuasion of the music from the thousand-voice choir that is doing the job. It must be the choir. It has got to be the choir because it can't be the preaching because preaching can't do that much. It is that thousand-voice choir that he got up there that is drawing those folk down the aisles, so much so that forty thousand folks came forward. It must be the choir that is doing that trick, because after all, more people get more gospel from the music than from the preaching in worship anyway, said one cullud pastor in fact, after messing up one Sunday morning.

The cullud pastor said this, knowing that I was sitting over there as the professor of homiletics. He said, "You know that I didn't do so well this morning but we had the choir anyway. And after all, more people get more out of what the musician does than what you do in your preaching class Doc." And the saddest part about that lying statement is that he did not even see that that statement was an indictment against him, talking about his insignificance.

Why should more people get more gospel from the choir than from the preacher, Your Honor? Why? Why would people get more out of the choir, untrained professionally, than from us who are supposed to be trained professionally, Your Honor? That was an indictment against preaching, not a compliment back to the choir.

It should be most obvious to this court that all those rationalized lies are supported by liars with nasty collars on backwards, so as to account for our preaching failure over against Graham's apparent success, Your Honor.

Now, Your Honor, and ladies and gentlemen of this jury, let me set the record straight about the prosecutor's personal attitude about Billy Graham. Let me set that record straight, Your Honor, because Billy Graham is not a specimen of a genuine prophet, as far as I as the prosecutor is concerned, your Honor. Billy Graham was too close to that lying Richard Nixon, and anybody friendly to Richard Nixon is automatically my personal enemy.

Your Honor, and ladies and gentlemen of this jury, we are not trying to prove that Billy Graham is the greatest and mostest. Your Honor, all that we are trying to prove by this witness is that most of our local members are spiritually hungry. Your Honor, and ladies and gentlemen of this jury, that is all that we are trying to

For Whom God Calls

prove by this witness. Not that we like Graham, but that what he is doing proves that people are hungry at the local level. And whether or not I like Billy Graham personally is not the issue, Your Honor. What really is the issue is that Billy Graham's apparent success proves conclusively that most people on the local level are being starved out spiritually by most local pastors. Those people are not getting enough, if anything at all, to eat spiritually in most local churches, Your Honor, and ladies and gentlemen of this jury. All those lies put out by lying local pastors and their lying seminary disciples against Billy Graham are simply not true, Your Honor. The simple truth of the matter is that those folks are simply starved at the local level. That is the most plausible explanation of all, Your Honor, and ladies and gentlemen of this jury.

Let me dramatize this spiritually hungry appetite of local folk to this court through a concrete personal illustration. Your Honor, and ladies and gentlemen of this jury, let me put this thing down on the ground so that everybody in this court can get it, so that you can reach a fair verdict on this issue of whether preaching is shallow and in the shadows. (Now this is the way you give examples in sermons.)

For example, where I once lived, my garbage cans were turned over almost every day by some hungry dogs, all because people in the neighborhood did not believe in feeding their dogs at home, Your Honor. They merely turned those dogs loose at suppertime to fend for themselves, Your Honor. So every day, Your Honor, every single day, every day, Your Honor, it was a sound being heard like this in my backyard. BAM DE BAM BAM BAMA BAMA LAMA RING RING RING with hungry dogs turning over my garbage cans looking for something to eat, Your Honor. Every day there were those hungry dogs looking for a meal and with garbage all over my back yard. Every day, Your Honor, BOOM DE BAM BAM, BAMA BAMA LAMA RING RING was in my backyard with garbage all over my yard. That was the way it was every day where I once lived, Your Honor, and ladies and gentlemen of this jury.

But where I now live, where I now live is an entirely different story. There are about twenty dogs in the community where I now live, Your Honor, so it ain't just about dogs. And up until last year, up until last year when the economic recession started, up until then, I did not have but six or seven incidents of overturned garbage cans in the past ten years in my present neighborhood, Your Honor, and ladies and gentlemen of this jury. Only six or seven overturned trash cans in ten years, but every day, every day before in my old neighborhood. Why, Your Honor? Why overturned garbage cans every day before? And why not the same story now? The explanation should be obvious to this court, Your Honor.

It is because people in my present neighborhood feed their dogs at home. At least they did until Nixon started a recession last year, with inflation for dessert with a steady diet of recession. They would give those dogs something to eat at home and those garbage cans in my present neighborhood stayed erect. And the garbage men, the garbage men in both communities will gladly come to this court to verify that fact, Your Honor. The garbage men in my old neighborhood will tell you that the garbage cans are all over the yard, and the garbage men in my present neighborhood will tell you that very seldom, if ever, do you see garbage cans turned over in my present neighborhood. If you don't believe me, I'll bring them into court, if you need them to testify.

So, Your Honor, and ladies and gentlemen of this jury, does that illustration not suggest a more plausible explanation of what is really happening in many, many local churches over against those lies put out against Graham by some local pastors? Those local pastors are frequently turning the hungry people loose Sunday after Sunday to turn over somebody's spiritual garbage cans, Your Honor, and ladies and gentlemen of this jury.

And like those hungry dogs in my past neighborhood, those church folks will head for anybody's spiritual garbage can to turn over looking for a spiritual meal. Also, Your Honor, and ladies and gentlemen of this jury, because like those hungry dogs in my past neighborhood, the present hungry folks in church know that there is nothing on the table. In fact, nothing is even cooking at home in the local parish with the local preacher. So, Your Honor, it is every man for himself.

And those hungry souls head for Billy Graham's or anybody else's spiritual garbage can to turn it over for some soul food for their starving selves. And those 930,344 souls at that Los Angeles crusade and those forty thousand souls streaming down

For Whom God Calls

those aisles who belong to our churches let the cat out of the bag about the spiritual poverty program in many, many local churches in this land, Your Honor, and ladies and gentlemen of this jury. That Los Angeles group let the whole world know what is happening in those spiritual dells on the local level, your Honor.

To tell you the truth, Your Honor, Billy Graham does not have to be in town to reveal the poverty in preaching in most local churches. You don't have to get a great big person like Billy Graham. Other lesser-likes, other people who ain't got no fame like Billy Graham can also let the cat out of the bag about the spiritual malnutrition in most local churches on the contemporary scene.

For instance, just let certain hummingbird clergy come to town, or get hold of a red-eyed drunken quartet from the alley, a bunch of bums with liquor on their breath hollering Mother, Mother, Mother, or just haul off a ten-year-old kid, doesn't even have to be a grown-up, a ten-year-old kid, just get a ten-year-old kid imitating
a jackleg and all those lesser-likes will outdo the average local pastor and will have most of our hungry people out there at those jackleg services. They will be out there turning over garbage cans for a desperately needed spiritual meal, Your Honor, and ladies and gentlemen of this jury.

And let me tell you something else, even after folks leave us every Sunday morning-in fact, before they get to us-they turn on the radio. They know if they are going to get anything. They have got to turn on the radio if they are going to get some spiritual food that day. They know ain't nothing going to happen when they get to church. And when they leave church, what are they going to do? At night, they are going to be saying where, where is so-and-so jackleg preaching? When people are hungry they will go anywhere to try and get something to eat.

Your Honor, and ladies and gentlemen of this jury, the prosecutor respectfully requests your forgiveness and your indulgence for bringing the dead into this nasty situation. But I am sure that the critical nature of this case warrants desperate efforts to get to the bottom of it. So please forgive the prosecutor's seeming disrespect for the dead at this juncture. It is also a known fact that most local pastors can be outdrawn by a dead corpse at a funeral. More people come out to turn over garbage cans at funerals than come out to hear us on the Lord's Day. Many of our local parishioners hope that even the dead can offer them more than we can as local pastors from that preaching stage. And that is the truth, Your Honor. Even the dead have more to offer hungry folk then most of us from the pulpit.

So this court should see why the prosecutor saw it necessary to bring the dead into this nasty affair. Please forgive me. For when our folks look in such unseemingly places as funerals for a spiritual morsel, you can be sure that there is much spiritual fasting going on in our local churches all the time. Your Honor, and ladies and gentlemen of this jury, there is definitely a Lenten season of spiritual fasting, going on 365 days a year, not every other day, but 365 days a year in most local churches with no spiritual food on this side of the Jordan for those hungry folks. And there is not even the hope of anything better on the other side of the Jordan River if what some of us proclaim about heaven is true, Your Honor. The way some jacklegs talk about heaven, they expect to have a jackleg on that preaching stage in heaven, Your Honor. The way they talk, it is going to be a funkmaker that is going to be sitting in the middle chair between those pearly gates. You are going to see a funkmaker up there in the middle chair. And then to top that off, every day, every day is supposed to be Sunday. You get the picture, with a jackleg running things on that heavenly stage with worship going on every day. Well, if that is the way that heaven is, Your Honor, and ladies and gentlemen of this jury, let me declare myself here and now, on this side of the Jordan about that situation. If heaven is going to be run by a funkmaking jackleg every day, then hell here I come, voluntarily. If heaven is like that, jacklegs running things every day, forever, then please Lord, remember me with the lost in hell, just reserve a place for me in hell.

Thus, Your Honor, and ladies and gentlemen of this jury, this court should now see clearly, I am not lying when I say that this sound is heard all over the land, BAM DE BAM BAM BAMA LAMA LAMA RING RING RING, all over creation now and supposedly in heaven later on, if heaven is like what those jacklegs are talking about.

For Whom God Calls

Your Honor, and ladies and gentlemen of the jury, the prosecutor respectfully asks this court for a recess. We are not resting our case, not by a long shot, but we are merely calling for a recess in the trial, because we want to bring to this court expert witnesses who are now on the way by jet to testify for the prosecution against contemporary jacklegs. Your honor, and ladies and gentlemen of this jury, can I get this recess?

Recess granted.

DELIVERABLES

REFLECTION PAPER & Questions

1. On average, how much study to you do and how much effort to you put forth when preparing a sermon?

2. What are your steps to preparing a sermon; or do you have a systematic approach or methodology to sermon preparation?

3. Do you have a sermon ready right now? If called to preached tomorrow, would you be prepared?

4. Why do you wait until the last minute to prepare your sermon given that you have ample notice to prepare?

5. Have you ever turned down a preaching opportunity because you weren't prepared?

6. If you have preached a sermon, recall one where you know you were ill-prepared and recall, how did you feel during and after the sermon and what was the reaction of the congregation to your message?

Chapter 3
The Black Congregation and the People Within

Whenever I witness a disconnect between minister and congregation, it almost always results from the minister trying to make the congregation see things the easy they do. Likewise, I've also seen the frustration when ministers believe they have preached or taught a highly effective sermon, only to get feedback that they missed the mark entirely. What is the reason for this, you might ask? What I've learned, and what this section is about, is the need to become familiar with the congregation and context you are ministering. Failing to make a connection with the people is the greatest failure of all. It doesn't necessarily have to be in a religious context that this happens. Any speaking or teaching engagement that doesn't consider the attitude, concerns, and location of the people could fall on deaf ears. Therefore, we must not only gain an understanding and appreciation of ourselves, but we must make a concerted effort to understand and appreciate our intended audience. I propose that this is done not according to some checklist but rather by a sincere undertaking to understand the historical and cultural ingredients that make up the physical and psychological makeup of the African American people.

I have on frequent occasions expressed my frustration with ministers who seem to walk in their light and not the light of God. These ministers preach what *they* think is essential, make the sermon about *them and their issues,* and are totally out of touch with the realities of their present environment. These are the type of ministers who feel that other people, namely the congregants, need to view the world as they do, express faith as they do, and experience life as they do. Unfortunately for them, they've done nothing more but establish ministries fraught with fantasies and disappointments. The consequences of transferring their "personal mess" disguised as a sermon onto the people serve no one, especially not God.

Finally, and don't perceive this the wrong way; just because you're African American doesn't mean that you somehow magically connect with your brethren. Every person is a unique creation of God, so no one formula works for all. Therefore, what you must seek out and ingest are the cultural similarities African American people share and embrace those similarities. And yes, you are a part of those cultural similarities as well, so you will also be in the process of discovering yourself! So I ask the question, to who are you preaching and ministering? When you're preparing a sermon, who is it precisely that your message is targeting? Read on as Na'im Akbar leads you through an encounter into the psyche of the Children of the Maafa.

BREAKING THE CHAINS OF PSYCHOLOGICAL SLAVERY

LIBERATION FROM MENTAL SLAVERY

Na'im Akbar, Ph.D.

Liberation From Mental Slavery

In order to address the problem of "breaking the chains of mental slavery," there is a simple but important idea that must be understood. This idea is actually true for all human beings but has special importance for the people in the current condition of Black people. This idea is that human beings are a very special form of creation; we have a very unique place in nature. We are the only life form in nature who operate based upon our self-consciousness. Every other form of animal life on this planet, no matter how gigantic or how small (whether it has the building precision of a termite or the destructive capacity of a rhinoceros) do what they do not based on what they know about themselves but guided by their instinct or innate programming. There is nothing which requires the worker bee to define itself as a worker bee in order for it to work in the hive. Insects, birds, and beasts do what they do based on instinct or training (adaptation). None of them acquire their abilities from any knowledge of who they are, at least so far as we have been able to observe.

This quality of creatures in nature has some drawbacks. On the one hand, these creatures are able to do what they do and not too much more other than what they are programmed to do. Ants have been building the same basic type of hills for thousands of years (with occasional modification to fit the changes which humanity has imposed on nature). They have not been able to progress beyond this form and they will probably be doing it the same way for thousands of years yet to come. Even though the form apparently serves them well, there is no evidence of any significant advancement in their hill-building skills over the centuries. We have no evidence that any other form of life on this planet has the capacity to make anything known as "progress" because they are locked into what they do very well but they can't do too much else.

As human beings, our limitations rest only in our ignorance. We are ignorant of who we are and what we can do. We have the need to gain consciousness (awareness) and only in consciousness is our true human capacity open to us. We are not a tabula rasa, (or blank slate) at the time of birth but we must have the access code in order to gain the creativity of our God-given genius. The access code for other animal life forms is simply the stimulation of the environment and some minor training experiences. We must acquire consciousness of who we are and what we have been in order to operate to our full human capacity. This is why cultures expend so much energy in creating the kind of environments and experiences which insure that each generation of will maintain the gains and acquire the consciousness which is necessary to preserve the human accomplishments. Human Beings clearly have the deadly potential to drop below even the most despicable forms of barbarism and endanger the entirety of human advancement, even the most basic human characteristics. We are the only life form who can engage in collective and individual self-murder for no apparent transcendent motive while knowing the consequence of the suicidal act. Instinct prohibits such conduct among other forms of life. The rare occurrence of other animals committing suicide (such as whales beaching themselves) is undoubtedly a result of ecologically insensitive humans disrupting the natural environment which fouls up the natural instincts, rather than these behaviors being conscious self-murder. We can go lower than any form of life, but we also can go higher. This is the mixed blessing of freedom.

If this is the nature and mixed blessing of freedom, what must we identify as the source of human power? The answer is obvious. As we have suggested above, this ultimate human power is our mental power, our consciousness, our awareness. Whatever the form that consciousness may take will determine our state and circumstances as human beings.

By no means is this an original formulation. This perception is as old as there has been any remnant of human civilization. This has been known by Homo Sapiens (knowing beings) for as long as we have been Homo Sapiens. Human beings have consistently worked to create the circumstances to maximize their consciousness and to insure that each subsequent generation will know fully who and what they are. On the other hand, whenever human beings chose to oppress or capture other human beings, they also did all that they could do to undermine any expansion of consciousness by the oppressed. So, when a group who has power wants to maintain that power or wants to take over the power of others; when people want to make captives of other people, they operate with the very same assumptions. They understand that ultimately the control of the people was in the control of their thinking, in control of their minds, in control of their consciousness.

The process of enslavement was not simply the brute force of overcoming people who were militarily weaker and forcing them to operate under your influence. It was not simply the outcome of barbaric treatment of captives by assault, brutality, restricted movement and activity. The process of human slavery is ultimately a psychological process by which the mind of a people is gradually brought under the control of their captors and they become imprisoned by the loss of the consciousness (awareness) of themselves.

It is this process which completely altered the human conduct of African people for the last four centuries. The disruption of our consciousness-building processes and the imposition of an alien consciousness has reduced Africans from being major builders and contributors to world civilization to becoming totally dependent on other's civilization for any guide to human conduct. African-Americans are most notorious for their self-destructive conduct, which is indicative of the process of destroyed consciousness that we are describing here.

The case history of African-Americans is a dramatic illustration of how this process destroys the human power. Africans were the builders of pyramids, now we destroy our own homes in frustrated explosions of rage and irresponsibility. We reached high civilization through the dignified leadership of African queens and many of us have now become contemporary abusers of Black femininity. We introduced medicine and healing on the planet. Now we have become drug abusers and destroyers of our own lives. We have descended from scientists who studied the heavens to become clowns who degrade and brutalize ourselves for the entertainment of our captors. These processes could only occur as a result of the loss of our higher human awareness.
"Let us make slaves ... "

How did the slave-makers accomplish this deadly feat? They engaged in a systematic process of dismantling any and all mechanisms that preserved the continuity of the African people. The African captives were separated from related language groups and were isolated from their most familiar selves. Any of the rituals which preserved the integrity of the African culture from marriages to funerals were forbidden and alien practices were substituted or none were permitted at all. They cut the tongues from the griots who tried in the quiet of night to remind the people that there was a continuity that reached beyond the fields which they had come to know in Jamaica, Bahia, Alabama, Georgia and Virginia. Griots tried to remind the people of difficult days which had already passed and how we had endured death from the environment and from the hands of our enemies of centuries past. They tried to keep the people reminded that there was hope even in the face of hopelessness. This story was stopped and the teller was called a trouble-maker and used as an example of the fate of those who dare to sustain the captive's story of salvation. Such storytellers were brutally killed or mutilated so that their story of African continuity could not be told.

For Whom God Calls

Slave owners frequently snatched suckling infants from their mother's breast for fear that the natural empathy of the birth mother might communicate a message of resistance that would undermine their process of captivity. There was a kind of conspiracy to create a race of orphans, to intentionally breakdown the Black family. (It is so ironical that contemporary social scientists make such an issue of the breakdown of the Black family which did not begin to break down until some white families began to break it down for their objectives). As we discussed in the previous section, families were broken up at the whim of the slave master. In addition, Black men were forced to watch their wives, daughters, sisters and mothers raped by their owners. Such experiences effectively disrupted the sense of connection and reciprocal protection that exists in the preservation of family systems. By undermining this loyalty and protective image for almost twenty generations or 400 years, one is able to create a painful alienation between men and women which continues to contaminate the reciprocal respect that men and women must have for each other in order to develop and maintain families.

As we have discussed in earlier parts of this volume, the personal character of the former slaves was distorted in ways that even 130 years from legal emancipation we still carry the scars. The processes of brutality, humiliation, and deliberate ignorance continue to plague the personalities of America's former slaves in such a way that make us our major enemies here at the turn of the century. The psychological process of slave-making remains an inadequately under- stood and appreciated phenomena for its impact on the functioning of African-American persons and our communities. The challenge for those who would choose to be healers of Black life must be the removal of these psychological chains.

Strategies to Break the Chains of Slavery

It is important to understand as a primary rule that the restoration of African consciousness is a process that must be accomplished primarily by African people. It is unrealistic to expect that the descendants of the slave masters will initiate and play the major role in the elimination of the mental shackles which were put in place by their ancestors. This is not a condemnation of European-American people. As was the case with the abolition of physical slavery, many white people played critical roles which facilitated the alleviation of the philosophical contradictions of legalized slavery in a "free" country. However, it was the impetus and the persistence of the former slaves themselves who took the radical posture to demand uncompromised elimination of the system of slavery. We are again reminded of the tension experienced between Frederick Douglass who was an escaped slave and his liberal white abolitionist friends who viewed many of his positions as being too extreme. Certainly, Nat Turner had no white allies in his forceful removal of the captor's boot from his neck.

So much of the European-American consciousness is based on its affirmation of greatness and superiority in contrast to the inferiority and wretchedness of Africans. This false security built into white supremacist culture clearly limits the role that European-Americans are capable of understanding or playing in the restoration of African consciousness. Whether whites play a role or not is not nearly as important as it is for Black people to understand that our ultimate mental liberation must be guided by our independent action and activity. We cannot operate with the expectation that our true liberation can only come when European-American people change their mentality. The elimination of white racism is not a necessary prerequisite for the liberation of the African mind. Black people cannot commit excessive energy to the effort to alter the attitudes and consciousness of white people with the assumption that this is the path to freedom. Certainly, the obstacles created by white supremacist institutions and attitudes cause great difficulties in the march to Black mental liberation. There is no doubt that if those obstacles were removed, progress would be much easier. It is evident after all of these centuries that it is unrealistic to expect this European-American white supremacist mentality is going to disappear anytime soon. White racism is a fact of life and we must strategize solutions which are independent of its initial elimination.

As we have discussed above, the primary objective to freeing the Black mind is to change the consciousness of Black people. This is not a simple nor a brief process. We must understand that the current consciousness of Black people is the consequence of over four centuries of direct intervention and even longer efforts to destroy the indigenous institutions of African people which developed and sustained their independent human consciousness. We cannot expect that this process; will be reversed at the end of a year or by reading a book. Once we embark upon the journey, change has already begun and will continue so long as the direction is maintained. We dare not surrender and declare defeat if we don't immediately see the massive results that we would wish. We must understand that generations of unborn African, people will be the true beneficiaries of this process.

Knowledge of Self

In order to change the African consciousness, we must change the information that is in the African mind. We cannot equate awareness with information though information is the road map to awareness and it is acritical part of the process. The "knowledge of self" which was the foundation of the highly successful Black reform program of the Honorable Elijah Muhammad {1965} and the premise of Ancient African teachers in the Nile Valley over 4,000 years ago, still remains an essential ingredient of this process of mental liberation. A fundamental component of the chains which continue to handicap Black minds is the excessive and distorted information about white people and the absence of information about ourselves.

Consistent with the argument we have already made in this discussion, European-American people have done an admirable job of insuring that the content of their consciousness was well-informed about their greatness. The great stories of Louis XIV, Columbus, Napoleon, Queen Victoria, Copernicus, Galileo, the Greeks and the Romans are fundamental elements of the information system that we are given about European-American people. This barrage of information about European and American greatness is systematically given to themselves to ensure that they maintain their consciousness of who they are. Quite accurately, they realize that unless their children are given information about themselves they will never develop the consciousness that will permit them to maintain their control and influence over the world's major resources and their actions of self-determination and survival within the human family. So the story about European accomplishments and the description of European culture and structuring the world's reality around European experiences are essential parts of building the European consciousness to insure its survival and maintain the freedom of European people.

We do not wish to argue in this discussion that European people are not in their rights to offer such information for the expansion and maintenance of their human consciousness in order to insure their self-interest. We do argue, however, that if this is the only information that African-Americans receive, then they develop an inordinate regard for the self-interest of European-Americans and inadequate or no regard for themselves or their own self-interest. Therefore, Black children need to know about Black accomplishments throughout history and throughout the world. They need to know about our heroes and heroines, our discoverers, scientists, teachers, artists, inventors and as much about the greatness of African accomplishment as Europeans are taught about the greatness of European accomplishment. Since our objective is not the captivity of Europeans nor the guiltless domination of them, this information about the African accomplishment should not exclude information about them (Europeans) and their accomplishments. We need to know about our great ideas, our great victories, but we need to also know about our great defeats and how those defeats were transitory and did not deter the forward progress of African people as a whole.

The great restoration project of especially the last 20 years has expanded and intensified the significant work that was begun by W. E. B. DuBois, J. A. Rogers, Carter G. Woodson, Martin Delaney, George G. M. James, and hundreds of others who realized the significance of reviving the history and telling the story of African accomplishment as a significant part of the Black liberation process. The continued work of the great scholars of the latter half of the 20th century such as Chancellor Williams, John G. Jackson, John Henrik Clarke, Yosef Ben Jochanon, Cheikh Anta Diop, Ivan VanSertima, Asa Hilliard, Maulana Karenga, Wade Nobles, Frances Welsing, Molefi Asante, and many, many others will be remembered for generations to come as significant contributors to the rebuilding of the information about African and African-American reality that was erased by the distortions of slavery and the slave makers. Though there has been considerable controversy about the work of these scholars because they have dared to reveal what had been systematically concealed, they have made an invaluable contribution to breaking the chains whose strength had been fortified by the ignorance about our history and ourselves.

    The demand for teaching about the Black experience is by no means a trivial consideration as has been claimed by white captors and Black captives alike. To change the content of the information is a necessary start to restoring the consciousness of Black people about themselves. It is not just a story of history, but a story of science and that every people have contributed to the progress of science and no one people has a monopoly on the accomplishments of science and technology. It is important that all people understand that the resources of the Earth are available to all of its inhabitants and the claims of superior knowledge, technology and circumstance is an accident of information and consciousness and not a Divine right given to some people and systematically kept away from others. The information about how Black people came to be in the state that we find ourselves is an important story to be told so that future generations will understand that it was not genetic deficiency and/or Divine decree! Which created our circumstances, but the advantage of human oppression that created the privilege of the few and the poverty of the many. This information begins to free our minds to let us know that there are no limits to our potential. When young Black boys learn that there are no limits to our possibilities on the basketball courts, we create the athletic genius of Michael Jordan or Magic Johnson and in their genius, they recreate the game of basketball. When our young people know that there are no limits to their potential in the world of manufacturing, communication, physics, chemistry or the science of the human mind, s: then those same young Black minds who create dances on the dance floor or compose music on their bodies with the "hand jive" will recreate these fields of human endeavor with the same incomparability.

    Information about the Black reality and experience must be transmitted as broadly and as intensely as is possible. Black singers must sing about it, Black researchers must identify it, Black actors must act it, Black scholars must conceptualize it, Black teachers must teach it, and Black preachers must preach it. From the cradle to the grave, we must submerge ourselves in information about ourselves; from books, pictures and whatever source that will bring messages to our minds. Each bit of information helps to mold the keys which will open the chains that remain on our minds.

"Cel-e-bration Time, Come on!"

The popular musical group Kool and the Gang popularized this song in the early 80's. Even though they were singing about a rather transitory party experience, the lyric captures the imperative of a morel generic process that is necessary to remove the chains of mental slavery. We must learn to comfortably celebrate ourselves. Self-celebration (we again emphasize) does not necessitate the degradation of others. It does, unapologetically, sing the greatness of our accomplishments and special blessings to the world. It tells each new generation something about the value of the fabric from which they are made. Cultures and institutions put considerable resources into creating images and opportunities to sing the praises of their accomplishments. This process is an essential part of maintaining a free mind, but it becomes even more fundamental in freeing a captive mind. Certainly one of the major strategies for enslaving the mind was the degradation of the Black/African self. The story of natural Black inferiority and ugliness were constant stories told to destroy the worth of the Black mind. The fantasies of African backwardness as incapable of technological development and characterized by superstitious and humanly regressive acts of cannibalism and savagery were all constructed in Tarzan stories, Little Black Sambo images and thousands of other derogatory ideas and illustrations to destroy the Black person's self-image and to further the idea of Black incompetence and deficiency.

Celebration then becomes a healing. If Europeans could comfortably identify themselves with every image from Santa Claus to the Son of God in order to celebrate who they are, why shouldn't we find images (both real and imagined) that communicate to Black African people something about our potential greatness. Perhaps, Kwanzaa is not an actual African Holiday, but why shouldn't we have a week-long celebration that brings pride and dignity to our culture. Why shouldn't the entire nation stop on the second Monday in January to celebrate the battle for human dignity by Martin Luther King, Jr. If Black people decide to call an assembly of one million Black men in Washington, D.C., on a Monday in October 1995, then why question the celebration since the very structure of the city of D.C. so emphatically celebrates the greatness of European American accomplishment. The hundreds of statues, museums, galleries, libraries, plaques and monuments which blanket the city consistently celebrate the greatness of being European- American. One could very easily walk around D.C. for an entire day and conclude that only European-American males built this great country. It is not accidental that European-American males continue to run the country in that the celebration and information they receive continuously reinforces their greatness.

    We must unashamedly display our images and great ancestral figures throughout our environments. From pictures on the walls to statues in the park and street names, we should celebrate our heritage and those people who have distinguished themselves as African people of greatness. We should have more than one street named for an African-American person, particularly in communities where we live; we should immortalize our great builders, thinkers, and warriors by constructing their images and placing their pictures systematically throughout our communities. Our churches should show pictures of great women and men of faith who endured to make a way for young Black people who had not yet been born. Although Biblical or Qur'anic heroes tell a distant story of the power of the faith, a greater story is told by our immediate ancestors who took the faith and changed not only the ancient world but our contemporary world as well. I would think that every Baptist church, at least, and every Black religious gathering place ideally should have pictures of Cynthia Westley, Addie Mae Collins, Denise McNair, Carol Robertson, these four Black girls who were killed when white terrorists threw a bomb through the window of 16th Street Baptist Church in Birmingham, Alabama, on September 15,1963. They should be the angelic cherubim who we think of since their lives were lost in innocent worship in a church that stood for the dignity of their people.

As we discuss in greater detail in the next chapter of this volume if we must have images of religious characters, let them look like us. If we must have Santa Claus entering our houses on Christmas Eve and occupying our malls from early November until December 24, then make sure that your Black child has a fantasy of a Black Santa Claus who comes with goodies and good cheer from black hands and hearts. The mythology of the culture must celebrate ourselves as do the facts of the culture. The persuasion for this argument is demonstrated by looking around the world in any culture where people's minds are free and they engage in self-determined action, you will find that they comfortably celebrate themselves in hundreds of ways.

The family reunions which were initiated in such large numbers during the late 70's were an excellent and creative way to celebrate the Black family's worth, survival and expansion. The decoration of mantles and walls in Black homes with pictures of their children and their ancestors, though simple acts were profound efforts to carry on the celebration process as best we could in environments that we had some control over. We need to gain broader control of the environments that we occupy so we can expand those images of self-celebration. We should comfortably celebrate in our own churches, schools, or communities-the birthdays and history of significant ancestors who have paid a great cost for our freedom. This celebration should and must go on independent of permission being given by the outside political figures. Black History Month must be a start for the celebration of our being. It cannot be an exclusive celebration, but must continue from February 1 until January 31 the following year. This must be a right that we guard and make apologies to no one for maintaining.

It is through self-celebration that we heal our damaged self-esteem. Yes, feeling good about oneself is a legitimate activity of cultures. In fact, any culture which does not make its adherents feel good about themselves is a failure as a culture. It is through the energy of self-worth that humans are motivated to improve and perpetuate themselves. The inspiration for the greatest of human accomplishments in architecture, science, poetry, art, industry, or any other human endeavor has been fueled by the octane of self-worth and a positive self-esteem. In the same vein, the low point of human degradation and even human self-destruction, both personally and collectively, is a consequence of the absence of self-esteem which demoralizes the very human spirit. To free ourselves, we must comfortably celebrate ourselves!

Only the Brave Need Apply

The process of mental liberation is not unlike many of the requirements of physical liberation. Freedom from captivity must be taken, not passively requested. It is never willingly given since the captivity has been in some way beneficial to the captor, so the captor gives up his captive only reluctantly. As our great Ancestral Saints, Harriet Tubman, Nat Turner, Ida B. Wells, Frederick Douglass, Medgar Evers and many others (now nameless) all found out, the decision to take one's freedom meets with resistance and even mortal danger. To take the captor's trophy could easily result in death to the captive. The lonely and ill-equipped road to freedom is one that will be wrought with all kinds of dangers. It is one thing to sing songs of freedom and to dream dreams of one day having it, but to take the responsibility to claim one's freedom is not for the faint of heart.

The nature of the alien consciousness has already created an atmosphere which justifies your captivity both to themselves and to your fellow captives. You are viewed with suspicion of your sanity to even raise the issue of wanting to be anything other than a well-kept slave. Both your fellow captives and your master cannot possibly conceive why you are not content to partake of his benevolence on his plantation. When you have earned the status of a "privileged" slave (economically, educationally or favor from association with the master), then it becomes even more incredible that you should want any more from this life in this world. The first designation is that you are "crazy" to think of freeing your mind. You are encouraged to compare yourself with your captive ancestors who suffered such great distress and so many of your fellow captives who continue to suffer great agony and this should be sufficient evidence of your blessed status. The fact that you no longer have literal chains on your body is more than sufficient evidence that things are "changing" and you are only a greedy and impatient step short of heaven.

Once you are designated as "crazy" then your credibility is seriously compromised. No one who wants to be respected as sane would dare pay any attention to you. What's even worse is that "crazy" people are not be trusted to care for themselves and they must be carefully watched for fear they may be a danger to themselves or others. Since your insanity has been defined by someone with another consciousness with another set of objectives, then what constitutes a danger fits into their frame of reference and not into the reference of your free consciousness. Courage is needed to deal with the isolation and vulnerability which results from this designation by your captors. The fact that they control the consciousness of most of your fellow captives means you have very few allies who can offer support and even protection as you seek to free your mind.

The process of beginning to think new thoughts in a new consciousness is a lonely process. It has been described as going into the desert by the newly liberated "Children of Israel" in the Old Testament and the Holy Qur'an. It is described as going into the wilderness as did Jesus Christ after he was baptized (liberated) by John the Baptist. Each of these scriptural images speaks to the sense of isolation which comes from newfound freedom. The loneliness and vulnerability which comes from the removal of your chains and trying out your new legs is considerable. As was the wilderness experience for both the Hebrew Children and the Christ, there are strong temptations to relapse constantly confronting the newly freed mind in the desert. The reminder of the security and companionship that you knew as a captive is constantly thrown in front of you. The possibilities for fame and fortune if you will abort your new consciousness and come back into the captor's mind set is almost a daily consideration. So it is for those who would dare to free their minds from slavery. They see their less competent and infinitely less accomplished fellow captives rewarded extravagantly with fame, fortune and celebrity status simply by their confirmation that the master's consciousness and his reality is the correct way to think. One can receive grants, tenure, promotions, movie roles, television shows, book contracts, or just the fame of being a prominent display on master's centerpiece simply by disavowing the consciousness of freedom and comfortably staying on the confines of the mental plantation.

This is why those who would choose to break the chains of mental slavery must be courageous. Only the very brave can resist the temptations or endure the isolation. Since the new consciousness can take a lifetime to begin to show tangible results, it takes a great deal of courage to persist in breaking the chains of the old consciousness and developing a new consciousness. This is another area where the new information and the self-celebration becomes very important. You cannot rely upon the encouragement of the multitudes running to your support and defense. The very nature of the slave's mentality insures that the majority of the slaves will be primarily committed to their master and his consciousness. Though your very life is committed to freeing the minds of the captives, you will be perceived by them as an enemy and they will gladly surrender you to crucifixion for the nature of the enslaved mind demands it. This requires you to be patient and comfortable that what you know is correct and even with so much consensus that you are wrong, you must be able to hold on to your right of freedom.

This Takes Great Courage

Rebellious slaves have always been dealt with in a very brutal fashion. In the days of the physical plantation, they were beaten, mutilated or killed. In later times, the same torture was the fate of those who threatened the status assigned to the former slaves. Even today, the possibility of imprisonment, police brutality, mysterious deaths from questionable causes is still the fate of those who challenge the master's consciousness. Of course, there are always the social murders of being unable to make a living, being publicly humiliated and accused of all kinds of horrendous crimes of reverse racism, anti-Semitism, un- American activity, etc., etc. The bottom line is that those who seek to get free are still dealt with severely and one should not take the decision to break the chains from your mind as a minor consideration. It will take courage.

How do we gain such courage? The more we know the braver we become. The stronger our pride and self-love, the greater our courage. We must maintain association with newly escaped slaves who know the price and the feeling of true mental liberation. There is strength in association. We must seek out colonies of maroons (or runaways) and gain solace from our association with like-minded souls. We must commune with the spirits of the ancestors who knew and took freedom before us and in anticipation of us. We must stand with the Paul Robeson, Marcus Garvey, Sojourner Truth, Fannie Lou Hamer, Elijah Muhammad, Harriet Tubman, and W. E. B. DuBois spirits who refused to settle for captivity in any form and whose entire lives were examples of the commitment to breaking the mental chains · and going into the desert until they were free. The ultimate weapon against fear is faith, which we will discuss below.

Umoja or Unity

There is strength in solidarity with others who are seeking to break the chains. As we have discussed in earlier sections of this book, "community division" was one of the major weapons used against the slaves. The fact that so much effort has gone into making sure the slaves do not form a common identity is indicative of the value of such a common identity. As was demonstrated during the civil rights struggles of the 60's as well as the successful Million Man March of 1995, the most potent weapon that we have in developing any kind of independent freedom is through unity.

Breaking the mental chains of the slave requires us to stand together despite the definitions of division that we have been given under the slave's consciousness. We have discussed in the previous chapter, the impact of William Lynch's "kit" for the control of the slaves. As we gain greater knowledge and information, many of those divisions will disappear because they cannot stand under the light of Truth and correct information. We must see our membership in religious groups, political groups, professions, academic groups, even in gender and class groups as being devices which can be and continue to be used to keep us divided and at war with each other. Although there are certainly issues on which we differ based upon the experiences in these various groups and categories, we must realize all of those differences are secondary when it comes to the reality of breaking the chains. We can do this more effectively if we begin by allying ourselves with other Blacks in the various groups where we find ourselves. When we stand together with other Blacks in our religious or political groups, professions, or even gender groups, we find that we have much more in common as Black members of those groups than we do with our non-Black colleagues. This realization brings the point home very clearly that we must stand together on the basis of our racial realities. Once we are able to see the commonality of our issues in the groups where we have strong identities, then we will be able to form coalitions with Black people who are apart of groups that we may know nothing about or feel hostile towards. So different fraternity men stood together as Black men at the Million Man March; Black Republicans, Democrats and Socialists stood together; Black graduates from the Naval Academy and West Point stood together when they realized that the unifying reality of being Black men brought them together. In a similar vein, Maya Angelou, Rosa Parks, Betty Shabazz all stood together in solidarity with Ben Chavis, Jesse Jackson and Louis Farrakhan in recognition that even being called a "man's" march required them to unite regardless of gender.

    This is the kind of unity which is critical to obtaining mental liberation. As we have noted above in our discussion of courage, it is not possible to get free alone. The chains are very heavy and are interconnected which requires us to free each other as we free our- selves. The frightening thing about unity for many of the slaves is the fact that they may lose special privileges they have been able to acquire by their uniqueness (e.g., they can sing, play some kind of ball, speak the language well, or they are one of those "only Blacks" in some kind of organization). We know that many of these kinds of concerns vanish once we make the commitment to break the chains in our minds. With that commitment, we are no longer interested in holding on to minor slave privileges. On the other hand, however, there are unique talents and qualities which we all have. In the process of liberation, it is important to recognize that unity does not require uniformity. We can stand together and preserve our separate qualities which serve to enhance further the objectives of freeing ourselves and all of our people. We cannot break the chains unless we appreciate our unique form of enslavement while not permitting that uniqueness to impede our unity with others who are trying to get free. At the same time, as we free ourselves, we must adapt our special gifts to enhance the liberation process.

In the process of uniting we bring our special gifts to the total process of breaking the chains. If you sing, then sing freedom songs; if you play ball, then play freedom ball; even if you tell jokes, laugh while breaking the chains as Dick Gregory and Bill Cosby have done. Never let your unique gift be used to keep yourself and the remainder of our people in slavery. In fact, this is one of the most popular strategies., There are so many musicians, comedians and scholars who are re- warded for bringing messages which continue to tighten the mental chains. The same special use that our captors make of our gifts, we can use to further our mental liberation. The key to the power of unity in this liberation process is that we must avoid the danger of letting ourselves be used to impede the freedom process. In these latter days of the 20th century, this is the major strategy of battle against our liberation. In a similar vein, we must appreciate the power of unity as the major instrument to break the chains which continue to inhibit our minds.

Evidence of Things Unseen

Probably the single most important quality used in the act of achieving physical liberation from slavery was the inner power to believe that freedom was possible. It took a strong compelling belief that even though you could not see freedom and how to reach it, you knew it was possible and you were willing to confront all odds to obtain it. This is the power of faith and it was the power of faith that took Harriet Tubman back and forth on her many trips on the underground railroad. It was faith that permitted the thousands who ran away and took their freedom and endured the dangers and the obstacles to reach their goal. It was faith that sustained those who did not run away to keep their spirit and dignity intact until (physical) freedom was achieved. It was faith that kept the brutalized slaves from not giving up. In much the same way, faith is necessary to achieve mental freedom as well.

The faith that we are describing does not apply to any particular religious expression, even though all religions are based on faith and are intended to cultivate faith. The faith must be a basic sense that "everything will be all right," no matter how things might appear. Whether this certainty comes from belief in a Supreme Being or in a process like Karma, the person looking to obtain mental freedom must find something to give them a sense of faith-that everything will be all right. This sense may come directly from a belief in the new conscious- ness and the freedom it will bring and a conviction that no matter how hard the battle, the progress towards removing the chains is worth it. I am certain that many physical slaves made the flight to freedom just on the basis of faith that anything would be better than captivity and this faith was strong enough to sustain them in their struggle for liberation. Without a strong faith in something bigger than your master and yourself there is no way to engage in the struggle that is necessary to achieve freedom.

As we have stated above, it is faith that provides a shield from our fears. It is the belief that "everything will be all right" that feeds the courage we described as being so necessary in obtaining this mental freedom. It is through the power of faith that the mentally enslaved person can, in the image of Samson, break the chains which confine us. This is another of those instances where qualities we already have can be transformed to serve the purpose of our freedom. If our faith is already in a concept of God, who has dominion over all things, then like Harriet Tubman, Nat Turner and many others, we can use the faith we already have to sustain us in our efforts to get free. Now, if that faith is in the god of the chains or in the god of the person who put us in the chains then of course, that faith will do you no good in getting free. In fact, it was that kind of faith which made many slaves fear to take their freedom or even to believe that freedom was in violation of God. Such can also be the case in seeking mental freedom. Of course, it is particularly difficult when the slave believes his chains are decreed by God and God, then, has become the chains. In the next chapter, where we discuss the impact of religious images on our psychology, we further analyze the potential dilemma created by faith in alien images.

Faith must be acquired from within. This is very much an individual task which must be accomplished by drawing upon the example and the inspiration of those who have faith. We can be taught about faith by those who know faith, but each of us must explore our inner self to discover the power of faith. We must be willing to search for the belief in a power higher than circumstance and to locate this "evidence of things unseen." One of the great discoveries which comes from gaining information about who we are as African people is the overwhelming and convincing evidence that faith has been the sustaining force which has brought us to where we are. Where other people may point to material or intellectual resources, our power has been in our spiritual resources and it is this realization that helps us to discover the power of faith and our potential for faith even if we have not yet discovered it.

The task of breaking the chains of mental slavery requires a great deal of faith. Faith gives us the patience to stick to the job of looking for our own reality. It gives us the determination to overcome the hold of the chains of the plantation mind which tend to increase their grip as we seek to free ourselves. Since the situation of slavery created such a void of information about the African reality and so effectively erased the African consciousness, then it requires a great deal of faith to pursue the restoration of this awareness. As we mentioned above, the ever-present opposition which says to the fleeing mental slave there is no reality other than the European-American consciousness, requires faith to keep us seeking and building. Certainly, it is faith that sustains us in the fear and loneliness of this lifelong search to help restore who we are.

"Let's Get to Work"

Each of us has to make the commitment to engage in the personal and collective job of freeing ourselves from mental slavery. The strategies we have outlined above which will assist us in changing our consciousness process We must work to re-educate ourselves and our young people be seeking and studying new information about ourselves. We must find every opportunity to celebrate ourselves and we must challenge the fear that caused us to hesitate in taking the chains out of our minds. We must work together and we must have faith that our struggle will be successful, regardless of the opposition

The first step is acknowledgement of our slave mentality and the fact that we remain limited in our effectiveness because of the slavery experience. There are many African-Americans who will be unable to do this because the very nature of the mental slavery creates an illusion that we are free. Hopefully, this publication and many of the experiences that inevitably we will have, will help us reach this realization. We trust in the natural love that human beings have for freedom that will motivate us to break the chains once we realize they exist. As we have discussed above, we will immediately understand we cannot be freed just as individuals, but must work to fee all of the mental captives. As we become aware of our captured mental state, then we will have to commit ourselves to join the mental liberation process for all Black people. The accomplishment of this task will become increasingly easy as we more and more people committed to this mental liberation struggle.

DELIVERABLES

REFLECTION PAPER & Questions

1. Have you witnessed the behaviors brought out by Dr. Akbar in your present context?

2. Where do you find yourself in this reading?

3. Do you see the potential to further connect your ministry with the people your ministry targets?

Michael H Sands

**Part Two – The What
Ministry and the African American Community**

CHAPTER 4
EXPECTATIONS AND MISCONCEPTIONS OF MINISTRY AND THE CALL

Now is the time to begin our transparent discussion about beginning this journey into and through being a minister of the Gospel. Let us delve into this transformative vocational commitment by examining two major pitfalls I've witnessed by new and associate ministers. Many new ministers have entered the ministry by declaring their "Call to Preach" founded on an epistemological misunderstanding of ministry that will forever impede their ministerial objectives.

The following reading by Virginia Samuel Cetuk serves as a prelude for a more pragmatic view of the motivations to answer the call to Christian ministry and the perils and pitfalls of that decision. You will demonstrate your understanding of this reading via the written exercise at the end of this chapter.

When engaging this material, you will see mention of seminary and think that the reading does not pertain to your situation because you have no desire to attend seminary, or at least not yet. Bear in mind that you can easily, and you should, substitute the references to seminary for the experience of approaching your local pastor and the beginning of a church-based ministerial training process. (Which is the case in the majority of Black Baptist churches I've studied whose transition to minister/pastor is a part of local church polity.) I can assure you that the emotions, concerns, questions, doubts, triumphs, failures, and frustrations are interchangeable to either setting. Likewise, I would also substitute "student" for the "candidate." However, when entering ministry, you should consider yourself a "student of the Gospel" since your ministerial sanctification should never be without capitalizing on every learning opportunity.

Michael H Sands

WHAT TO EXPECT IN SEMINARY: THEOLOGICAL EDUCATION AS SPIRITUAL FORMATION - THE CALL TO MINISTRY

Virginia Samuel Cetuk

And he said to them, "Follow me...." Immediately they left the boat and their father, and followed him. (Matthew 4:19, 22)

As Matthew tells the story of the calling of the first disciples, Peter, Andrew, James, and John did not hesitate to leave all they had and follow Jesus. The Gospel writers disagree about the order in which the disciples were called. They also disagree about the setting of the first call to ministry: Matthew and Mark place it at the Sea of Galilee while Luke places it at the Lake of Gennesaret; John does not say where the call took place. There is one thing that the Gospel writers do agree on, however: without fail those whom Jesus called immediately said, "Yes." Without an apparent thought about the fishing businesses they had worked so hard to establish or the families that depended upon them, they left everything behind and followed Jesus on down the shore. With each step they moved farther and farther away from the people they had been and came closer and closer to becoming the people God had created them to be. As they discovered, to live with Jesus meant by definition that one would change.

Peter, for example, underwent a tremendous transformation while living with Jesus. In the Gospels, early on we see the arrogant Peter who vows his undying allegiance though all else should fail (John 13:37). At the end of John's Gospel, we see a different Peter. When Jesus asked Peter if he loved him, Peter responded a quiet "Yes, Lord; you know that I love you." Gone were the boasting and bravado, and in their place was a humble spirit that was born when the cock crowed (John 18).

In the book of Acts, we read about Paul's call to ministry and his conversion on the road to Damascus. Known for his prowess in persecuting Christians, Paul met the living Christ while on his way to Damascus to arrest more Christians (Acts 9). His encounter with Christ left him a changed man, on his way to do great things for the Lord. Once converted and called, Paul did not look back he simply followed the risen Christ

True discipleship, as Bonhoeffer pointed out, means that the disciple will be at odds with former beliefs and old lifestyles. True discipleship causes us to question our motives as well as our practices; it causes us to become restless with the way things are when justice and mercy are not the order of the day. True discipleship means that when Christ is done with us we will not be the same people we were. True discipleship involves openness to the future and the expectation that we will change as we walk closely with God.

Given the nature of true discipleship it has been interesting and somewhat disconcerting for me to find that by and large seminary students do not come to seminary expecting to change or be changed through the experience. While most expect to leave seminary with more knowledge than they had when they arrived, many students resist the kind of soul searching and wrestling with issues that is part of theological education.

Of course, people entering seminary are no more likely to seek change than the general population. Seminarians come with a variety of theological perspectives and expectations. Some come with the same reluctance to change and the same misunderstanding of the true nature of God's grace that is seen throughout society. Others come expecting and hoping to change and counting on the grace of God to see them through. In short, seminary students are a reflection of humanity.

Considering the realities of today's enrollment patterns, however, one might expect people who decide to become seminary students to have an even greater difficulty given the magnitude of changes wrought in their lives by the decision to enter seminary. When I went to seminary, I was with peers of the same age; most of us had come to seminary three months after graduating from college in our early twenties. We had come with firm convictions about the direction we wanted our professional lives to take; most of us had wanted to be in the ministry at least since adolescence and had not longed for any other kind of work. Few of us had any life experience beyond college life, and most of us had not worked in any jobs besides summer jobs while in college.

This clarity about life's direction coupled with an uninterrupted path into preparation for ministry is not often seen today. The majority of students now come to seminary after leaving [or still actively engaged in their] first professional careers. That means that many students come having known some satisfaction and dissatisfaction in their lives personally or professionally. They come with conviction about the rightness of their decision because they have known other, less satisfying work prior to enrolling. They are seeking something, and expect to find it in seminary.

Research done by the Association of Theological Schools (ATS) is useful for showing trends in enrollment in theological schools in recent years. A quick look at some of the research illustrates the age diversity of people entering seminary today. The ATS Fact Book for the 1995-1996 academic year reports that the largest percentage of men and women enrolled in theological schools that year were in the 40-49 age range. Furthermore, 58 percent of all enrolled students in ATS schools were 35 years of age or older.[1]

This description was also seen in research done by ATS on the 1994 entering classes in twelve out of the thirteen United Methodist theological schools. From those data we see that at eleven out of the twelve schools, at least half of the entering students were 32 years of age or older.[2] My own school mirrors this data. In 1994, the average age for both male and female students entering Drew Theological School was 40.

In addition to this increase in the average age of students, theological schools have seen a dramatic increase in the number of women attending in the past 25 years. In 1973, ATS reported that 11 percent of all entering students were women. In 1995, the same body reported that 33 percent of all entering students were women.[3] Some schools have a much higher percentage of female students. In 1994, for example, 49 percent of students entering Drew Theological School for all degree programs were women. In the Master of Divinity degree alone (the degree leading to ordination) 55 percent of the entering class were women. Although this percentage is somewhat higher than we have seen for the past several years, women have made up approximately 49 percent of our student body for more than the past decade.

As the above data shows, theological school student bodies today are gender and age inclusive. Some years ago I met with one of our students a few short weeks before she was to graduate. When she asked me what the mandatory retirement age was in The United Methodist Church, I told her it was 70. Observing her crestfallen expression, I learned that she would soon turn 72! This student was not alone; in fact, she had several contemporaries in the student body at that time.

Such a diversity of age leads to a rich mix within the student body and in classroom discussions ... My purpose here in noting this change in makeup of theological schools is simply to point out the corresponding difficulty some students have leaving former lives in order to enter seminary. They often come from established careers and have owned their own homes. Some students move with their families from larger homes into small apartments on campus while others choose to commute long distances in order to avoid such disruptions in family life. Many students wonder how they will pay their own tuition bills alongside those of their college-age children. Unlike the first disciples, many seminary students today do not have such an easy time disengaging from former lives to follow the call.

Students' Reasons for Coming to Seminary

Students come to seminary for a variety of reasons. In the fall of 1994, 794 students entering twelve United Methodist theological schools were asked to respond to a series of questions relative to their entering seminary. One of the questions asked was: "How important were the following in your choice of a profession or calling?" The categories were rated in the following way: 1 of no importance; 3 somewhat important; and 5 very important. The categories and the rate at which they were ranked as being very important were the following:

    Experienced a call from God 88%
    Desire to serve others 77%
    Opportunity for study and growth 75%
    Desire to make a difference in the life of the church 71%
    Intellectual interest in religious/theological questions 70%
    Experience of the community life of a local church 58%
    Promise of spiritual fulfillment 57%
    Desire to contribute to the cause of social justice 53%
    Encouragement of clergy 52%
    Experience of pastoral counseling/spiritual direction 43%
    Desire to celebrate the sacraments 43%
    Search for meaning in life 43%
    Influence of family or spouse 33%
    Desire to preserve traditions of the church 31%
    Influence of friend(s) 23%
    Experience in campus Christian organization 16%
    A major life event (e.g. a death, divorce) 15%[4]

    As the above data show, there are many reasons given for coming to seminary. These reasons are legitimate and believable. My experience of seminary students over the last fifteen years is that they are generally kind and compassionate people who want to make the world a better place and to spread the gospel message of love, justice, and reconciliation. In addition to the reasons stated above, which are the conscious reasons for coming, students enroll in theological degree programs for unconscious reasons as well. These reasons must be discovered and explored while you are in seminary, for they will exert pressure on your ministry in powerful ways unless you are aware of them.

    I once was asked to attend the final evaluation session for a student in supervised ministry. His time at the church had been an unsatisfactory one for the supervisor and the lay people on his teaching committee. They had experienced the student as pleasant to be with but lacking energy and enthusiasm for ministry. Despite clear agreements that he would be working in close contact with the people of the church, he spent most of his time working at his computer and doing publicity for various programs of the church. His forays into the written word were taking him away from contacts with the people. The student's supervisor and Teaching Church Committee members agreed before the meeting to speak honestly with the student about their concerns about him as a future pastoral leader.[2] As the conversation developed and moved toward the end point of the evening, I asked the student why he had come to seminary in the first place. In the quiet moments that followed I believe he came to reframe his self-image: he told the group that his father had been a minister. One day, a few years before the student came to seminary, his father left his church to walk across the street to the local deli for lunch. On his way across the street, which he had crossed hundreds of times, he was hit by a truck and killed instantly. Of course the student knew that he was mourning the loss of his father with whom he had been close. What he did not realize until those quiet moments at the evaluation session was that he had come to seminary to continue to be close to his father and to thereby avoid the full force of his grief. Though this was not part of his conscious decision to enter seminary, it was the driving force behind his decision.

    In a recent conversation with students at Drew Theological School, Bishop Neil Irons of The United Methodist Church said that an alarmingly high number of persons in the ministry today are wounded and in need of healing. To an unhealthy degree they need and expect their parishioners to provide the kind of loving acceptance they did not get elsewhere.

    His observation matched one of my own, namely that a large number of students come to seminary from troubled backgrounds of one kind or another. In conversations with students about their families of origin, I have been told stories of physical and emotional abuse; sexual abuse by parents, siblings, and extended family members; and unresolved grief from earlier losses. Some students are quite candid about being drawn to the church because it was the one place where they received unconditional love and felt valued in their own right. While I celebrate the healing effect such outreach on the part of the church has for these individuals, I believe that some students come to seminary confusing the love they have found in the church with a call to the ordained ministry. The one does not necessarily follow from the other.

Some students come to seminary, it seems, because they want to be taken care of; they want (and need) to an unhealthy degree the respect, the authority, and the power afforded clergy. Such people are candidates for the codependent relationships that cripple effective ministry by preventing the pastor from offering genuine prophetic and pastoral leadership in the church.

I have known some students over the years who came to seminary because they wanted to explore deeper faith issues and better understand the relationship of faith to life in contemporary society. I once talked with a student who was ready to begin supervised ministry. This young woman had come to Drew three months after finishing college and was bright, enthusiastic, and eager to learn. As we talked about the kind of church that would be the appropriate placement for her, I asked her to tell me what her reasons were for coming to seminary. She said that she wanted to be in a church that was as theologically diverse as possible. I asked her what she hoped to gain from such an experience. After a lengthy silence she said that she was seeking certainty about her own faith. When we talked further about her life prior to coming to seminary, I discovered that she had become a Christian only two years before coming to Drew. Her family had never been churchgoing, and it was only while in college that she had felt drawn to God and the church. She had no real desire to be ordained, but did expect that her faith would become clearer and at the same time strengthened through attending seminary.

After she left my office, I continued to think about her placement in supervised ministry for the next year. I concluded that, instead of the usual supervised ministry experience in which she would try on the role of pastoral leader under close supervision, she needed a type of confirmation experience in which she would be assisted to wrestle with issues of faith as she would have done years earlier had she been in the church at the time.

As these examples show, people come to seminary for highly individualized reasons, which are both conscious and unconscious. Regardless of your reasons for coming to seminary, the decision to enter a program of theological education is an important one with life-changing implications. I hope that you will look at yourself objectively as you read this chapter and allow yourself to think more carefully about the reasons you have come. It is of paramount importance for you to know yourself well if you want to become an effective and helpful pastoral leader. Without such intimate knowledge of yourself, you will not be able to sustain the kind of relationships with others in ministry across the years that are the bedrock of the church. This kind of introspection and self-awareness is at the heart of ministry and will be required of you as you meet your denominational review committee if you choose to pursue ordination.

The sacrifices students make in order to come to seminary, coupled with the conscious and unconscious reasons they come, can serve to create an atmosphere in which expectations of an assured outcome are high. While not every student who has decided to enroll in a theological school is intent upon being ordained upon graduation, many students are. In most Protestant theological schools, the Master of Divinity is the primary degree offered; hence, the majority of students are on the path to ordination.[3] [... except in the setting of the traditional Black Baptist church.] The convictions they bring about themselves and the church often serve to shape their ideas about the timeline for their ordination and foreclose their wondering about the rightness of their vocational choice.

The decision to come to seminary is viewed by some students as the end point of a journey to vocational fulfillment. Because of the strength of their conviction about the rightness of this step for their lives, they assume that upon completion of the degree they will be ordained. Some students are confused about the role of the seminary in ordaining people for pastoral leadership. While there is usually a collegial working relationship between theological schools and the denominations they represent, theological schools (unless they are Jewish theological schools) do not ordain people. It is their role to assist students to think critically about issues of ministry within the Christian tradition and the contemporary world. Although such work is obviously relevant to the work of the ordained pastor, it is not a substitute for a thorough process of review administered by the appropriate church body. Each denomination reserves the right to determine whether a given candidate is suitable to be ordained and exercise pastoral leadership within that part of the Body of Christ. Put simply, just because you have come to seminary and are a Master of Divinity student does not mean that you will one day be ordained.

Students' Expectations of Theological Education

… In addition to the previously noted conscious and unconscious reasons people come to seminary, students come with multiple expectations about what their seminary experience will be like.

I began seminary three months after I graduated from college at the age of twenty-one. The night before I left for seminary, I was at once excited and frightened about what lay ahead of me. I had wanted to be ordained since I felt called to ministry at the age of thirteen. Although I had enjoyed my college years immensely, I was always aware that they were only a means to an end: I wanted to be ordained. My excitement in going to seminary lay in the reality that in seminary I was several steps closer to my goal. Further, I had been challenged and invigorated by my study of the Bible and philosophy in college and was eager to continue to study in these areas. Finally, I expected that I would enter a community that would welcome me and share my enthusiasm for Christianity and ministry in the contemporary world. I expected my seminary experience to confirm my already firm faith, round out my knowledge in necessary ways, and prepare me for almost any situation in ministry. I did not know it then, of course, but I was about to embark on a difficult, and at times, exhausting journey. I also did not know at the time that I had come to seminary with a set of flawed expectations. I expected to be prepared for all eventualities in ministry through the experience. That was my goal. I did not realize that goal was an in appropriate one at the time and was confused when I was frustrated by the experience.

Many students come with similar expectations: they view seminary as the place where they will learn the "how to's" of ministry; a place where they will find their faith deepening automatically; a time when they will be confirmed and affirmed in their desire to be ordained. Perhaps you have come with similar expectations.

The problem with these expectations is that they contain a view of theological education that is flawed in multiple, serious ways. They suggest that seminary is a place with enough and definitive answers to specific as well as universal questions and that it is possible to prepare people to face any and every situation in life and ministry.

This view of seminary is flawed both in its anthropology, and its theology. It views humanity as static, and civilization as unchanging. I can only expect to arrive at a state of preparedness for all situations if things never change and tomorrow is predictably like yesterday. If that were the case, I would be able to learn a series of responses to the limited situations that will arise in the future.) Such a view is based upon an anthropology that says that you and I are not influenced by the world around us in new ways every day, that there is nothing new under the sun. The issues facing the church today, it follows, are the same issues that have faced the church since Pentecost. Were this view true, the people in the church would think the same predictable thoughts, feel the same feelings, and conclude the same things as did their forebears in the faith. Any student of humanity knows, however, that this view is not reality.

This anthropology is also, of course, theologically flawed. It says that it is possible for us to know all we need to know once and forever, and it thereby forgets the lesson of the Garden of Eden: that God alone is omniscient. Further, it denies the truth of the church doctrine of sanctification: namely that the life of the Christian lives closely with God is one in which it is possible to become more Christlike through use of the spiritual disciplines. In other words, it denies what Peter and Paul knew to be the truth, namely, that the encounter with Christ causes one to change.

You may think at this point that my critique of students' expectations is itself flawed. You may say in response something like the following: "Well, of course, I know I can't be prepared for everything that will come my way." I don't doubt that you know that reality on some level. And yet, I have heard many students (and seasoned clergy) complain about the inadequacy of their theological education in preparing them for ministry. The assumptions behind these complaints are that the seminary could have and should have done a better job preparing them for ministry. The charge against the seminary, then, is dereliction of duty. I have also heard judicatory officials wonder about the kind of candidates presenting themselves for ordination today and imply that the seminary did not "do its job" because the candidates are inadequate in some significant way. This complaint implies that the seminary could have done more than it did to prepare candidates for the realities of church life and leadership today.

While no curriculum is perfect, these complaints would only serve as a legitimate critique of theological education if it were possible to prepare students for every situation that will arise. In a world that changes quickly, is complex and ambiguous, and has technological capability which far outdistances its moral maturity in our world, it is simply not possible to cover everything or prepare for all that will come your way in ministry.

To critique theological schools on the grounds that they did not prepare you adequately is, therefore, unfair and misses the point. It is neither possible nor theoretically desirable for theological education to prepare you for every occurrence in ministry. Instead it is the job of theological education to teach you how to think critically and theologically about issues of faith and life and ministry. The faculty of your school no doubt view themselves as being able to teach you not so much what to think, but how to think. That critical thinking is of greater value in the long run because it will help you face the issues confronting you with insight and integrity.

I return to the work of Paulo Friere in Pedagogy of the Oppressed. It is his contrast of "bank deposit" education and "problem-posing" education. The former consists of the teacher sharing necessary knowledge with the students who then remember that knowledge to be used during tests. In this kind of education, the students are dependent upon the insights, wisdom, and under- standing of the teacher. They are not challenged to think for them- selves or to be actors in their own history.

Friere argues for the necessity of pedagogy being instead the "problem-posing" kind, in which the teacher is a co-learner with the students and all are called upon to think critically, utilizing the intellectual and experiential resources available. In this type of education, all parties share the roles of student-teacher. It is this type of pedagogy that is more often the norm in theological education today.

You will be expected to think critically about yourself and for yourself. You will have to assimilate vast amounts of material at the same time that you critique its applicability to your life and ministry. I raise the issue now because I hope you will reframe your expectations about what your time in seminary will be like.

… A common metaphor for theological education for many students is that of arrival. Seminary is seen as the place to which they have been propelled by a variety of things. Because it is so closely linked to the destination of ordination, students view themselves on some level as having arrived when they enter seminary.

Although in a certain sense it is true that coming to seminary seems for many students like a homecoming (especially if they have come after years of thinking about ministry or having left other careers that were unsatisfactory), arrival is a dangerous metaphor. It suggests an end point instead of a beginning, and short circuits the kind of wondering about vocational choice that is a part of the spiritual formation needed in pastoral leaders. Adopting arrival as the predominant metaphor for your seminary experience can lead you to foreclose the kind of spiritual, psychological, and intellectual wrestling that is a necessary part of the formation of pastoral leaders.

Theological Education: A Journey

A more appropriate tack would be to reframe this view of your seminary experience and adopt instead the metaphor of journey. The metaphor of journey is a beloved one in the Judeo-Christian heritage because it is so very representative of the truth about our lives and our relationship with God. To be alive is to be always changing and growing; to be spiritually alive is to be continually deepening one's relationship with the Transcendent and to God's "good creation" and at the same time to be shaped by these relationships. Both of these statements reflect movement from one place or state of being to another. They also reflect the truth at the heart of the universe, namely that it is in the nature of creation that life is complex, mysterious, and dynamic, not static. That this is so has been evident from the beginning of time, for the Genesis account of creation records the movement from chaos to order, from the void to the garden.

The Judea-Christian heritage acknowledges Abraham as the father of the faith. It is interesting to note that the history of salvation and covenant relationship with God begins with God's calling Abraham to a journey into the unknown: "Go from your country and your kindred and your father's house to the land that I will show you. I will make of you a great nation" (Genesis 12:1-2a). Abraham is asked to follow God into the future by giving up the familiar, setting out into the unknown, and to do so trusting God to supply his need. Because of the nature of Abraham's call into the unknown, he is a good model for seminary students who are also called away from the familiar and into the unknown.

The story of the Exodus marks the salvation of the Jews from the tyranny of Pharaoh. You may find yourself identifying with the Jews in some ways as you learn about their journey from oppressive security, through forty desert years, into the promised land because you have left a life that must have been unsatisfactory in many ways in order to journey on to a better life. Throughout the difficult journey through the desert, the Israelites experienced God as the One with them: "My presence will go with you, and I will give you rest" (Exodus 33:14).

After the Exodus accounts, the spirituality of journey that is so evident in the Old Testament is best exemplified in the Psalter. The book of Psalms is, in its essence, a love story about the people of Israel and their God. Full of their everyday struggles as sometimes faithful, sometimes unfaithful people, the Psalms contain the whole human drama of misery and redemption. If you have not already studied the Psalms, I hope you will do so while you are in seminary. They contain every known emotion, are wonderfully earthy and passionate, and resound with hope in God and humankind. It is their unqualified honesty and their raw candor with God that makes them my own favorite part of scripture. They contain the journey of the Israelites from faith to greater faith. They express the fears and hopes, the despair and salvation of the psalmists and the conviction that wherever they are on this spiritual journey, God is with them. "Where can I go from your spirit? Or where can I flee from your presence? If I ascend to heaven, you are there; if I make my bed in Sheol, you are there" (Psalm 139:7-8).

In the New Testament, the theologies of journey are central in the interpretation of God's saving work in Christ. Following his baptism in the river Jordan (Matthew 3:13-17), Jesus is led by the Spirit into the desert to share the wilderness and temptation experiences of his people. The forty days Jesus spends there parallel the forty years of the Israelites in the desert in that the spiritual journey contained in both is one of testing and desolation. Jesus is victorious as he is resolutely faithful to God, and he is able to begin his public ministry following his time of testing.

Continuing the metaphor of spiritual journey, we see that Jesus' life was a journey from Galilee to Jerusalem. His public, ministry was one in which he moved from place to place pro- claiming the kingdom of God. In Luke 9:58 we read about his nomadic existence: "Foxes have holes, and birds of the air have nests; but the Son of Man has nowhere to lay his head." His movement from place to place, unencumbered by mortgages or rent, both fostered and expressed his utter reliance upon God for his material needs and thereby served to daily deepen his intimacy with God.

When he finally journeyed up to Jerusalem and faced the inevitable horrible end to his earthly life, he chose a course from which he would not stray. In the agonizing struggle in the garden of Gethsemane, the triumph of his spiritual journey was revealed when he prayed finally, "Yet, not my will but yours be done" (Luke 22:42). His acceptance of and preference for God's will over his own was the apex of his spiritual journey. He died to himself and was indeed one with God.

We have seen how the people of God have used the metaphor of journey to express the reality of their walk with God since the beginning of covenant history. This simple metaphor, so common in our experience of secular life, is eminently useful for theological school students with the twin goals of faith formation and preparation for lifelong service in ministry. Your time in seminary should be a time of soul searching and exploration, of wondering about yourself and about God, and of pursuit of meaning in life related to vocational choice. Properly understood, it is a time of discernment in which you discover with greater clarity the exact nature of ministry to which you are being called.

I have often asked students beginning their supervised ministry requirement to suspend for the time being any convictions they may have about their belonging in the role of pastoral leader. Instead I urge them to use their experience in the church under supervision to test their call and to wonder with each act of ministry about the "fit" between them and the ministry in which they are engaged. This suspension of their convictions about their call allows them to be more open to feedback and evaluation from others. It also helps them to become more attuned to the still small voice within that can guide them to firmer and more appropriate decisions about vocational direction in the future.

I urge you to do the same as you move through your [training] program. Understand yourself as being on a journey

For Whom God Calls

with God in which you will discover who you are and where God is leading you. Know that with God's help you will gain clarity about the nature of ministry to which you are being called: ordained or lay. Allow yourself to lean on God and your community and receive from both the encouragement and insight about yourself that you will need to make important decisions about your life.

DELIVERABLES

REFLECTION PAPER & Questions

Even though you may have no desire to enter Seminary, the training experience offered in the local church is equally demanding of an intimate encounter with self to be of benefit to you and the congregation. Pay close attention to that portion of the reading that emphasized that the pastor, local church leader, or ministerial training facilitator cannot and will not be able to answer your questions or provide solutions to all of life's dilemmas. That is ultimately up to you and your willingness to let God be your guide. Be honest when addressing the call portions of this reading. As mentioned previously, in the Black Baptist tradition, the questioning of the "Call" is not typical, a practice that I hope pastors and local church leaders will slowly reassess. The Black Baptist church is unique because it is the only *major* denomination in which the "Call Declaration" is accepted or rejected with little to no resistance. The determining entity is singularly in the purview of the pastor and their recommendations to the congregation.

1. *What are your expectations of ministry?*
2. *What are your misconceptions about ministry and how have they changed after engaging the reading?*
3. Outline the process of ordination in your church setting. Describe the requites for each step and the timeframe you would expect following these processes. If you are not familiar with this process in *your* church setting, now is the time to find out. In the Black Baptist church, it usually best to seek out the pastor, for it is the pastor who has total control over the ordination process. Alternatively, if the

sitting pastor has recently ordained a minister in the church, consult with the candidate to learn from their experience. This is especially true if you have not yet shared your Call to Ministry with your pastor.

4. Have you taken into consideration that as a minister of the Gospel, there is a strong possibility that you will change? How might you see yourself changing?

5. As part of your decision to enter ministry, have you taken into consideration why? If you have been called to ministry, why have you accepted that calling now? What are you hoping to gain and what are you searching for in this process? What questions are you trying to find answers for?

6. When looking at categories of why you believe you have been called to ministry, which ones do you relate to? Give examples for each situation. This step is very important. Here is part of the discovery process by which you will begin the authentication process of your calling.

For Whom God Calls

Chapter 5
Is There A Need For An Edified Ministry?

Few subjects are more controversial in the Black church as the argument for or against the necessity for formal religious education as a qualification to be an effective minister of the Gospel of Jesus the Christ. Even as you engage this book and its readings, there is a debate within you deciding to what extent an "education" is necessary to fulfill your ministry calling. If not, I'm confident that external forces try to influence you one way or the other.

In my experience, the attitudes and opinions of formal religious education, such as seminary or bible college, are directly related to incentives for ordination. In other words, if your pastor says you need formal education for ordination, you will seek and be an advocate of it even if you previously disagreed with its necessity. In essence, you'll do whatever is necessary to attain the title/reward of ordination. Conversely, if your pastor does not believe in the need for such preparation as the seminary of bible college, you'll likewise be a mouthpiece against the need for education.

No matter where you stand on the subject, now is the time to challenge your beliefs. I've encountered many ministers whose opinion waivers on the issue according to the company of people they're surrounded by at the time. As you engage this reading, you will find yourself in agreement with many of the points Dr. Pitts is making. My recommendation is to take the time to examine your stance thoroughly and why you take the perspective, you're taking.

Many ministers fall victim to the opinions of others versus what God has placed on their hearts. Here would be another excellent place to begin your authentic "self-speak" to arrive at the root of your motivations for ministry and whether or not you need more than what your local context is providing. Savor this moment of reflection.

"A STUTTER AND A STICK"
THE (NON-)VALUE OF EDUCATIONAL CREDENTIALING

Richard N. Pitt

Competence in ministry became tied to one's educational pedigree, and that pedigree could be earned, in certain religious traditions, only by attending these institutions. These schools were attractive to many Congregationalist ministers who were losing their hold on local congregations and being forced to become itinerant preachers. Without the status inherent in being head of a congregation, they needed some other way to separate themselves from the laity. The seminaries gave them "new bases of professional status; where revivalists distinguished themselves from the laity by fiery preaching, the new breed of Congregational ministers would seek this distinction in a learned and autonomous elaboration of theology." The belief in seminary's importance was so strong that when their status was threatened by itinerant preachers, seminary-trained clergy succeeded in passing laws making it illegal for parishes to call a pastor without a college degree.

The Resurgence of the Untrained Revivalist

This practice of requiring a degree was effective when most colonists were members of Presbyterian, congregational, and episcopal congregations; in 1776, 55 percent of religiously active Americans belonged to one or the other of these denominations." As new religious sects born in the late eighteenth and early nineteenth centuries-the Methodist Episcopal church, the Baptist Triennial Convention, the Latter-day Saints, and others-began to blossom and challenge more established denominations, the preeminence of seminary training began to falter. These new sects ballooned in size as a result of the ministry of effective, energetic, but uneducated itinerant preachers. This brought them into open conflict with mainline clergy such as Timothy Dwight, the Congregationalist president of Yale College (1795-1817) and founder of Andover. Dwight denounced followers of the upstart denominations, using an argument that equated the clergy with other classical professions. He said:

> They demand a seven years' apprenticeship, for the purpose of learning to make a shoe, or an axe [yet] they suppose the system of Providence... maybe all comprehended without learning, labor, or time. While they insist, equally with others, that their property shall be managed by skillful agents, their judicial causes directed by learned advocates, and their children, when sick, attended by able physicians; they were satisfied to place their Religion, their souls, and their salvation, under the guidance of a quack.

In spite of the charges leveled against them, the new denominations decried the need for formal religious education well into the mid-nineteenth century. They argued that seminary education would "make them dependent on their books and written sermons rather than the movement of the Spirit which was central to the revival experience."

There were clear benefits for not depending on seminary-trained ministers. At the organizational level, denominations could grow quickly without the lag between someone's professing a call and their ability to start operating in it. Clergy shortages were almost unheard of. Training for new preachers occurred in short apprenticeships, often while those preachers co-led smaller units of larger local congregations. There were also benefits to the ministers themselves. Men from non-elite backgrounds could claim a calling and pursue ministry, with all of the authority and autonomy that comes with the title. They assumed the status of professionals, at least within their own religious denominations, without one of the most important trappings of professionalism:

formal religious training. Most importantly, they seemingly maintained some level of effectiveness at their craft, which enabled them to continue to attract adherents.

While the Baptists, Methodists, and other new denominations fought credentialing for many years, once their prominence made them the new protectors of the clergy's professional status, these now-mainline institutions began to turn to seminaries as a means of patrolling the borders of that status. Today, a non-seminary-trained member of the clergy in the mainline denominations is the exception rather than the rule. If not a requirement, seminary or seminary-like training is becoming a clear expectation for ordination in these formerly "new" American sects. In the contemporary mainline denominations, ordination usually follows some evidence that the aspirant has mastered specialized knowledge. While internships in a local congregation or chaplaincy position along with some kind of denomination sanctioned examination may constitute part of that evidence, neither is a strong substitute for an advanced degree in religion. Consider that there are seventeen seminaries or schools of theology affiliated with the United Methodist Church and its predecessor denominations. Similarly, twenty seminaries are affiliated with three of the largest Baptist denominations. Not surprisingly, like their nineteenth-century antagonists, these denominations are beginning to experience the very clergy shortages they warned against.

Both the memberships and the clergy pools of many mainline denominations (including former upstarts like the Methodists) are being dwarfed by sects born in the latter part of the nineteenth century. These include the Jehovah's Witnesses and Pentecostal-Holiness sects. Zikmund's study of clergy determined that less than half of the ministers in (predominately White) Pentecostal denominations attend seminary. While not being stridently anti-seminary, these denominations have returned to the apprentice- style of training that characterized early versions of practically every new American religious tradition.

Joining them have been what sociologist Donald Miller calls "new paradigm" congregations: nondenominational churches and innovative religious movements like the Vineyard Church and Calvary Chapel, which train their ministers in similar ways. In

Miller's study of the leadership of these pre- dominantly White and moderately charismatic ministries, he encountered the kind of emphasis on calling above all else which was present in my interviews with Pentecostal ministers. Rejecting the need for seminary, the founder of the Calvary Chapel network is quoted as saying, "God does not call those who are qualified, but qualifies those who are called;" In listing the kinds of qualities that guide the selection of leaders, Miller points to characteristics like "passionate commitment to God" and "a Spirit-filled life" as the only prerequisites for effective ministry according to these movements. "After all; he adds, "they say, Jesus used a group of fishermen to establish his kingdom".

The Black Church and Educational Credentialing

Formal religious training has been a factor almost from the beginning for the Black church in America. In fact, barely three years after its founding in 1816, the African Methodist Episcopal (AME) Church had created a publishing house that produced study materials for young ministers. Soon, they began to develop Sunday school programs, a development that helped to solidify the Black church's position at the heart of many Black communities. In the absence of opportunities to do so in any other way, former slaves and their descendants were learning to read in these classes, with the Bible as a counterpart to the "New England Primer".

In 1844, while the AME's White Methodist peers were still debating the Congregationalists about the value of seminary training, this new sect created the Union Seminary in Ohio. The seminary's objective was explicitly to educate "young men who propose to enter the Christian ministry". Soon after Union Seminary became what is now Wilberforce University (the oldest private degree-granting historically Black university), the church organized the Payne Theological Seminary. Alongside Atlanta's Gammon and Turner seminaries, which were also founded by AME bishops, Payne is one of the oldest historically Black seminaries in the country. In many ways, the AME church has been the only one of the Black denominations to fully embrace the value of formal religious training as an important component of credentialing. While there has been a considerable increase in the numbers of Black clergy graduating from accredited divinity schools or seminaries, much of that growth has been in the AME denomination, which has the highest percentage (48-51 percent) of "trained" clergy. They are also the only historically Black church that has made the degree of master of divinity a requirement for pastoring.

The majority of Black clergy do not have seminary training. According to most studies, it is believed that about one-third of all black clergy have had some religious training beyond the college level. Only 10-20 percent of Black clergy are estimated to have completed their professional training at an accredited divinity school or seminary. Of the largest Black Protestant denominations, the Church of God in Christ has the smallest percentage of ordained clergy with graduate degrees (19 percent). Certainly some of this trend is a function of cost and time. Many Black pastors are bi-vocational, splitting their time between full-time secular employment and part-time pastoring. But there is also a cultural angle: as in the "new paradigm" congregations, most of the religious talent in Black Pentecostal and Baptist churches is homegrown. For the majority of clergy in these denominations, apprenticeship training with a senior pastor is often the only educational requirement for ordination.

Specialists without Spirit, Sensualists without Heart

In many Black denominations, the same arguments that White Methodists and Baptists used to reject training at Andover are still being used to reject seminary degrees today. These arguments, when based on scripture at all, are often drawn from passages like 1 John 2:27, which reads "the anointing which you received from [Christ] abides in you, and you do not need that anyone teach you ... the same anointing teaches you concerning all things". The message implicit in this warning about false teachers, a label occasionally used to describe seminarians, is that anything a religious leader needs he can get directly from God; everything else is counterfeit. The historians C. Eric Lincoln and Lawrence Mamiya explain that contemporary efforts to mandate seminary training collide with these long-held attitudes…

For Whom God Calls
COGIC and Educational Credentialing

While the current leader of the COGIC, Bishop Charles Blake, has earned a master's and a doctoral degree in divinity, no other COGIC Presiding Bishop has earned more than a bachelor's degree. The founder of the denomination, Bishop C. H. Mason, was admitted to and attended the Arkansas Baptist College. While considered a talented student by the college's leaders, Mason withdrew after three months because of frustrations with both non-scripture-centered teaching methods and the doctrinal perspectives of the faculty. In spite of this, Mason was a strong advocate for education, encouraging education-leader Dr. Arenia Mallory to found the denomination's Saints.

Industrial and Literary School (now Saints Academy) in 1926 in Atlanta. His successor, Bishop J. 0. Patterson Sr. later established the C. H. Mason Seminary and the system of jurisdictional colleges that have since become the Jurisdictional Institutes discussed earlier. The jurisdictional college for the Memphis area became the All Saints Bible College in 2002 and offers a bachelor's degree in religious studies. The COGIC denomination now owns both undergraduate and graduate institutions designed to train aspiring ministers but still has no requirement that aspirants possess degrees of any kind. While some of my respondents have taken at least one Bible college or seminary course, many ministers maintain a fairly negative appraisal of seminary and seminary-trained clergy.

This is not to say that COGIC ministers are anti-education; nearly two thirds of those I interviewed have some college experience. In fact, the educational range of these ministers is a broad, and likely surprising one. A little more than a third of the ministers have no college experience at all. Three of those all women have less than a high school diploma, with one having attended formal schooling only to the fifth grade. Even if they wanted to, these ministers (half of whom have terminal clerical licenses) would not qualify for seminary admission because they don't hold bachelor's degrees. About 43 percent of the ministers are college graduates. Only two of my respondents have undergraduate degrees in religion or theology.

Consistent with the norms for Blacks, the men in my sample are less likely to have gone to college or received bachelor's degrees than the women. One in every five ministers has received some kind of post-baccalaureate degree, but most of these degrees are in something other than religion: either business, education, or social work. Two female ministers were pursuing law and medical degrees. Only eight ministers, five men and three women, have master's degrees or doctorates in divinity. In addition to these eight, twelve other ministers report spending time in some kind of formal religious training.

Hidden in these numbers is a more surprising finding. Half of the ministers without any college experience currently hold either an Elder's or Evangelist's license. One of these is a pastor. Of all the ministers who have these terminal credentials, only one-quarter indicate having spent any time in a seminary or Bible college; less than half of those have degrees. Of the pastors I interviewed, only half have seminary degrees. These numbers make clear the role that educational credentialing plays or, more precisely, doesn't play, in the ordination process of Black Pentecostal ministers. Not only is seminary or Bible college training not a requirement of ordination, it could not even be considered normative. It is the rare COGIC minister who has pursued or completed such training.

There is a structural reason for this. The most likely explanation would be that most Black ministers, regardless of denomination, come to recognize a call to ministry late in life. These "late-career" clergy are, understandably, less likely to pursue seminary degrees. While this trend is especially prevalent in Black churches, studies of other religious communities suggest that many clergy decide to pursue callings at a later age than in the past. Compared to their counterparts who have been in ministry for ten to twenty years, clergy in both mainstream Protestant and historically Black denominations are getting ordained six to seven years later. According to religion Jackson Carroll, the median age at ordination was thirty-nine for Black clergy who have been in ministry for less than ten years. That number ranges from twenty-one to thirty-two for clergy who have been ministering longer than that.

For Whom God Calls

One can see from my sample that many COGIC ministers are also late-career clergy. The average age of Aspiring Ministers and Missionaries is forty-five, with men claiming a call to ministry two years later than women. Concomitant with their late-career decision as clergy is that every one of my respondents would be considered second-career clergy as well. Accordingly, for many of them, their educational training is more closely aligned with their pre-call occupation than with a clerical one. This too is becoming the norm, regardless of race and denomination. While young men and women are still coming into the ministry directly from college, they are in the minority. Most new clergy, including those who have attended seminary, are coming to ministry from another career path. While the second career trend is not abnormal for mainline and conservative (White) Protestant denominations, where nearly half of the clergy are second-career, it is more significant in Black churches. Almost 80 percent of Black pastors had a different occupation before actively pursuing a call.

In terms of both late-career and second-career entrants, the clergy is quite different from medicine and law. The age for entry in these professions still hovers around twenty-four to twenty-six; the decision to pursue a law or medical degree generally happens at age twenty-one. The average age at which aspirants seek ordination is thirty-one. Compare that number to the average in my sample (forty-five years), and it is clear that pursuing a call by seeking additional educational credentials is prohibitive, based on the disruption to one's life that decision might cause. This disruption is exacerbated by the twin challenges of finding and affording an appropriate seminary.

While the structural barriers are quite real, the church does not see them as insurmountable for someone claiming a call to ministry. The pressures to have appropriately trained ministers weighs heavily on many congregations, especially those in urban areas. As COGIC leadership changed, they launched new priorities for the church as it moved toward the new millennium. One of those priorities was responding to the need for a more professional clergy.

In 1995, the COGIC Assembly mandated that anyone seeking professional status via ordination must complete the denomination's two-year certificate program. Part of the curriculum for the certificate can be found in the Understanding Bible Doctrine as Taught in the Church of God in Christ textbook and workbook. The book is "designed to acquaint the candidate [for ordination] with the biblical teachings which constitute the doctrines of the Church of God in Christ". Aspirants are trained in eleven doctrinal areas: The Bible (Bibliology), God (Theology), Christ (Christology), the Holy Ghost (Pneumatology), Angels (Angelology), Demons (Demonology), Man (Anthropology), Sin (Hamartiology), Salvation (Soteriology), the Church (Ecclesiology), and the Last Things (Eschatology).

In addition to doctrine, the other pillars of training (i.e., those tested in written/oral examinations) for ministers are church history and organization. They are required to know COGIC history, COGIC polity and structure, and church protocol. Some training is also offered in Bible study techniques and homiletics (sermon preparation and delivery). The assumption (stated in the introduction to the handbook) is that "all candidates for ordination must complete the catechism before receiving ordination". In spite of this mandate, few of my sample's recent licentiates or ordinands had even seen, let alone completed, the catechism in the back of the training manual. As with many mandates in the Church of God in Christ, the decision to require completion of the seventy-six-page catechism belongs to the Jurisdictional Bishop alone. If he does not require the catechism as part of the credentialing process, it may or may not be used. In larger COGIC churches, the training in catechism is facilitated by in-house courses overseen by a, usually, seminary-trained Elder or Evangelist. The courses themselves are often taught by clergy, but many churches draw on expertise wherever it may reside in their congregation. As a result, licentiates and ordinands may be taking courses taught by lay-members and lay-leaders.

In order to receive a terminal license or to be ordained, female Deaconesses and male Licensed Ministers must pass both an oral and written test created by each jurisdiction's ordination board. The jurisdiction's Commissioner of Ordination uses these tests as the key qualifiers for his recommendation to the Jurisdictional Bishop (and for women, the jurisdiction's Supervisor of Women) that the aspirant be given their final credential. This test, based largely on the catechism, can be a stumbling block for some. Ordination committee members gave examples of ministers who could competently give stirring sermons and served the church passionately, but could not pass the written test. In some cases, the minister had to retake the test multiple times until he or she could pass it. Again, as with most COGIC mandates related to training and credentialing, the final decision resides in the hands of the Jurisdictional Bishop. If the recommending pastor can make the case, as one ordination committee member quoted, that "no number on some test should get in the way of this young man's destiny," the bishop may waive the test as a requirement.

    It is important to note that these are requirements for ordination. In most cases, the local requirements for licensing (which are entirely controlled by the local pastor) are much less structured. In addition to offering some suggestions for aspiring licentiates (e.g., "write one message or lesson each month and present it to your pastor"), one jurisdiction's training manual for aspiring ministers informs them of how the process might proceed: Wait for the day that your pastor tells you that he will bring you before the church to be licensed. The process may differ from pastor to pastor. You may desire to ask your pastor to tell you his manner. This is not to question his manner or to tell him how someone else does it. You are asking that you may [sic] know how best to wait with patience. Some pastors will have you preach on a given evening and after you have preached he then will go forth to issue you the license. Other pastors will license you based on your faithfulness alone. The manner is left to the local pastor and you will be licensed based on your fitting into his system.

    This description is a very real example of how imprecise the local-licensing process is for Licensed Ministers and Deaconesses. Much of this flexibility is a result of COGIC's (and, more broadly) Pentecostalism's tensions with what historian Grant Wacker refers to as a "primitive" otherworldliness and a very practical and realistic "pragmatism." Pentecostalism, more than any other Christian religious tradition, is practically defined by non-predictability and lack of standardization – a sovereign God demands the freedom to act, unconstrained by human rationalism. However, Pentecostal religious leaders are working under the same pressures to maintain professional standards of competence that their less Spirit-oriented counterparts are. These pressures have created long-standing tensions, with which Pentecostalism has had mixed results.

Webers Priests, Prophets, Charisma Priestly Professionals

To some degree Wacker's description of those two poles- the pragmatic and the primitive-finds a corollary in Max Weber's description of two kinds of religious leaders. The clergy can be divided into two ideal types, priests and prophets, the first being the pragmatic professional and the latter the primitive personality. Weber suggests that "priests" are, essentially, religious bureaucrats whose primary duty is to patrol the borders of religious ideology. They protect religious institutions by sacralizing certain actions, texts, and interpretations of those texts, drawing clean lines between the traditional values of the community and the tendencies of laity to reject that orthodoxy. The danger here is amplified as religious communities interact with other communities or expand via conversion.

Whether labeled priest, pastor, or cleric, religious professionals represent the religious establishment. Their professional status is intrinsically bound to the success of the "corporate enterprise of salvation" they protect. Like any professional, Christian priests' claims to authority are tied to their monopoly of some body of knowledge and the practice associated with it. This is not just a question of claiming exclusive rights to mediate man's communication with God. Weber argues that not only do they claim to "monopolize the regular management of Yahweh worship and all related activities" but they also claim "a monopoly in the employment of certain oracular formulae, priestly teaching, and priestly positions". In essence, they seek to control the methods by which God communicates with mankind.

Of course, in order to control knowledge, a professional group must standardize that knowledge. In this way, people who stake a claim to knowledge can be tested and deemed legitimate. Physicians have done this by embracing empiricism, moving farther away from seeing medical practice as "art" and beginning to depend more on the efficiency produced in scientific and technical discovery. This move has been effective. Beyond first aid, few laymen would consider themselves competent to meet their own health care needs. "Priests" have been less successful, even with the advent of professional schools, at retaining a monopoly over the arcana of religious practice. Inasmuch as most Protestants take seriously the New Testament principle of the "priesthood of all believers," the doctrine of priestly mediators between man and God loses much of its meaning. As a result, mainline churches are losing members as congregants find themselves fully capable of meeting their own religious needs.

Consider, for example, one of the most sacred religious traditions in the Christian church: administration of the Eucharist. While still mystical in some ways, its management by contemporary priests has become as rationalized as any other priestly duty. Many churches use pre-filled communion cups advertised as "a communion wafer and grape juice in one sanitary, single-serving container". Laymen can buy these in the same stores where they purchase other paraphernalia once reserved for clergy. In fact, the book by the Pentecostal evangelist Perry Stone, The Meal That Heals, encourages readers to take communion at home as a kind of prophylactic against illness.

The idea of a trained clergy, already firmly embedded in largely bureaucratic organizations, points to the rationalization of ministry. It might be argued that such training promotes the rational over the traditional, a preference for logical answers over mystical ones. Thus the work of religious professionals becomes formulaic: evangelizing a new convert? Just teach them their "ABCs"-A(dmit your sins), B(elieve in Jesus), C(onfess Him as Savior). A congregant is ill? Just "PRAY"-P(raise), R(epent), A(sk), and then Y(ield). Preaching? Wash your mouth out with "SOAP"-S(cripture), O(bservation), A(pplication), and P(rayer). This development has the potential to lead to the kind of "too much education in ... and too much spirit exits" phenomena that Tavis Smiley warned about at his 2003 conference. Weber, too, warned of this possibility when he spoke of "specialists without spirit". While he was speaking of any worker who gave into the bureaucratization of life, the larger context of his comments make this relevant to the question of religious professionalism as exemplified in "priests:'

Charisma and Prophets

While the priest still plays a critical role in religious communities, he is not the only game in town. While much of the priest's influence is tied to his position in the church, that position and its authority rides on the personal holdings of the priest himself. Weber describes these as "his professional equipment of special knowledge, fixed doctrine, and vocational qualifications, which brings him into contrast with sorcerers, prophets, and other types of religious functionaries who exert their influence by virtue of personal gifts (charisma) made manifest in miracle and revelation". In this summary, Weber introduces readers to another trait held by religious leaders – specifically, prophets – a trait whose meaning is as contested as that of the word "professional".

Indeed, charisma has the power to make a lowly carpenter the "savior of the world" even more than two thousand years after his death on a cross. It made a German shoemaker able to take a distorted version of that cross and make it the most hated symbol in the world. Its power took four young musicians from Liverpool and gained them crowds of crying, fainting followers in America and around the world. For Weber, the chief distinction between priests and prophets is the prophet's holding of "charisma," which he defined as a certain quality of an individual personality, by virtue of which one is "set apart" from ordinary people and treated as endowed with supernatural, superhuman, or at least specifically exceptional powers or qualities. These as such are not accessible to the ordinary person, but are regarded as divine in origin or as exemplary, and on the basis of them the individual concerned is treated as a leader.

Those endowed with charisma gain legitimacy as authority figures because people believe them worthy of being followed. As a result, churches led by charismatic leaders are initially characterized more by followship than by fellowship. The charismatic prophet's authority is freely given to him or her, and this legitimates them in a very different way than the traditional or bureaucratically determined authority of the priestly professionals. Weber argues that the legitimacy of true charismatic personalities resides in the followers' belief that the leader just has "it" and that it is their duty to be devoted to the individual. There is rarely any evidence of this kind of genuine charisma, that is, charisma not catalyzed by some evidence supporting a belief that the person has exceptional qualities. Weber focuses more on the kind of charismatic authority granted as a result of one's magical abilities, prowess on the battlefield, or ability to enthrall and manipulate. In order for these actions to legitimate someone's leadership, they must be perceived as worthwhile or important themselves.

In this way, most charismatic communities are, at least initially, governed by an emotional action orientation. Unfortunately, emotional social action is tenuous and is easily undone. If there is a weakening of the evidence of charisma, the followers may rescind their "offer" of legitimacy and the charismatic's following would minify. Traditionally, this evidence was based in some magical or heroic ability that was usually not sustainable. Defeats in war, droughts, and locust attacks were easy proof that the charismatic leader may have fallen out of favor with the gods. Today, something like a terrible selection of songs or poor reviews of a movie can just as easily bring a charismatic leader down.

Weber describes the prophet's powers as the source of his appeal, his charismatic authority. The "anointing" may operate in this same way, granting one the ability to perform in the prophetic role, making the absence of priestly "vocational qualifications" irrelevant. But what is this "anointing" and how does it function?

The Anointing: Defined

The clearest description of "the anointing" comes from COGIC Missionary, Kenya. She describes it as "a special impartation through the Holy Spirit to give you the wisdom, the know-how, the revelation to do what it is you need to do from a spiritual perspective. The things that I go forth to do, I know that me and my own ability wouldn't come up with the ideas, the creativity, the understanding that I have. That doesn't come from a natural ability." Kenya's description of her abilities as unnatural are, in some ways, surprising. From an outsider's perspective, one might look at the religious labor she does-teaching in and helping to administer the church's youth Bible study- as fairly routine and manageable. This is especially the case given her secular training and employment as a program coordinator in the local school district. She says she has a gift to teach and a gift to administer, but in order to be effective in her calling, she must be anointed to do it. She explains:

> Like with [Vacation Bible School]. A curriculum was set before me. So now I need the anointing from the Lord to tell me how to teach this so it would fit this particular group of people. I don't perceive me getting that from just regular intellect. I need the direction and guidance of the Holy Spirit who knows the needs of the people, who knows how it needs to be set up, who knows what needs to be done. The Holy Spirit gave me the creativity on how to map it all out.

Even though a minister might appear to have the requisite skill set to perform church tasks, they downplay those skills. Kenya certainly has the ability to organize a classroom and teach a set of materials given to her by her church's education coordinator; she does similar tasks every day as a middle-school administrator. But from her perspective, religious labor requires some skills she does not naturally have. When she speaks of needing to know how to "teach this so it would fit this particular group of people;" she's referring to something other than being able to teach at a grade-appropriate level. She is speaking of needing a kind of supernatural insight into what approach might best be used to have an impact on her students. This "revelation to do what it is you need to do" is attributed to divine intervention via this anointing that she describes.

When this anointing is activated, the ministers claim to be supercharged. Again and again, they used the word "power" to describe what they felt the anointing gave them. Their abilities to do ministry are not just unnatural; they're supernatural. For example, Amy goes farther than Kenya in describing what she is capable of doing when anointed. She is not just more creative or more capable
of understanding complex theology. When in "preaching mode" she says, "even the state that I'm in at the time is not a normal state to be in because I'm hyperaware of my surroundings and what's going on in the room. I can hear things I couldn't normally hear; I

can see things that I couldn't normally see. And so that's not me. I know that that's not me".

In the absence of any seminary training to perfect their skills as preachers or teachers, ministers pointed to the impact of their anointing. Even when they described working for hours on sermons, ultimate credit for the success of the sermon went to the anointing. Consistently, ministers described the anointing as empowering them to preach. As Carl says, "Right now, if I were suddenly asked to preach, I feel the Lord's anointing will come on me to be able to preach. That's the power of God that comes on you and allows you to do whatever He calls you to do." At the time Carl said this, he had been an Aspiring Minister for just one year, and yet he believed wholeheartedly that, with very little training, he would be capable of successfully preaching a sermon on the spot. Nothing in his professional training as a baker could prepare him to do that. Prior to having a call (and having it endorsed by his pastor), he likely would not have considered himself capable of such a thing. But he understands the calling and the anointing as a package deal. With one, he has access to the other.

Because most ministers serve in some capacity alongside people who neither claim a call nor claim to "operate under an anointing;' they must have a way to distinguish themselves from other religious laborers. One way they do this is by speaking of the anointing as something different from talents, skills, and gifts. Essentially, they argue that someone might have a set of gifts or talents – which they are as likely to attribute to hereditary origins as divine ones – that enable them to be effective as a religious laborer. But, they explain, the gifts or talents can be absent, and the anointed person can still be effective. The most common example used to explain this phenomena was musical ministry. The comments of one Evangelist, Katherine, capture this idea:

> See, the calling and the anointing go together, but a gifting and an anointing may not. I can be gifted to sing, hitting all the right notes. And you're the person that cannot sing. But if God has anointed you, I believe God does something not just to the giver but to the receiver. Although you sound like junk, because the anointing is on your life, they're not even hearing your bad notes. What they're hearing is what

you're singing and the message that you're giving. But if I can sing, but there's no anointing there, I believe that nobody's receiving anything from that.

While many describe the anointing as enabling them to do the kinds of tasks one might be otherwise trained or skilled at, like teaching or singing, they also describe its importance in managing other tasks. Many COGIC ministers, both men and women, ordained and licensed, are expected to do more than preach sermons, teach classes, and administer the sacraments. Additional responsibilities that some ministers claim to be anointed to do are drawn from a list of gifts found in Ephesians 4:11-13 that includes serving, encouraging, contributing to the needs of others, giving, leading, and showing mercy. Like teaching, many of these responsibilities are shared by lay-members in the COGIC church. Ordained and licensed ministers participate in these tasks but don't consider them the exclusive domain of someone who is called. That said, many believe these tasks are important enough that anyone doing them should be anointed. Essentially, they believe that everyone who does ministry, including what many might consider lay-ministries like choral music, ushering, and hospitality, should be anointed for it, even if they have not been called as a minister.

There is another set of tasks, though, that COGIC ministers argue requires both a calling and an anointing. In some cases, both COGIC doctrine and the Bible explicitly charge clergy with these tasks. According to the COGIC manual, the church believes in and practices divine healing. It describes scriptural commands for spiritual leaders to heal, pointing most directly at the quotation compelling a sick church member to "call for the elders of the church, and let them pray over him, anointing him with oil in the name of the Lord. And the prayer of faith will save the sick, and the Lord will raise him up." (James 5:14-15). Healing is still practiced widely and frequently in the Church of God in Christ and, according to the manual, "testimonies to healing in [the] church testify to this fact."

My respondents believe that the list of supernatural abilities enumerated in 1 Corinthians 12:8-10 and other places, which include giving prophecies, discerning and subduing evil spirits, speaking in or understanding unlearned languages, and having special insight into or knowledge of circumstances, are real and actively practiced by COGIC clergy. In fact, many ministers listed one or more of these attributes as a function of their own call to ministry. While one might imagine not needing any supernatural powers to give a sermon or distribute meals to the homeless, these forms of religious labor would certainly require something more than a course in homiletics. Believing themselves responsible to carry out these tasks, ministers find in those responsibilities their biggest premise for requiring an anointing. For example, Paulette describes her ability to heal parishioners:

> The anointing of God comes in and empowers you to do certain aspects that He has called you to do. I couldn't lay hands on the sick and they recover if I didn't have the anointing of God. If He calls you, He's going to empower you to do what He's commissioned for you to do. The anointing is when it is not you yourself operating. You realize that you could not have done that and it's not you. You are now operating at a point that you know it is only God himself.

Anointing Carriers and the Anointing Infused

When it comes to understanding how the anointing operates in their lives, ministers seem to come in two types. While some ministers blur these distinctions in their descriptions, the vast majority of them tend to fall into two clear categories. The first, and smaller category of ministers, are "anointing-carriers." They consider the anointing to be something they always have, making them certain that whenever they have an opportunity to do ministry, they will be effective. In light of this, some believe they carry their anointing with them in non-religious environments, such as shopping malls, as well as religious venues.

Some ministers believe that their anointing is useful for what we might consider secular tasks, but which they see through a spiritual lens. For example, Courtney claims to use her anointing when shopping:

When I go shopping, my thing is I need God to lead me. I pray and ask Him first for the parking space, then I pray and ask Him to guide me to be a good steward over what He has blessed me with. Once, I had to buy something for my daughter and the thing was like $700, but I found it in this little obscure place for $30. I consider He led and He guided me. He anointed me to spend the money that He blessed me with. For others, the anointing is not used to function in these situations.

As Katherine says, "it's not that deep with me. I don't use the anointing in the mall. I rather use my natural abilities when it comes to certain things. Not to say that I don't need the Lord or the guidance of the Holy Spirit in my everyday life. Yes, I do. But it's just certain things that I feel capable of." Most carriers argue that the anointing's presence within them makes them capable of operating in their calling at any given moment. In fact, some claimed to be anointed during the interview, suggesting that this power would ensure that they said what God needed them to say in response to my questions.

Anointing-carriers tend to describe the anointing as "rising up" in them or "coming out" of them, almost as if it lies dormant until they have a ministry opportunity. Natalie says:

> I would say that there is an anointing on my life, but I don't believe it's activated except when I have to step before God's people to do ministry. Sometimes I can be on my way to prison ministry and just be fleshly Natalie, driving in traffic trying to get there on time, screaming at the other drivers to get out of my. But I know that as soon as I get behind the podium, there's no more flesh there. It's all just anointing then.

Like Natalie, the anointing-carriers describe feeling anointed from the very moment they begin to do ministry. Raquel says, "it's there in me. It's part of me. I don't have to wait to get up behind the podium. It's in me before I even leave the house, so I know it's in me as I'm doing the work:'

For Whom God Calls

The second set of ministers refers to the anointing as something that comes upon them during an act of ministry. Like the "carriers; they expect the anointing to operate whenever they are doing ministry, but they were more likely to talk about the anointing as something they can feel descending on them at some point during the ministry act. For example, some would describe being in the middle of a sermon and feeling their "help coming on," This "help"- the anointing – was described as something they could literally feel, either as a flush or tingling of the skin or as a kind of head rush. Often this moment was accompanied by outbursts of glossolalia (or "tongues") or involuntary muscular tics ministers referred to as "quickening." Whatever the particulars of the) infusion, ministers claim to know precisely the moment when the anointing is activated.

Mylisha described the moment this way:

> God, how can I explain it? I can feel the presence of the Lord and I can feel the change within me and how the Word of God is just coming up, as the scripture says, "out of your belly shall flow rivers of living water"? I know it's God because of the things that are happening, how the Word of God is coming and coming, and then it's just overflowing. I can tell that the spirit of God is just taking over and I'm operating under the anointing.

It became clear in ministers' descriptions that this infusion of the anointing tended to occur only during acts of ministry they might consider needing to be "empowered" for. The moments most often given in examples were preaching, praying, and teaching-in that order. Ironically, no one mentioned "feeling the anointing" while participating in sacramental tasks (i.e., administering the Eucharist or baptism) reserved only for ordained clergy. The anointing may also be activated, in a felt way, only during those parts of one's religious service that they feel a particular call to.

Tasha, a Deaconess who also sings on her church's praise team, feels called to preach but doesn't describe herself as called, specifically, to music ministry. While she might not feel any particular infusion of the anointing while singing, she describes feeling something when asked to introduce a song to the audience:

> It's like this sensation'll come over me. And then I'll get up there, not having practiced anything, and it's like I can just, I'll get to talking, and the words aren't scattered. They're just flowing and they're connecting and they're ushering in the spirit of praise, and by the time I'm done, I'm like, wow, what did I say? When the anointing comes on me, I just know something's happening to me at that moment. I know this level of authority that comes on me, and it just takes me to another level.

Just as they can describe the moment when they receive the anointing, ministers seem to know when the anointing is withdrawn. They describe the circumstances of the anointing's infusion and withdrawal almost as one might describe an adrenaline rush. Amy says that "when that moment passes and that anointing kind of subsides, you're drained, you're tired, you feel like a wet towel." Again, they seem to experience the anointing as something physical and real. Kelly describes this moment the same way:

> When you're up ministering and stuff like that, you're highly anointed to do that. And you can go and do stuff like that, sweat like crazy, and don't pass out. And then as soon as you finished, then you're drained. Because that anointing's lifted off you. It's a supernatural ability that comes on you to do something at a particular time.

The Role of Audiences

Just as congregants play a role in legitimizing a minister's calling, they are also part of the process whereby one's anointing is confirmed. In some ways, the audience's response to a minister's preaching or teaching is, at once, a confirmation of both their calling and their anointing. To the extent that ministers believe that an anointing is evidence of a calling, they depend on a response to their anointing to legitimize their sense that they are called. This was not only evident in their statements about their own calling but in their evaluations of other ministers' callings as well.

Many anointing-carriers spoke of "fruit" as an important component of their belief in their anointing (see Jn. 15:1-8). In fact, their past experience with effective ministry seems to have led many of them to the belief that are always anointed. Katherine exemplifies a common anointing-carrier perspective when she explains:

> I know I'm anointed because everything that I do, everything that I set out to do, I see the fruits of it. I see the fruits in other people's lives. And I see the fruit in my life. I see the things that I've done in Christ based on what my calling is and my anointing. I see the fruits. It's like the seed is planted and here's the fruit of it.

A history of positive audience responses to her religious labor strengthened Katherine's belief that she had the ability to be successful in future exercises of her calling. Audiences help give meaning to the ability to do ministry just as they give meaning to the motivation for it. That said, anointing-carriers didn't always require a response in order to maintain their belief that they were anointed. Some described situations when they would pray for someone and nothing seemed to happen in that moment. These are the kinds of moments described earlier that might otherwise appear to be a test of one's calling and, pertinent to this chapter, anointing. In the absence of positive outcomes, they stated that their belief in their calling and anointing never wavered. They have reasons for this, backing up their claims using examples from the ministry of Jesus himself. While in most cases, Jesus' ministry had "immediate" effects, ministers made the case that his anointing didn't always operate that way.

Their primary argument was that every act of anointed ministry does not have an immediate effect, describing those situations as "as they went" encounters. Most describe these moments in terms of the biblical accounts of Jesus healing ten leper (Lk. 17:11-19) or healing a blind man (Jn. 9:1-7). In both accounts, the healing did not seem to happen in Jesus' presence. Instead, the lepers were cured as they went the priest and the blind man was only able to see after washing mud out of his eyes in the pool of Siloam. The ministers pointed to similar examples from their own ministry where they might tell someone to go to their doctor to confirm the effectiveness of a prayer for healing. Alternately, they extend the "fruit" metaphor to these circumstances, explaining that they are only "planting a seed" and that it takes time for the anointing to fully produce whatever outcome it is intended to produce.

They also read these two biblical stories as parables about deference to spiritual authority, essentially arguing that the healings required the lepers and the blind man to trust Jesus and follow his instructions. They suggest, for example, that the lepers' healing would not have happened had they not had faith in Jesus' power to heal them. Paulette argued this point exactly, extending it to her own preaching ministry:

> In that same way, God anoints the Word, but that Word has to land on good ground. People have to be receptive to it, and you can't always do something if somebody's not receptive. If they're not open to it, if they're not open to the will of God, you can have all the anointing in the world. It's not going to change their situation.

This is one of the ways that the anointing is different from charisma. Anointing-carriers like Paulette do not require a positive response from the people she ministers to. Charisma requires a response and is measured by its effectiveness at drawing followers. Paulette doesn't measure her effectiveness that way. When followers don't see results, she sees the problem as theirs: she would be more effective if the followers weren't so flawed. In this way, she can still maintain her belief in her anointing even if it doesn't engender a response.

Those who experience an "infused anointing" depend as much on their own physical sensations as the responses of an audience, but even they are clearly affected by audience interaction. In fact, they are more likely than anointing-carriers to speak of outcomes as a determinant of anointed ministry. Justine, a Deaconess at the time of her interview, spoke of the common occurrence of being drafted to do ministry without preparation and how much she depended on the anointing:

> So often in my experience I get surprised by chances to preach. There's no   real chance to do a lot of study and preparation before I have to get up there. I believe that that's why He does that; so that I don't try to make my whole purpose be to get up and to preach the people crazy. Half the time I'm not feeling anything but fear when I get up there. And I don't always get effects. One time I thought I was a bad preacher because the people just sat there.

This feeling of uncertainty, of wondering if the anointing will (or did) "show up" was describe by many as an important, and even desirable, attribute of the phenomena. For example, Joel defends his lack of certainty about the anointing, claiming that this uncertainty keeps him humble:

> Most of the time I know I've been operating in the anointing only when I'm walking away from a time of ministry. Because, see, I think that's where the flesh will come in if you say, "I'm walking in here and I'm going to blow these people away with my anointing:' It's not like you can turn the anointing on or off. I have to go in thinking I'm going in here to do what God has me to do. Then whatever happens, happens.

Obviously for ministers like Joel, the goal of any ministry opportunity is success at it. These ministers often measured their success both in the degree to which they "felt" anointed and on the level of response they got from their audience. These measures of success were more readily available in certain specific ministry situations. While anointing-carriers occasionally spoke of their anointing's activation in the absence of an audience (e.g., while praying alone or even doing the dishes), those who experienced anointing infusions almost always gave examples of ministry interactions with other people. In those cases, the audience's response played an important role in confirming their sense that even if they weren't on track with their plans for the lesson or prayer, they were still operating in an effective manner.

Reflecting on this, George described how he feels when he comes prepared to minister and God chooses to do something different:

> I have my objectives and all the key points that I want to hit. But when He begins to sidetrack me, make me deter from that, that's when I can see where people's hearts are being touched and the tears begin to flow. It's not me doing it. I don't think I'm saying something so amazing. I don't think it's just emotion either. I consider it the anointing of God working through me destroying that yoke, breaking those chains and those binds in the people's lives.

When the Anointing Falls

While George suggests that he is able to reflect upon his in-the-moment experience of ministry, some ministers claim to be so overtaken by the anointing that they go into a kind of dissociative fugue state. In that state, they are incapable of measuring their success by audience response. They suggest that under the anointing's influence, they are no longer in control of their bodies and have little recollection of the events that took place while ministering.

In some cases, they were very clear that they were lucid when this was happening. In explaining a moment when the anointing enabled her to pray with a congregant, Sharon said, "I don't know what I said to her after that, but I know it was words of encouragement. A whole different tone. I'm not saying I went into a trance or nothing, but God just spoke directly through me like in the movie Ghost with Whoopi Goldberg. That's how I knew it was the anointing." While Sharon knew the point when the anointing started to affect her, she had no recollection of what she said after that point. This phenomena seems to occur in a variety of situations. Monica says:

For Whom God Calls

> When I'm speaking, I'm not there. When I'm praying for somebody, I'm not there. I guess I just zone out for lack of a better phrase. I do things and have no idea that I did it. So I know it's not me because I'll have no recollection of saying or doing what people tell me I've done.

Monica describes various ministry opportunities where she was overcome by the anointing, experiencing it so powerfully that she describes herself as not even being conscious. A more dramatic version of this was relayed by Jeff who was also required to minister with little preparation:

> We have a model here where you need to be ready when called. One time they just called me up because the guy whose time it was didn't come. I got up there and I didn't have any idea what I was going to say. To tell you the truth, even now I can't tell you what I said. Afterwards I had to ask my wife what I said because I was gone. I remember standing up behind the podium and leaving the podium, but all that in between? No clue, Doc.

The most common element in these explanations of the anointing's function was these moments when ministry was required but the minister had no time to prepare. In a practical sense, this is no different than a lawyer having to think on his feet as his opponent changes course in the midst of a trial or a physician suddenly being called on to render first aid. But imagine that same physician having to do an emergency procedure and claiming, once done, that he "zoned out" and doesn't remember doing the operation. While our trust in that physician would be shaken by such an admission, similar admissions by ministers are intended to strengthen the hearer's trust in them as someone who is truly dependent on God for their successes.

Just as ministers resisted any suggestion that their calling was self-initiated, they consistently spoke of their actual religious labor as being outside of the scope of their own abilities. Unlike other professions, personal inadequacy and even lack of knowledge or skill authenticates one's membership in the corps of called and anointed ministers. Jimmy spoke of his ministry on the street team:

> To be able to have people crying in the street and accepting Christ? That ain't me. That's when the anointing's going. I'm just being used by God. So you know it's Him that draws everybody to his self, not me. I'm just there. Like I said, I'm not the smartest guy in the world, but Lord I'm available. Once again, I depend on Him and I trust Him to give me what to say and to do the work.

While charismatic leaders are often assumed to be outsiders-rabble- rousers who seek to usurp priestly authority-that is rarely the case. The prophet is often a member of the traditional organization who, through normal means, probably could not attain a leadership position at all. They could not make any claim to power based on position or purse. So, in a way, the possibility of charismatic authority allows nobodies to rise up and lead. The anointing enables seemingly unqualified men and women to do the same. For example, Jimmy's assertion that he's not the "smartest guy in the world" is one that was repeated in different ways by many of my respondents. They would often say things like "I know it wasn't me" or "I'm not smart enough to come up with that" as a way to underscore the authenticity of their calling. By claiming non-elite status (i.e., "I don't deserve to be used this way"), they strengthen the claim that their ability to effectively play out I the prophetic role isn't a function of origins, training, or even hard work. Instead, they argue, they depend fully on God's favor and His anointing. Success in ministry is not theirs to claim; the credit- or as they describe it, "the glory"- remains His.

When the Anointing Fails

An important rationale for only recognizing one's successes in ministry as a function of an anointing, rather than one's talents, training, or even preparation, is that sometimes the anointing fails. One of the most surprising characteristics of the anointing, and one that makes it quite different from the skills/knowledge one might gain by training, is the possibility that someone could "lose their anointing". For many of my respondents, a person could find themselves disempowered. Some had biblical examples for this possibility. The two most common examples were the biblical judge and strongman Samson and the first king of Israel, Saul.

In most cases, people were adamant that disobedience- whether in your use of your anointing or in your character-was grounds for losing one's anointing and that this loss could hinder one's effectiveness even if they are called. Apparently, an important aspect of access to this anointing, this power source, is the required absence-figuratively-of the body. Referred to as "the flesh" by many respondents, the body seemed to be a hindrance to the full activity of the anointing. The body, or "flesh;' is considered to be the locus of sinful behaviors and motivations; it is profane. As a result, it must be managed in order for the anointing, a sign of the minister's sacredness, to be fully activated. Amy speaks of this management, "Like at work, I'm having a hard time staying out of flesh. I really got to get that under subjection. When I know I ain't been right all week, I feel like God can't use me. My anointing can't be as high as it should be."

While some speak of having to actively manage their flesh, claiming to tamp it down or bring it into submission, others suggest that the anointing itself does the work of managing their flesh. As Jeff argues, "having the anointing is knowing that the spirit of God is there upon you. You're out of the way. The flesh is out of the way and it's the anointing of God, the spirit of God that has taken over with the power."

Ministers are adamant that even if a person is called to do ministry, there is the possibility that they could fail in that ministry if they haven't managed their flesh. They tend to describe the problem as the sociologist Emile Durkheim did when he described sacred things as "par excellence, that which the profane should not touch, and cannot touch with impunity." It seems that the profane "flesh" and the sacred "anointing" cannot abide in the same vessel. This idea was expressed more plainly by Mona:

I just don't see how God can bless mess. Now understand me. They may look effective. The people might shout and things, but if the ministers' life ain't holy, there's not going to be any real change going on because the anointing won't be there. God's anointing can't rest in an unclean vessel. Even David. He was a man after God's heart, but when he did that dirty thing with Bathsheba even he was praying, "Lord don't take your anointing from me."

Seminaries: Not Really "A School of the Prophets"

My respondents claim to have supernatural gifts and talents-an anointing. Why not do what other "prophets" like Jeremiah Wright or mega-pastor Rick Warren did and take those gifts to seminary? Why don't they become priests? The answer came early in the interviews when I asked some of my respondents a seemingly simple question: "Without any additional information, if you had to place your children in a Sunday school class taught by a teacher who claimed to be called to the ministry or one taught by a teacher who also claimed a call and had been trained in seminary, which teacher would you choose?" In every case but one, the respondents paused for a moment and then answered, often shyly, that they would choose the non-seminarian. Their answers came with critiques similar to this one from Deana, a forty-year-old teacher with both a bachelor's and a master's degree in education: "I would say the one who hasn't gone to seminary. Personally, I think if you need to go to school to learn how to do ministry, that's a crutch. You can tell the difference between someone who was schooled by man and someone who was schooled by the Holy Ghost."

In different ways, ministers seem to share Deana's rejection of seminary or other formal (i.e., outside of their local church or jurisdiction) training as part of the formula for effective ministry. They are likely advocates for general education, not only for themselves or their children but also for members of their congregations. But while they believe education is necessary for success in other occupations, most see ministry differently. They argue that the important ministerial skills cannot be taught and that people trained in seminaries are either "handicapped" or inauthentic ministers.

Seminaries Can't Teach It

As our discussion of the anointing shows, the primary reason for rejecting seminary is ministers' beliefs that the knowledge required to do most religious labor cannot be learned in the classroom. Claims to be able to heal illnesses, prophesy, and exorcise demons have long been central to Pentecostalism's understanding of itself as distinctive among Protestant religious movements. The historian Grant Wacker describes the testimonials of early American Pentecostals who sought the kind of power my respondents claim comes with the anointing: "Many, perhaps most, spiritual memoirs began by referring to years of intense yearning for an 'enduement of power: For some it meant the ability to perform apostolic miracles of healing and exorcism, for the others the ability to witness for Christ with extra-human boldness and effectiveness."

What is notable about this description of the Pentecostal's desire for supernatural ability is its inclusion of both "miracles" and of what might appear to outsiders as more natural, and trainable, achievements. It is not enough for Pentecostals to depend on the anointing to be able to do miracles. They also consider the anointing to be critical for witnessing, preaching, and other tasks that are taught in seminary courses. As such, they find seminary training in these areas irrelevant to one's effectiveness as a minister. While this was consistently voiced by ministers without any seminary training, it was echoed by some who had attended Bible colleges. Kelly explains:

> I went to Bible school. I learned the facts about the Bible and the history of the Bible and all that kind of stuff. But there wasn't much that they could teach me that I could really use to change people's lives. The revelation that I get directly from God is something different. When the anointing's there, it's like a supernatural ability to take that Word and really use it.

Michael H Sands

Seminarians Are Handicapped

Ministers' critique of seminary training goes farther than this. Not only do they consider such training unnecessary but they also describe it as problematic. Thus they would not just avoid prescribing seminary training for aspiring. Ministers, many offered proscriptions against it. One reason they denounce seminary training is their sense that seminaries hamper effective ministry. They worry that material taught in most university settings, but particularly in seminaries, is likely to be contrary to their beliefs. Their evidence for these suspicions are, in some ways, dependent on their own experience in these environments. Some point to courses in religious studies, sociology, anthropology, or English literature (e.g., "the Bible as literature") they had taken as undergraduate students at secular institutions. Tanya, a Deaconess, told us that "the professor told us on day one that he wasn't a believer and that we were just studying it as a book just like any other book. I should have known what I was getting into just from that, but I stayed anyway. I admit it caused me to question some things."

Some ministers state that they took these courses prior to receiving a call to ministry, and that these courses made them wary of similar training they expected to get in seminaries. Others, who had taken courses in Bible colleges or seminaries, reported similar experiences. Kathryn, a fifty-five-year-old Deaconess who has gone to seminary part-time over the course of three years, made the case that COGIC ministers need to be prepared to go to seminary. She discussed arguments she had gotten into with Sunday school students who had taken non-credit courses offered by a local Lutheran-affiliated seminary: "I've had some seminary training and I got caught up in it too. There was a way of thinking when I came out that made me look at things different. I think there's a danger in seminary. The Bible says 'lean not on your own understanding' and I think seminary can really take you away from that".

The harshest critiques against religious training came from a third group. Most ministers who criticized seminary training had had no experience at all with religious training outside of either their local church or their COGIC jurisdiction's training institutes. Their apprehensions were based on the testimonies of other ministers or on their own impressions of ministers who had pursued seminary degrees. Sheba, another young Deaconess, says she still occasionally considers taking courses at a local seminary but is skeptical of the benefits that training is supposed to provide. She worries that the courses might "take [her] backwards," a fear based on conversations with a seminary-trained mentor: "My old pastor-who had a degree, mind you- said that when you go to seminary, most of the teaching is contrary to what the Word is and what you believe. So if you're going to go to seminary, you better know your Word."

Curtis, who has been an ordained Elder for nearly twenty years but holds only a high school diploma, is not only critical of seminaries but of their product as well. He, like most of my respondents, maintains a belief that the anointing-more than training or preparation-is the key to a successful performance as a minister. He explains why he believes training is not only futile, but the lessons learned there might hinder effective ministry:

> I never prepare a whole lot because I've learned the hard way that you're never going to use that. Why? Because if God gets his opportunity, what he's going to reveal is revelation. It's going to be direct from him. That right there is one of the things you see a lot with people who have been [uses quotes with his fingers] "trained." They try to plan out their whole message. I think a lot of people who been taught in seminary are being taught how to do that and not relying on God to do it. The anointing's coming if you are relying on God to do it.

The emphasis on preaching is perhaps related, to some degree, to the accessibility that both trained and untrained ministers have to that particular form of religious labor. For example, at the church attended by a subset of my interviewees, one of their colleagues had been to seminary to be trained in pastoral counseling. The consensus about that minister was that her roles as preacher and counselor were different. At the time, she was serving as a counseling intern at the church, in preparation for receiving a chaplaincy at a local hospital. They believed that both jobs required an anointing, but the counselor position required the kind of training she received in seminary. In fact, they didn't criticize her at all, even after rendering more abstract criticisms against seminaries and seminarians. The specific task her training was being applied to had an impact on their acceptance of her training. Again, this suggests that there is no wholesale rejection of education. Instead, it may be the case that training which is attached to one's professional employment, even if ultimately religious in nature, is acceptable.

Seminarians Are Inauthentic

Curtis's statement denouncing "trained" ministers also points to another problem Pentecostals have with seminary training: it produces inauthentic ministry. Because so much of the called identity is tied to the idea that ministers cannot take credit for their successes, seminarians' ability to claim a learned set of skills seems anathema to their untrained peers. Even in those cases where ministers respect the skills of trained ministers, they still disparage them as less authentic than themselves. Carl, a forty-four-year-old aspiring minister with no college experience, does this when he says:

> It's not easy to preach. I can share my testimony, but to outline a sermon and really give God's people God's Word? That's not easy. We have some people here who are truly Bible students. They been to school and learned things I would never be able to get. So to stand before them and give them God's word, you have to come correct. But I know one thing, they can't hold a candle to someone really flowing in the anointing. Even without a degree. I know where God guides, he provides.

Untrained ministers, especially those without college degrees, resisted any suggestion that they needed seminary training to serve as ministers. Tequia, who has two years of college but no degree, argues that "ministry can't be like a vocation where you go to school and learn it like a trade, like some skills. I know what I have comes from God. I can't help wondering when some Dr. Such-and-Such preaches what book he got that message from."

For Whom God Calls

This was a common theme among these ministers. They argued that seminary-trained preachers were fakes, mimicking what they learned in classes, drawing on sermons they've read or watched as inspiration for the sermons they deliver. They spoke of religious labor as having technical aspects that accompanied good ministry but which weren't always necessary in order for that ministry to be effective. It was those aspects that they ridiculed as easily learned and copied by seminarians. Eric, a fifty-seven-year-old Aspiring-Minister whose full-time job as a human resource manager made pursuing seminary training difficult, pointed out the difference between his anointing and others' ability:

> I think that someone can have technical abilities to do certain things and not be anointed to do it at all. Like we can learn the mechanics of something and go through the motions of doing it but it doesn't mean that we're really called to do it; it's just that we can mimic doing it. You see that a lot in seminary-trained preachers. They learned how to do the technical work of ministry, how to talk, how to make sure you have three points, but they don't really have any real impact because they're not anointed.

This criticism was not just reserved for seminary training. A number of the ministers complained about being required to go to the jurisdictional courses on homiletics, those courses designed to teach techniques, principles, and standard practices in the delivery of sermons. Angela, an Evangelist with an associate's degree, argued that these classes simply become showcases for ministers' abilities to imitate their favorite preacher: "You can learn to do things in those classes. You can learn all the body language and it's just theatrics to me. I find today a lot of people emulate other big preachers. You'll know who they really like because you can see part of them in their stance or, their presentation. God don't make copycats."

The COGIC ministers' reliance on "the anointing" over seminary training as the source of their knowledge or skills need not be viewed as global anti- intellectualism. In some cases, while their defense of the anointing may have left little room for the possibility of training's impact on the core tasks of ministry, my own survey of popular books sold in their churches' bookstores told a different story. Entire shelves were heavy with books on intercessory prayer, expository teaching, counseling, leadership, spiritual warfare, healing, and even prophecy and divination. While these books were likely being purchased by clergy and laymen alike, it stands to reason that some of the clergy were using these books to supplement and reinforce their understanding of these phenomena. Indeed, some of the minister's homes had book collections that rival those of any seminarian.

These books are clearly written as how-to books. For example, there is a hugely popular book by the Black Pentecostal evangelist John Eckhardt titled Prayers That Rout Demons. The book claims to teach readers how to preach, prophesy, heal the sick, and cast out demons, the four major tasks my respondents say requires the anointing-not training-to accomplish. The publisher's description of the book says that it "combines powerful prayers with decrees taken from Scripture to help you overcome demonic influence and opposition in your life. It includes an introduction to spiritual warfare and biblical principles for praying along with specific declarative warfare prayers for every circumstance. Prayers That Rout Demons is your reference handbook for defeating the devil." The popularity of this book and a host of others points to the likelihood that Pentecostals believe that there is some room for instruction when it comes to even "supernatural" religious labor. It is likely that this belief is played out by my respondents and other non-seminarians in the church.

It is somewhat counterintuitive that having more education might decrease one's status in the minds of these Pentecostal ministers and the congregants they serve. But we see a similar dynamic in the ways self-taught artists and musicians describe themselves and the status given to them. The "authentic" artist is the one whose craft is uninfluenced by the established institutions, born of instinct rather than color-by-numbers-trained sensibilities. By producing this "primitive art," they gain status, not despite their lack of training but because of it. Gary Fine, a sociologist, quotes the art critic James Yood's description of this inverted status system:

> Intuitive [self-taught] art is seen then as the sole art of Arcadia, all else is fraudulent, mired in intellectual corruption,

needlessly obscure and pretentious. What was low now becomes high, what was high now becomes debased. New York is Gomorrah, education causes loss of originality.

Knowledge is insidious and we could easily replace the word "art" here for "ministry" and "New York" with "Harvard Divinity School" and find this an apt description of the beliefs about seminary training that many Pentecostals seem to hold. While we might expect untrained ministers to use such criticisms to counteract any damage to their own reputation or sense of themselves as serious pursuers of a call, this doesn't explain why even those ministers with religious training or even secular, but relevant, training provide the same appraisals. Again, we see the tension between pragmatism and primitivism, the priest's reason and the prophet's revelation. Although reason and pragmatism may be more valued in non-Pentecostal denominations, that is not the case among members of the Church of God in Christ. If there are only two explanations for a spiritual problem, "we figured out a solution" and "your faith has made you whole," the more appropriate answer in a denomination that considers its leaders prophets and not priests falls into the latter case.

It is for this reason that many professionally trained teachers in my sample don't claim the "logical" explanation for their success in Sunday school, claiming instead that their talents would be ineffective without the anointing. In this cultural context, the pragmatic or technical solution to spiritual problems – and every problem is, ultimately, spiritual in nature – is simply insufficient. It would be like trying to fix a crooked nail with a spoon.

There's nothing wrong with the tool; it's just the wrong one for the job. A Caveat on the Value of Seminary Training It would be unfair to suggest that all of my respondents were ill-disposed toward seminary or other formal Bible training. Some spoke quite eloquently about the evolution in their perspective about seminary training, an evolution that started at the same place that many of their peers remain. In contrast to those who saw seminary training as a handicap, these ministers spoke of the training as a possible asset. Like their peers, they still retained the sense that the ability to do successful ministry was dependent on the anointing", but they also recognize that outside of Pentecostal circles, a profession an anointing might be insufficient for some opportunities. Angelo, a twenty-nine-year-old Elder, has recently begun to pursue his bachelor's degree in hopes of eventually earning a master's degree in divinity. The son of a Baptist pastor and a COGIC Evangelist, he is well aware of the benefits of seminary training; his father has a doctorate in divinity.

Angelo, who was called to the ministry as a teenager, originally believed the anointing was all he would need to be effective in ministry. Using the apostle Paul as a model, he described how he came to realize it might not be enough:

> Initially I thought there were some things I had to work on like stage presence or people skills. When I was younger, I felt that while I needed to work on that, the anointing would help me through those deficiencies. But I've come to believe there's a greater quantity of people you can reach with the skill that comes from an education. Paul said we need to be all things to all people. He was trained in the religious seminaries of his time. He was a Jew but also had learned the culture of the Greeks and Romans, their language, their culture. Even though he had this undeniable experience with God, he was able to minister to the Gentiles because he had this education. While God can definitely give me the skills without a degree, there might be a need for it so I can identify with a greater number of people. There are some people who won't listen to me preach because I don't have a degree.

In his description of Paul, Angelo draws on a statement in 1 Corinthians where Paul proclaims "to the weak I became as weak, that I might win the weak: I have become all things to all men, that I might be all means save some" (1 Cor. 9:20-22). While Angelo suggests that seminary would be instrumental in enabling him to "be all things to all people," three of the ministers mentioned earlier-T. D. Jakes, Paula White, and Joel Osteen-are experts at shaping their messages to reach different audiences, and none of them learned those skills in seminary classrooms. Shayne Lee, a sociologist, and the historian Phillip Sinitiere, in describing T. D. Jakes's particular talents state, "Some may call this God's anointing, others may acknowledge it as the preacher's craft; but however one frames it, Jakes radiates the kind of energy that leaves audiences spellbound." Lee...details moments when Jakes, literally, follows Paul's example by "speak[ing] in the place of those hurting and longing for relief,' sometimes reviewing his own struggles before audiences in a way that makes his message more persuasive, more "touchable;' more "real."

These talents, shared by Osteen and White, are described as effective because of their conformance to sound psychological principles. Yet, we are also reminded that these powerful models of effective ministry, for example Osteen's "simple, pragmatic, and positive message ... the force behind his mass appeal" come from "unlettered evangelical innovators."

Deprofessionalizing Religious Professionals

It stands to reason that many Pentecostal ministers, and possibly many of those I interviewed, do not give much thought to the professional clergy's "seminary project." The religious labor that most of them engage in on a regular basis does not require study of systemic and philosophical theology, homiletics and liturgics, or even pastoral care and counseling. In most cases, licensed and even ordained COGIC ministers are completing tasks shared with lay-members of their churches. In fact, these ministers engaged in many of these very tasks-from praying for other congregants to directing church auxiliaries-before they ever considered pursuing a clerical credential. Certainly some kinds of religious labor require considerable skill or talent (e.g., instrumental ministry), but to be blunt, most ministry really isn't brain surgery. As a result, few ministers see any incongruence between their claims to be called to do ministry and their ignorance of the not-so-esoteric knowledge their seminary-trained peers might possess.

In a way, this approach to credentialing makes the clergy very different from the other classical professions. As noted in the introduction to this chapter, both professionals and paraprofessionals may work in the same environments, contributing to the same cases, and even possessing similar knowledge. The distinction between the paralegal and the lawyer is both training and credentialing. The lawyer's educational background is substantially different, and she has earned that legal credential certifying her possession of that knowledge. Can we truly consider even the layman-clergy, let alone deacon-clergy, distinctions analogous to the paralegal-lawyer or nurse-physician ones?

Certainly, ordained clergy have reserved some legal authorities (e.g., to solemnize weddings) that are not available to laymen or lay-ministers, but even those authorities aren't tied to a foundation in any truly "esoteric" body of knowledge. In many ways, the clergy in these "new paradigm" denominations are more like certified public accountants (CPAs) than lawyers or physicians, but barely so. Even CPAs are required to pass a national standardized test (the Uniform CPA Exam) and prove that they have 150 credit hours of post-secondary training in accounting or in a field related to it. In COGIC, the intermediate licenses- Licensed Minister and Deaconess-give possessors of those licenses many of the rights and most of the responsibilities of their terminally licensed peers, the Elders and Evangelists. Because COGIC ministers, like accountants, never have to pursue the terminal license in order to do most of the profession's essential tasks, pursuing either a terminal license or ordination becomes optional. As CPA's do not need to hold an MBA in order to be licensed as accounting professionals, so Pentecostal ministers do not have to hold a master of divinity degree or its equivalent to be licensed (or ordained) as religious professionals.

This new reality, at least for this portion of the clerical population, certainly brings into question how professional these professionals may actually be. Because the success or failure of many religious tasks-prayer, evangelism, preaching-is determined by congregant response, ministers can measure one's anointing the way social scientists might claim to measure charisma. If an Evangelist preaches a sermon that moves people, she considers herself anointed. On the other hand, COGIC "prophets" don't have to have big followings; they're not movement starters. They see themselves as people with a message. If people hear that message and are changed by it, they believe they've done the work of the prophet. But in their minds, it isn't charisma that moved the followers. They consider charisma to be a gift, something Barack

For Whom God Calls

Obama or the motivational speaker Les Brown might have. For them, the work of the prophet is done through the anointing.

What's particularly fascinating about the anointing and makes it quite different from charisma is that one can continue to claim to be anointed even if no one else believes it; even if there is no response. Charisma is an almost explicitly social phenomena; we know someone has it because people respond to it. In that way, it is like "status." While you can take power, you must be given status. One's charisma is evident only if an audience buys the message.

As discussed earlier, though, ministry doesn't always have an immediate response. In fact, sometimes there is no apparent response at all. Congregants move forward with divorces; no one joins the church at the end of a sermon; prayers are prayed, but the child still dies. In these circumstances, these ministers take the same pragmatic response to seeming failure that other professionals do. In spite of years of training, physicians have patients that die, lawyers lose cases, professors have to give some students failing grades. If these situations happen continuously, any professional might doubt his competence. Even if he didn't, others would.

But if these situations happen only infrequently, it is easier to attribute that failure to other culprits. For the physician, it may be the body. For the lawyer, it may be the system. For COGIC clergy, it seems to be the follower himself. They invoke Jesus. Weber's favorite example of prophetic charisma, for support of this decision: "But Jesus said to them," A prophet is not without honor except in his own country, among his own relatives, and in his own house: Now he could do no mighty work there, except that he laid his hands on a few sick people and healed them. And he marveled because of their unbelief." (Mk. 6:4-6). They argue that even Jesus wasn't always effective in attracting a following. In spite of ample evidence of his charisma or, in the words, anointing-elsewhere, this hometown "prophet" was not received a religious authority and his usual abilities to do charismatic miracles fail, because of potential followers' flawed faith.

Jesus was still competent; all, he laid hands on some people and healed them. But his inability to perform his usual raft of miracles raising the dead, casting out devils suggests to some that even anointed leaders have their bad days. Their belief that person's anointing and their own when their anointing fails remain unabated.

DELIVERABLES

REFLECTION PAPER & Questions

1. Where do you stand on the idea an anointing as it relates to the authenticity of ministry?

2. What is your opinion of the need for formal religious education as a precursor to an effective ministry?

3. If given the choice, would you pursue formal religious education, why or why not?

For Whom God Calls

**Part Three – The How
The Ministry Declaration – "The Call" Paper**

Chapter 6
Reflections of The Self

A natural expansion to the discernment of the expectations of ministry explored by Cetuk, we turn attention to another phase of this pre-ministerial journey; reflections of the self. The use of this term refers to you, the reader partaking in an intimate exploration into the "whys" that undergird your "call" motivation. Cetuk spoke of expectations and external stimuli that may cause one to question the authenticity of their call to ministry. Dr. Wimberly discusses the psychological reasoning behind embedded theologies, which ultimately influence the motivation, or superficially, the perception of being called, by God, to Christian ministry.

The truth one must wrestle with in this Wimberly reading is that *each of us has a story* that influences our perceptions of the world, ultimately affecting our view of ministry and the call to ministry. Our stories shape who we genuinely are and steer us towards accepting our call to ministry and how we can be part of God's omniscient plan.

It is here where the controversy beings, especially in the Black Baptist Church, which regrettably lacks a formal methodology for those desiring to enter the ministry. It is here that motivational factors that cause one to declare a special calling to be a minister of the Gospel may be a sign of some other external catalyst rather than the call from God.

The majority of the mainstream denominations enjoy a group of people who assist the declarant in discerning these feelings to assist them in determining whether there has been a genuine call to ministry or not. As Cetuk pointed out, these external factors distort what many genuinely believe is a call by

For Whom God Calls

God, to be a call to service in some other capacity. Dr. Wimberly, in this reading, will place us in a narrative where we will answer the tough questions about the motivations behind the call. Just to reiterate, in the Black Baptist church, such calls, even if the pastor senses that the declaration is unfounded, are seldom challenged. This unfortunate circumstance results in superficial or placated training just to keep the declarant hopeful that at some juncture, they will realize on their own that their call to this type of ministry is false. No one is blessed if the people are treated as therapeutic aides rather than recipients of God's word.

It will be tough to read this information because you will sometimes see yourself and often not in the best light. It will be even tougher to step back and take a ruthless assessment of your call and humble yourself to what you discover, even if that discovery informs your "self" to question your call to ministry. Failing to make such an admission will result in years of frustration, aggravation, and bitterness that will influence your ministry, mental health, family, and ultimately, your relationship with God. Do not take this for granted, as I've witnessed such denials destroy people, families, and faith.

RECALLING OUR OWN STORIES
(SPIRITUAL RENEWAL FOR RELIGIOUS CAREGIVERS)
SUZANNE: ALLOWING THE TRUE SELF TO SURFACE

Edward P. Wimberly, Ph.D.

Hiding one's gifts in order to please others and be feminine is a major strategy that some women use to make the transition from adolescence into adulthood. Under pressure from family-of-origin expectations, roles, and dynamics, as well as cultural gender notions, many young adult women have learned to hide their true selves and identities. This can be particularly devastating for ministry as well as to the sense of identity of the religious caregiver.

This chapter is about a religious caregiver, whom I call Suzanne, and how she developed a personal mythology based on her feelings of rejection and hiding her gifts and talents. It describes how she moved from being unaware of her personal myth, and the influence that the myth had on her life and ministry, to awareness and the start of reauthoring her personal myth to benefit self-formation and her ministry. Suzanne's story shows how hiding one's true self in order to please others hampers ministry and why it is important to revise personal myths that hinder our effectiveness.

Suzanne

Suzanne is a single African American in her mid-twenties. She is a senior in seminary and struggling to develop her confidence in her ministerial gifts. Taking off a year from seminary to do an internship in ministry, she hopes to learn to claim her gifts for ministry and demonstrate them with- out hesitation or apology. As a member of a mainline, predominantly white denomination, she knows she needs to be less bashful in claiming her gifts and allowing her light to shine more.

Suzanne faces a major problem: her reluctance to assume leadership roles in ministry. While her calling to ministry is clear to her, there is something holding her back from exercising her gifts and leadership ability in ministerial roles. She comes across as preferring to remain in the background, keeping her light hidden from others. At times she appears to be an adolescent, just trying to get along and not ruffle too many feathers. She is the epitome of the good girl. She likes being liked, and if assuming leadership roles means she might not be liked, she will hesitate in taking those roles.

In a year-long group therapy class prior to her senior year in seminary, she received feedback from her peers concerning her gifts, especially her people skills. She was told that she was very approachable and likeable and that people liked being around her. She was also very intelligent and had much insight into things that she kept to herself most of the time. Her peers also delineated her growing edge: her reluctance to assume her uniqueness on the basis of her gifts. It appeared to them that she would rather be one of the group than stand out. Realizing that these comments were accurate and could have a negative impact on her future ministry, she decided to explore why she behaved the way she did.

I gladly steered Suzanne toward the model of reauthoring her personal mythology, believing that part of the problem she was facing related to convictions about herself. She began the reauthoring process because she was motivated by a desire to be more effective in ministry; learning to share her gifts and talents was one way to do so.

Suzanne points out that the dominant theme running through her personal myth is her relationship with her mother. She was the youngest child and had many rebellious ideas; therefore, she was labeled the black sheep by her mother. While birth-order studies would explain her behavior in that light, her mother's constant remarking on her rebellious behavior left Suzanne permanently scarred. In truth, she felt rejected in believing she was a rebel; the seeds were sown for her to suppress that side of herself later in adolescence to win her mother's favor.

Her mother would also regularly accuse her pejoratively of resembling her father's side of the family. Suzanne viewed this too as a loss, as further rejection by her mother. Her parents were divorced, and her mother had many unresolved issues with regard to her former husband. When- ever Suzanne's mother was displeased with her, she would say, "You're definitely your father's child." Because of such negative attributions about her behavior, Suzanne felt alienated from her mother and alone in the world. She felt rejected as well as misunderstood.

Suzanne indicates that her mother's attitude toward her resulted in a great need to try to meet her mother's expectations. She tried to please her mother, but nothing she did seemed to make a positive difference. She also believed she had to work very hard to overcome the childhood badge of dishonor of resembling her father's side of the family. Hence at some point in her early life, she decided to hide her true self, thinking this would please her mother.

At the point of Suzanne's exploration of the major themes in her personal myth, she revealed that her mother's attitude has affected her relationships with men. She is not sure of the connection between her mother's attitude and her behavior, but she believes that she is attracted to men who are like her father.

The rejection that Suzanne feels began when she was caught up in the marital difficulties and pain of her parents. The dominant themes of her personal myth took shape. She believed she was expected to be the savior of her parents' relationship; but as a result, she was pulled in two different directions. Her mother suspected she was more supportive of her father, which added to her feeling of alienation. In turn, her mother said that Suzanne had deserted her for her father, and so Suzanne felt she had lost her mother's love as a consequence. From this loss of relationship with her mother, Suzanne formulated her goal in life of winning her mother's favor, but that primary motivation, to do things that would win her mother's approval, never seemed to result in returned love. Unrequited love became another important theme for Suzanne. It fed the myth of rejection, because she concluded that if she were different, she would be loved.

Suzanne's desire to win her mother's love became one of the commanding forces shaping her own view of who she is as well as how she relates to the world. She has always been recovering from multiple love losses, beginning with loss of her father's love as a consequence of the divorce. Suzanne decided not to connect with her father after the divorce, for fear that that would further alienate her mother.

Because of the several losses of significant others in her life, Suzanne has suffered significant emotional wounds. She says she is always seeking salvation. She looks for people to replace her parents or replace the void left by her parents.

Given the major themes of rejection and loss in Suzanne's personal myth, it is important to explore the different dimensions of her personal myth to envision how other themes have combined with the dominant theme of rejection to shape her life.

Identifying Suzanne's Themes, Birth Mythology, The Earliest Memory

In response to one item on the questionnaire, regarding her personal myth, Suzanne realized that her earliest memories relate to themes she is currently dealing with. She believes her early memory of hugging was an attempt to hold on to her mother and get her mother to return affection:

For Whom God Calls

My earliest memory that I have in my family of origin was lying and sitting in my mother's lap in church and at home. Sleeping with my mother, anxiously waiting for her to come to bed, yelling, "Ma, you coming?" Finally, playing at home with my cousin while other siblings were away in school, I found my father in bed with another woman. I was always very comforted by my mother. I stuck very close to her. I imagine this came as a result of being the youngest. I believe this is the earliest memory that I have. I see this theme still present today. That is, my mother often tells me to stop hugging her so much. I felt close to her and I also felt close to my father. At the time I saw him with this woman in bed, I did not understand exactly what was taking place. As I got older, I realized that my father betrayed my mother.

I realize now that the hugging and the affection I showed my mother and the betrayal of my mother by my father are related to themes that are present in my life today. I see myself seeking out parental figures in my life, and my hugging them is a way to win their favor.

She also realizes that her father's infidelity contributed to her eventually losing his love and affection. Ultimately, it was the marital difficulty between her father and mother that made youthful life miserable for her. This marital pain made it difficult for Suzanne to connect with either parent. Her mother expected her to feel the way she felt about Suzanne's father, and this left her feeling ambivalent toward him.

There is still a void in Suzanne's life. She has not found Mr. Right. All of the men in her life seem to resemble her father; specifically, they have the same inclination to womanizing. She does not want to lead the same kind of miserable marital life that her mother had. Even in associating with mentors in her ministry, she attaches herself to those who are like parental figures. She has been fortunate to find some mentors who recognize and nurture her gifts of ministry.

Suzanne believes that her mother felt the timing of her conception and birth was bad. Her parents were having grave marital difficulties, and her mother did not want to conceive then. This sense of being rejected by her mother continues in the present because her mother has been unable to accept her decision to be a minister. Suzanne's father, she has learned from relatives, was excited about her birth. He was proud to have a daughter.

God plays an important role in her birth story. Exploring her birth myth, she says she learned to depend on God and God's acceptance of her. With so much rejection in her family of origin, her God image has much to do with the degree to which she feels welcomed in this world. Whereas she feels let down by her parents, she feels lifted up by the presence of God in her life. She says she has felt God's presence in her life from a very early age.

Birth Order

There were nine children connected with Suzanne's parents. Her father had five children from a previous marriage, and her mother had one child prior to marrying Suzanne's father. There were three children born of that marriage; Suzanne is the youngest.

In many ways, Suzanne's behavior is consistent with that of the classic youngest child. She went her own way and has developed her life in ways other family members have not. She chose ministry as a profession, differently from any family member. In some ways she was and is a rebel; her mother often reacted to her as such. Despite her mother's warnings not to have much to do with her father, she rebelled at times and sought him out for a relationship.

Gender and Sex

Suzanne speculates that her mother must have been happy that she had a girl. She reasons that if she had been a boy, her mother would have been even more rejecting of her, by identifying the child with his father.

Names and Nicknames

With regard to names and nicknames, Suzanne says that her mother did not name her; a friend of her mother's did. What makes matters worse in Suzanne's mind is that the name came from a TV show the friend had been watching at the moment she was asked. Suzanne has remained offended by her parents' not thinking enough of her to have chosen a name themselves. Her mother did give her a nickname: Suzanne was the "Mason baby." This was her father's family name. That fact intensified Suzanne's child-hood feelings of rejection, because she knew the negative connotations that Mason had for her mother.

Peer and Sibling Relationships

Peer and sibling relationships have helped to prepare the ground for her ministry. It was her mother who labeled her the black sheep in the family. However, as Suzanne grew older, her brothers and sisters became aware of her special interests and gifts and came to her for spiritual guidance and religious perspectives. They looked up to her and gave her a leadership role in their lives regarding these concerns.

She says her role as religious confidante for her brothers and sisters came with a price. Having always sensed she was different, she felt even more like a misfit with them. They had different standards, values, and religious outlooks, although they respected her religious insight. "I never really engaged in girl talk or talk about sex, and they accepted me in this role," she says.
Roles

Suzanne played two different roles in her family. With regard to her mother, she was the black sheep. With her brothers and sisters, she played a religious role. Their acceptance of her in the religious role helped her feel wanted to some extent; it helped her deal with the rejection she felt with her mother and father.

Parental Discipline

As for parental discipline, Suzanne believes she was punished more than her brothers and sisters, she resigned herself to such treatment, reasoning that she might as well do what she wished since she was going to get disciplined whether she deserved it or not. About punishment, she says, "It made me bitter; I felt that my mother did not like me." Discipline in school was similar to what she received at home. She showed a bad attitude and teachers did not put up with it. Once she was suspended from school. She has some guilt over her youthful rebellious attitude, and she deduces that maybe she deserved disciplined treatment because of her poor attitude. She is only now connecting her misbehavior with her feelings of being rejected.

Story Identification

Suzanne's story identification relates more to her role with her brothers and sisters, but it laid the ground for her ministry:

My favorite fairy tale is the "Mother Hen," who was cooking and could not find anyone to help her cook. When it came time to eat, everyone wanted to come and eat. My favorite character is the mother hen, because she was able to handle the situation alone. Throughout the story, she was asking for help and busily doing all of the work. At the end, I believe, she fed everyone and told them of how they needed to correct their selfish behavior. The characters I dislike the most are all of the baby hens and other characters, because they all made excuses not to help. Throughout the story, they sat on their behinds and did nothing. At the end, the mother hen told them the lesson of the need to give and not just receive, and she fed them.

This story identification affirms a major effort that Suzanne made to please her mother. Taking over the mothering role for her brothers and sisters, she hoped she would receive acceptance for doing this. But her mother was never pleased. Suzanne says her mother has still not really accepted her in the ministerial role. Suzanne continues to feel that the theme of rejection dominates her life.

Mapping and Assessing

Suzanne's dominant theme of rejection relates to her mother's conviction that she favored, and resembled, her father's side of the family. As a result of this belief, Suzanne has spent most of her life trying to please her mother and win her affection. She also believes that her attraction to the wrong kind of men relates to her father and the pattern he established with her mother. She is attracted to men who will not be faithful to her, and this of course fuels her sense of rejection. Suzanne has identified with her mother and how her father mistreated her mother. This identification often happens with the same-sex offspring when there is spousal misconduct. She has come to believe that mistreatment is all she can expect in life.

Suzanne also believes she is still caught in the triangular relationship with her mother and her father. In triangulation, a third party is drawn into a troubled marital relationship in order to lessen the pain and conflict (Nichols, 1984). Suzanne wanted desperately to have a father-daughter relationship, but she did not pursue it aggressively for fear of losing her mother. As a result, her pursuit of her own self-interests and personal goals was and has been reluctant. Her stronger motivation remains to fulfill what others expect of her. At times, however, she still rebels and is uncooperative. This rebellion is self-destructive and self-defeating, of course; she feels it has affected her academic performance throughout her life. She sees herself as the classic underachiever, who has not really developed her true self or her true abilities. The positive side of her rebellious- ness is that it helps her identify her true self (even if she fails to carry through on that development); she does feel the need to bring into better harmony her rebellious self and her approval-seeking self. The real self, she senses, lies somewhere between these two extremes.

At first, she was reluctant to map the influence of the theme of rejection on her ministry. She resisted because it could mean facing real change. Finally, she gave up as she discovered that her reluctance to let her light shine in ministry related so strongly to her family-of-origin dynamics. She understands that not being affirmed by her mother in her ministry con- tributes greatly to lack of confidence in her own ministerial gifts. Although her sisters and brothers recognized and affirmed those gifts, throughout her younger life it was as if the gifts did not exist just because her mother failed to acknowledge them.

These observations have come as Suzanne traces the influence of the dominant themes of her personal myth on her life. In pursuing the impact of these themes, she sets the stage for altering the hold that her personal myth has over her life. She believes that having been triangulated and rejected contributed to a growth-inhibiting personal myth that has locked her into negative patterns of behavior. She recognizes the need to alter her personal myth.

Discernment

The third stage of the reauthoring process is discerning the transforming forces at work, to seek a more growth-facilitating personal myth.

Suzanne has had a sense of God's presence in her life since she was a small child. She felt the presence with her as she walked through the house as a little girl. She used to tell her mother, "I feel God following me, and every time I turn around to see him, he's not there." Because God was present in her childhood, she believes God is present now as she attempts to rewrite the dominant themes that make up her personal myth.

One way in which she has sought discernment is through prayer. She sees that God is working in her, trying to help her heal her relationship with her mother. From this revelation, she has found encouragement to begin doing work that may eventually help that relationship.

In seeking to renew her relationship with her mother, she finds that reading books helps her understand how God is guiding her through the journey of renewal of broken relationships. She sees God at work in her life helping her release harmful memories. She feels she has an unforgiving spirit and holds onto the hurt and pain of those who hurt her. God is leading her to see that she only hurts herself and prevents her own growth by not letting go of things from the past. She feels she has to learn to let go if she is to mature and have an effective ministry.

She is learning how holding on to painful memories is self-destructive. She is giving the hurt feelings over to God for healing. She finds that God is helping her understand the true meaning of forgiveness, and she sees how her life improves when she does not hold onto past hurts.

For Whom God Calls

Making Plans

The goals in reauthoring our personal myths are to revise the story that determines personal behavior, to heal wounds, and to transform them into service to others. The identification, assessment, and discerning phases of the reauthoring process are all essential components to altering the personal myth. Making plans is the final phase, where we outline specific steps for future modification of the personal myth.

Suzanne has outlined her planned steps for reauthoring: (1) to seek spiritual and professional guidance beyond seminary, to explore further the themes in her personal myth, (2) to explore how the themes perpetuate themselves in her behavior, and (3) to allow God's presence to heal the hurts and wounds that continue to influence her life.

Cultural Factors

Suzanne traces her feelings of rejection to her mother's indifference to her gifts and interests, and to the fallout of her parents' marital conflict. Rejection is clearly rooted in how Suzanne has interpreted and attributed significance to her parents' behavior. Her own loyalty to both mother and father left her caught, because her mother believed Suzanne's commitment was more to her father and so her mother withdrew affection from her.

Suzanne could have responded in any number of ways to perceiving rejection. She could have protested, ignoring her mother's expectations and becoming the very opposite of a model daughter. Rather, she chose to become a "conforming angel," who tries to please her mother in every way, even denying her gifts and graces. The decision to hide her talents under a bush (to use a biblical metaphor), thinking this would win back her mother's love, contributed greatly to the development of her negative personal mythology.

The strategy of hiding our talent brings to mind the cultural strategy girls use in making the transition from childhood to adolescence. When the girl experiences tension between her inner needs and what is deemed good and valuable under the influence of cultural messages, she may seek to dissociate from those inner qualities that are regarded as undesirable (Taylor, Gilligan, and

Sullivan, 1995). With this maneuver, the girl loses touch with her own voice and her inner sense of vitality and strength.

What is significant about the dissociation strategy in dealing with dis- sonance between self-perception and the perception of others is that it is culturally sanctioned. Suzanne's choice was not idiosyncratic; this hiding strategy is long-standing and culturally blessed. Cultural and family-of- origin dynamics combined to shape Suzanne's interpretation of reality and her responses to what she experienced.

Important Changes for Suzanne

Suzanne's response to her feelings of rejection, namely, to hide her talents, was a self-destructive move. The biblical metaphor of burying talents points to the reality that buried talents leads to human atrophy (Matthew 25: 14-30 and Luke 19: 12-27). Suzanne's approach to winning her mother's love was a way of sabotaging her self-development. To grow and become an effective person and minister, she needs to make some changes in her personal mythology. Her peers sense that her hiding tac- tic makes her ineffective in the ministry she wants to pursue. How can she change?

Suzanne came to seminary unaware that there was anything amiss with hiding her true self. However, when she enrolled in the group therapy course for a year, she began a slow process of coming to awareness of her hiding pattern. Her peers and the teacher enabled her to get a first glimpse of the pattern. The course was in the second year of her seminary pilgrimage; she then took a one-year internship to work on reclaiming her true self while engaging in ministry. After that, she returned to seminary to complete her senior year.

In the first semester back from her intern year, she registered in a course I entitled "Pastoral Care and Inner Healing." The course was intended to enable students to use the model of reauthoring presented in this book. Suzanne was ready to look systematically at her personal mythology; she brought to the course some awareness that she had gifts of insight and caring that she often hid. Wanting to explore why she chose to hide these gifts, she used the course to formally engage in the reauthoring process. The results of her work are evident in this chapter.

Suzanne's reauthoring was truly a "process"; it took place over nearly two and a half years. She was not alone in the process; she had significant companionship from her peers, supervisors, and teachers. Gradually, she was able to replace the internalized, intimidating expectations (from both her mother and from the larger culture) that had led her to hide her talents. She used the available support to risk being herself.

The expectations of others are often internalized and become a set of unrealistic standards calling for sacrifice of self. Merle Jordan deems this internalization of unrealistic demands religious idolatry. Idolatry is the elevation of a secondary value to primary status in our life, to the extent that this elevated figure becomes the primary means of self-evaluation Jordan, 1985). When this happens, we give over the self to a tyranny of expectations that destroy it. To overcome this tyranny, we must replace the internalized expectations with a more accepting and realistic expectation. That comes from caring others, who are committed to helping us realize our true self.

Suzanne found these others in her peers, supervisors, and teachers. They were all committed to her growth and development, and they made themselves available for her to carry out her positive internalization. When she internalized others (peers, supervisors, and teachers), they became an enduring source of nurturing expectations that sustained her as she slowly allowed her true self to emerge from hiding.

Suzanne's story teaches us that changing a personal myth takes time. It is aided by being in relationship with significant others who care. Without such caring relationships, the reauthoring process is almost impossible.

What Suzanne Found Helpful in Others

Suzanne found help from others as she engaged in the reauthoring process. They told their stories after she told hers. They listened to her stories. They showed interest in her welfare. They were willing to gently challenge her when she hid her experience. They were patient with her as her true self slowly emerged. Suzanne's peers, supervisors, and teachers were willing to share their own experiences, and she found that their sharing facilitated her growth. She understood these persons w genuinely committed to her growth. Their interest in her, their willingness to consistently confront her hiding, and their acceptance of her own pacing in the self-realization process were all essential help in her reauthoring process as well.

The Role of Reconnecting with the Call

Suzanne's call has been a continuing factor in her reauthoring process. Reconnecting with it has helped her make a decision not to bury her The reconnection gives her permission to claim her gifts and to render mother's expectations of her secondary. Getting back in touch with call has helped her to discern the priorities for her life and ministry:

> Deep down inside, I always had a desire to share the Gospel. As a youth, I sat down and thought about the most effective ways to do it. I noticed that the company that I kept was always with women in ministry, and I would continuously be concerned with how they carried out their ministries and wondered when they knew they were called. Soon after I began to realize that God was also calling me to the preaching ministry. My call is a major motivating factor in my life today. As I endeavor to use my gifts for ministry, I feel my call is the only thing that has. Sustained me as I seek to make the changes I need to make in order to be effective.

Suzanne's call reminds her that ministry is her vocational choice that her growth as a person and as a professional depends on developing her God-given gifts. The remembrance of the call helps sustain her give her courage to take the necessary risks she must make to reauthor her personal myth.

Conclusion

Suzanne brought to seminary a personal myth of rejection that caused her to hide her talents for ministry. It was hindering her ability to be effective in relationships and ministry. With the aid of peers, teachers, and supervisors, she was able to enter and carry out the reauthoring successfully. Her deep feeling of rejection led to self-rejection, but reauthoring her personal myth allowed her to reclaim her true self and a willingness to manifest that self in ministry. The process has been a long one, immensely meaningful for her.

DELIVERABLES

REFLECTION PAPER & Questions

1. What aspects of Suzanne's story mirror your own? Be as specific as necessary to unravel underlying similarities.

2. Has your view of your call changed since reading Suzanne's story? What changed specifically, if anything, and why?

Chapter 7
Becoming the Authentic Me

As we get closer to completing the actual call paper, the necessity for total transparency and authenticity at this juncture of the book should elevate your ability to speak frankly will benefit you as you seek God's voice in this process. Whisperers in your head trying to distract you will silence as you begin to respond with what you know God has placed in your spirit.

It is tempting at this juncture to take the easy way out and simply avoid the difficult moments, the difficult decision, the complex realities that arose as a result of your surrendering to God's call. I know it is freighting and intimidating to feel that you've; come this far on your feelings and emotions, but now it is time to put those feelings and emotions into action.

This reading by Parker J. Palmer, as it was for those who take my Foundations of Ministry class, is the last before undertaking the task of completing your call paper. For students who have faithfully challenged the status quo in and around themselves, you are ready to start. However, take Palmer's words to heart as he shares the vocational choice of ministry with you as experienced in his journey. His narrative is compelling, and if your heart truly desires to proceed on the path set before you by God, Palmer's words will ring true and remain in your psyche for the remainder of your life. This reading will also bring to the forefront the need to clearly define your motivations for entering the ministry and help you reconcile those motivations in a way that serves not only God but yourself and the people whom you desire to serve.

For Whom God Calls

LET YOUR LIFE SPEAK: LISTENING FOR THE VOICE OF VOCATION
NOW I BECOME MYSELF

Parker J. Palmer

With twenty-one words, carefully chosen and artfully woven, May Sarton evokes the quest for vocation-at least, my quest or vocation-with candor and precision:

> Now I become myself.
> It's taken time, many years and places.
> I have been dissolved and shaken,
> Worn other people's faces ....

What a long time it can take to become the person one has always been! How often in the process we mask ourselves in faces that are not our own. How much dissolving and shaking of ego we must endure before we discover our deep identity-the true self within every human being that is the seed of authentic vocation.

I first learned about vocation growing up in the church. I value much about the religious tradition in which I was raised: its humility about its own convictions, its respect for the world's diversity, its concern for justice. But the idea of "vocation" I picked up in those circles created distortion until I grew strong enough to discard it. I mean the idea that vocation, or calling, comes from a voice external to ourselves, a voice of moral demand that asks us to become someone we are not yet-someone different, someone better, someone just beyond our reach.

That concept of vocation is rooted in a deep distrust of selfhood, in the belief that the sinful self will always be "selfish" unless corrected by external forces of virtue. It is a notion that made me feel inadequate to the task of living my own life, creating guilt about the distance between who I was and who I was supposed to be, leaving me exhausted as I labored to close the gap.

Michael H Sands

Today I understand vocation quite differently-not as a goal to be achieved but as a gift to be received. Discovering vocation does not mean scrambling toward some prize just beyond my reach but accepting the treasure of true self I already possess. Vocation does not come from a voice "out there" calling me to become something I am not. It comes from a voice "in here" calling me to be the person I was born to be, to fulfill the original selfhood given me at birth by God. It is a strange gift, this birthright gift of self. Accepting it turns out to be even more demanding than attempting to become someone else! I have sometimes responded to that demand by ignoring the gift, or hiding it, or fleeing from it, or squandering it-and I think I am not alone. There is a Hasidic tale that reveals, with amazing brevity, both the universal tendency to want to be someone else and the ultimate importance of becoming one's self: Rabbi Zusya, when he was an old man, said, "In the coming world, they will not ask me: 'Why were you not Moses?' They will ask me: 'Why were you not Zusya?'"

If you doubt that we all arrive in this world with gifts and as a gift, pay attention to an infant or a very young child. A few years ago, my daughter and her newborn baby came to live with me for a while. Watching my granddaughter from her earliest days on earth, I was able, in my early fifties, to see something that had eluded me as a twenty-something parent: my granddaughter arrived in the world as this kind of person rather than that, or that, or that.

She did not show up as raw material to be shaped into whatever image the world might want her to take. She arrived with her own gifted form, with the shape of her own sacred soul. Biblical faith calls it the image of God in which we are all created. Thomas Merton calls it true self Quakers call it the inner light, or "that of God" in every person. The humanist tradition calls it identity and integrity. No matter what you call it, it is a pearl of great price.

In those early days of my granddaughter's life, I began observing the inclinations and proclivities that were planted in her at birth. I noticed, and I still notice, what she likes and dislikes, what she is drawn toward and repelled by, how she moves, what she does, what she says.

For Whom God Calls

I am gathering my observations in a letter. When my granddaughter reaches her late teens or early twenties, I will make sure that my letter finds its way to her, with a preface something like this: "Here is a sketch of who you were from your earliest days in this world. It is not a definitive picture-only you can draw that. But it was sketched by a person who loves you very much. Perhaps these notes will help you do sooner something your grandfather did only later: remember who you were when you first arrived and reclaim the gift of true self."

We arrive in this world with birthright gifts-then we spend the first half of our lives abandoning them or letting others disabuse us of them. As young people, we are surrounded by expectations that may have little to do with who we really are, expectations held by people who are not trying to discern our selfhood but to fit us into slots. In families, schools, workplaces, and religious communities, we are trained away from true self toward images of acceptability; under social pressures like racism and sexism our original shape is deformed beyond recognition; and we ourselves, driven by fear, too often betray true self to gain the approval of others.

We are disabused of original giftedness in the first half of our lives. Then – if we are awake, aware, and able to admit our loss-we spend the second half trying to recover and reclaim the gift we once possessed. When we lose track of true self, how can we pick up the trail? One way is to seek clues in stories from our younger years, years when we lived closer to our birthright gifts. A few years ago, I found some clues to myself in a time machine of sorts. A friend sent me a tattered copy of my high school newspaper from May 1957 in which I had been interviewed about what I intended to do with my life. With the certainty to be expected of a high school senior, I told the interviewer that I would become a naval aviator and then take up a career in advertising.

I was indeed "wearing other people's faces," and I can tell you exactly whose they were. My father worked with a man who had once been a navy pilot. He was Irish, charismatic, romantic, full of the wild blue yonder and a fair share of the blarney, and I wanted to be like him. The father of one of my boyhood friends was in advertising, and though I did not yearn to take on his persona, which was too buttoned-down for my taste, I did yearn for the fast car and other large toys that seemed to be the accessories of his selfhood!

These self-prophecies, now over forty years old, seem wildly misguided for a person who eventually became a Quaker, a would-be pacifist, a writer, and an activist. Taken literally, they illustrate how early in life we can lose track of who we are. But inspected through the lens of paradox, my desire to become an aviator and an advertiser contain clues to the core of true self that would take many years to emerge: clues, by definition, are coded and must be deciphered.

Hidden in my desire to become an "ad man" was a lifelong fascination with language and its power to persuade, the same fascination that has kept me writing incessantly for decades. Hidden in my desire to become a naval aviator was something more complex: a personal engagement with the problem of violence that expressed itself at first in military fantasies and then, over a period of many years, resolved itself in the pacifism I aspire to today. When I flip the coin of identity I held to so tightly in high school, I find the paradoxical "opposite" that emerged as the years went by.

If I go farther back, to an earlier stage of my life, the clues need less deciphering to yield insight into my birthright gifts and callings. In grade school, I became fascinated with the mysteries of flight. As many boys did in those days, after school and on weekends, designing, crafting, flying, and (usually) crashing model airplanes made of fragile balsa wood.

Unlike most boys, however, I also spent long hours creating eight- and twelve-page books about aviation. I would turn a sheet of paper sideways; draw a vertical line down the middle; make diagrams of, say, the cross-section of a wing; roll the sheet into a typewriter; and peck out a caption explaining how air moving across an airfoil creates a vacuum that lifts the plane. Then I would fold that sheet in half along with several others I had made, staple the collection together down the spine, and painstakingly illustrate the cover.

I had always thought that the meaning of this paperwork was obvious: fascinated with flight, I wanted to be a pilot, or at least an aeronautical engineer. But recently, when I found a couple of these literary artifacts in an old cardboard   I suddenly saw the

For Whom God Calls

truth, and it was more obvious than I had imagined. I didn't want to be a pilot or an aeronautical engineer or anything else related to aviation. I wanted to be an author, to make books-a task I have been attempting from the third grade to this very moment!

From the beginning, our lives lay down clues to selfhood and vocation, though the clues may be hard to decode. But trying to interpret them is profoundly worthwhile-especially when we are in our twenties or thirties or forties, feeling profoundly lost, having wandered, or been dragged, far away from our birthright gifts.

Those clues are helpful in counteracting the conventional concept of vocation, which insists that our lives must be driven by "oughts." As noble as that may sound, we do not find our callings by conforming ourselves to some abstract moral code. We find our callings by claiming authentic selfhood, by being who we are, by dwelling in the world as Zusya rather than straining to be Moses. The deepest vocational question is not "What ought I to do with my life?" It is the more elemental and demanding "Who am I? What is my nature?"

Everything in the universe has a nature, which means limits as well as potentials, a truth well known by people who work daily with the things of the world. Making pottery, for example, involves more than telling the clay what to become. The clay presses back on the potter's hands, telling her what it can and cannot do-and if she fails to listen, the outcome will be both frail and ungainly. Engineering involves more than telling materials what they must do. If the engineer does not honor the nature of the steel or the wood or the stone, his failure will go well beyond aesthetics: the bridge or the building will collapse and put human life in peril.

The human self also has a nature, limits as well as potentials. If you seek vocation without understanding the material you are working with, what you build with your life will be ungainly and may well put lives in peril, your own and some of those around you. "Faking it" in the service of high values is no virtue and has nothing to do with vocation. It is an ignorant, sometimes arrogant, attempt to override one's nature, and it will always fail.

Our deepest calling is to grow into our own authentic selfhood, whether or not it conforms to some image of who we ought to be. As we do so, we will not only find the joy that every human being seeks-we will also find our path of authentic service in the world. True vocation joins self and service, as Frederick Buechner asserts when he defines vocation as "the place where your deep gladness meets the world's deep need." Buechner's definition starts with the self and moves toward the needs of the world: it begins, wisely, where vocation begins-not in what the world needs (which is everything), but in the nature of the human self, in what brings the self-joy, the deep joy of knowing that we are here on earth to be the gifts that God created.

Contrary to the conventions of our thinly moralistic culture, this emphasis on gladness and selfhood is not selfish. The Quaker teacher Douglas Steere was fond of saying that the ancient human question "Who am I?" leads inevitably to the equally important question "Whose am I?"-for there is no selfhood outside of relationship. We must ask the question of selfhood and answer it as honestly as we can, no matter where it takes us. Only as we do so can we discover the community of our lives.

As I learn more about the seed of true self that was planted when I was born, I also learn more about the ecosystem in which I was planted-the network of communal relations in which I am called to live responsively, accountably, and joyfully with beings of every sort. Only when I know both seed and system, self and community, can I embody the great commandment to love both my neighbor and myself.

Most of us arrive at a sense of self and vocation only after a long journey through alien lands. But this journey bears no resemblance to the trouble-free "travel packages" sold by the tourism industry. It is more akin to the ancient tradition of pilgrimage - "a transformative journey to a sacred center" full of hardships, darkness, and peril.

In the tradition of pilgrimage, those hardships are seen not as accidental but as integral to the journey itself. Treacherous terrain, bad weather, taking a fall, getting lost-challenges of that sort, largely beyond our control, can strip the ego of the illusion that it is in charge and make space for true self to emerge. If that happens, the pilgrim has a better chance to find the sacred center he or she seeks. Disabused of our illusions by much travel and travail, we awaken one day to find that the sacred center is here

For Whom God Calls

and now-in every moment of the journey, everywhere in the world around us, and deep within our own hearts.

But before we come to that center, full of light, we must travel in the dark. Darkness is not the whole of the story every pilgrimage has passages of loveliness and joy-but it is the part of the story most often left untold. When we finally escape the darkness and stumble into the light, it is tempting to tell others that our hope never flagged, to deny those long nights we spent cowering in fear.

The experience of darkness has been essential to my corning into selfhood, and telling the truth about that fact helps me stay in the light. But I want to tell that truth for another reason as well: many young people today journey in the dark, as the young always have, and we elders do them a disservice when we withhold the shadowy parts of our lives. When I was young, there were very few elders willing to talk about the darkness; most of them pretended that success was all they had ever known. As the darkness began to descend on me in my early twenties, I thought I had developed a unique and terminal case of failure. I did not realize that I had merely embarked on a journey toward joining the human race.

The story of my journey is no more or less important than anyone else's. It is simply the best source of data I have on a subject where generalizations often fail but truth may be found in the details. I want to rehearse a few details of my travels, and travails, extracting some insights about vocation as I go. I do so partly as an offering of honesty to the young and partly as a reminder to anyone who needs it that the nuances of personal experience contain much guidance toward selfhood and vocation.

My journey into darkness began in sunlit places. I grew up in a Chicago suburb and went to Carleton College in Minnesota, a splendid place where I found new faces to wear-faces more like my own than the ones I donned in high school, but still the faces of other people. Wearing one of them, I went from college neither to the navy nor to Madison Avenue but to Union Theological Seminary in New York City, as certain that the ministry was now my calling as I had been a few years earlier about advertising and aviation.

Michael H Sands

So it came as a great shock when, at the end of my first year, God spoke to me-in the form of mediocre grades and massive misery-and informed me that under no conditions was I to become an ordained leader in His or Her church. Always responsive to authority, as one was if raised in the fifties, I left Union and went west, to the University of California at Berkeley. There I spent much of the sixties working on a Ph.D. in sociology and learning to be not quite so responsive to authority.

Berkeley in the sixties was, of course, an astounding mix of shadow and light. But contrary to the current myth, many of us were less seduced by the shadow than drawn by the light, coming away from that time and place with a lifelong sense of hope, a feeling for community, a passion for social change.

Though I taught for two years in the middle of graduate school, discovering that I loved teaching and was good at it, my Berkeley experience left me convinced that a university career would be a cop-out. I felt called instead to work on "the urban crisis." So when I left Berkeley in the late sixties a friend kept asking me, "Why do you want to go back to America?" -I also left academic life. Indeed, I left on a white horse (some might say a high horse), full of righteous indignation about the academy's corruption, holding aloft the flaming sword of truth. I moved to Washington, D.C., where I became not a professor but a community organizer.

What I learned about the world from that work was the subject of an earlier book. What I learned about vocation is how one's values can do battle with one's heart. I felt morally compelled to work on the urban crisis, but doing so went against a growing sense that teaching might be my vocation. My heart wanted to keep teaching, but my ethics-laced liberally with ego-told me I was supposed to save the city. How could I reconcile the contradiction between the two?

After two years of community organizing, with all its financial uncertainties, Georgetown University offered me a faculty post-one that did not require me to get off my white horse altogether: "We don't want you to be on campus all week long," said the dean. "We want you to get our students involved in the community. Here's a tenure-track position involving a minimum of classes and no requirement to serve on committees. Keep working in the community and take our students out there with you."

The part about no committees seemed like a gift from God, so I accepted Georgetown's offer and began involving undergraduates in community organizing. But I soon found an even bigger gift hidden in this arrangement. By looking anew at my community work through the lens of education, I saw that as an organizer I had never stopped being a teacher – I was simply teaching in a classroom without walls.

In fact, I could have done no other: teaching, I was coming to understand, is my native way of being in the world. Make me a cleric or a CEO, a poet or a politico, and teaching is what I will do. Teaching is at the heart of my vocation and will manifest itself in any role I play. Georgetown's invitation allowed me to take my first step toward embracing this truth, toward a lifelong exploration of "education unplugged."

But even this way of reframing my work could not alter the fact that there was a fundamental misfit between the rough-and-tumble of organizing and my own overly sensitive nature. After five years of conflict and competition, I burned out. I was too thin-skinned to make a good community organizer-my vocational reach had exceeded my grasp. I had been driven more by the "oughts" of the urban crisis than by a sense of true self. Lacking insight into my own limits and potentials, I had allowed ego and ethics to lead me into a situation that my soul could not abide.

I was disappointed in myself for not being tough enough to take the flak, disappointed and ashamed. But as pilgrims must discover if they are to complete their quest, we are led to truth by our weaknesses as well as our strengths. I needed to leave community organizing for a reason I might never have acknowledged had I not been thin-skinned and burned-out: as an organizer, I was trying to take people to a place where I had never been myself-a place called community. If I wanted to do community-related work with integrity, I needed a deeper immersion in community than I had experienced to that point.

I am white, middle-class, and male-not exactly a leading candidate for a communal life. People like me are raised to live autonomously, not interdependently. I had been trained to compete and win, and I had developed a taste for the prizes. But something in me yearned to experience communion, not competition, and that something might never have made itself known had burnout not forced me to seek another way.

So I took a yearlong sabbatical from my work in Washington and went to a place called Pendle Hill outside of Philadelphia. Founded in 1930, Pendle Hill is a Quaker living-and-learning community of some seventy people whose mission is to offer education about the inner journey, nonviolent social change, and the connection between the two. It is a real-time experiment in Quaker faith and practice where residents move through a daily round of communal life: worshiping in silence each morning; sharing three meals a day; engaging in study, physical work, decision making, and social outreach. It is a commune, an ashram, a monastery, a zendo, a kibbutz-whatever one calls it, Pendle Hill was a life unlike anything I had ever known.

Moving there was like moving to Mars-utterly alien but profoundly compelling. I thought I would stay for just a year and then go back to Washington and resume my work. But before my sabbatical ended, I was invited to become Pendle Hill's dean of studies. I stayed on for another decade, living in community and continuing my experiment with alternative models of education.

It was a transformative passage for me, personally, professionally, and spiritually; in retrospect, I know how impoverished I would have been without it. But early on in that passage I began to have deep and painful doubts about the trajectory of my vocation. Though I felt called to stay at Pendle Hill, I also feared that I had stepped off the edge of the known world and was at risk of disappearing professionally.

From high school on, I had been surrounded by expectations that I would ascend to some sort of major leadership. When I was twenty-nine, the president of a prestigious college visited me in Berkeley to recruit me for his board of trustees. He was doing it, he joked, because no one on that board was under sixty, let alone thirty; worse still, not one of them had a beard, which I could supply as part of the Berkeley uniform. Then he added, "In fact, I'm doing this because some day you'll be a college president-of that I'm sure-and serving as a trustee is an important part of your apprenticeship." I accepted his invitation because I felt certain that he was right.

For Whom God Calls

So half a dozen years later, what was I doing at Pendle Hill, a "commune" known to few, run by an offbeat religious community that most people can identify only by their oatmeal which, I hasten to add, is not really made by Quakers? I'll tell you what I was doing: I was in the craft shop making mugs that weighed more and looked worse than the clay ashtrays I made in grade school, and I was sending these monstrosities home as gifts to my family. My father, rest his soul, was in the fine chinaware business, and I was sending him mugs so heavy you could fill them with coffee and not feel any difference in weight!

Family and friends were asking me-and I was asking myself – "Why did you get a Ph.D. if this is what you are going to do? Aren't you squandering your opportunities and gifts?" Under that sort of scrutiny, my vocational decision felt wasteful and ridiculous; what's more, it was terrifying to an ego like mine that had no desire to disappear and every desire to succeed and become well known.

Did I want to go to Pendle Hill, to be at Pendle Hill, to stay at Pendle Hill? I cannot say that I did. But I can say with certainty that Pendle Hill was something that I couldn't not do. Vocation at its deepest level is not, "Oh, boy, do I want to go to this strange place where I have to learn a new way to live and where no one, including me, understands what I'm doing." Vocation at its deepest level is, "This is something I can't not do, for reasons I'm unable to explain to anyone else and don't fully understand myself but that are nonetheless compelling."

And yet, even with this level of motivation, my doubts multiplied. One day I walked from Pendle Hill through the woods to a nearby college campus, out for a simple stroll but carrying my anxiety with me. On some forgotten whim, I went into the college's main administration building. There, in the foyer, hung several stern portraits of past presidents of that institution. One of them was the same man who, as president of another institution, had come out to Berkeley to recruit me for his board of trustees-a man who, in my imagination, was now staring down at me with a deeply disapproving look on his face: "What do you think you're up to? Why are you wasting your time? Get back on track before it is too late!"

Michael H Sands

I ran from that building back into the woods and wept for a long time. Perhaps this moment precipitated the descent into darkness that has been so central to my vocational journey, a descent that hit bottom in the struggle with clinical depression that I will write about later in this book. But whether that is the case or not, the moment was large with things I needed to learn-and could learn only by going into the dark.

In that moment, all the false bravado about why I had left academic life collapsed around me, and I was left with nothing more than the reality of my own fear. I had insisted, to myself as well as others, that I wanted out of the university because it was unfit for human habitation. It was, I argued, a place of corruption and arrogance, filled with intellectuals who evaded their social responsibilities and yet claimed superiority over ordinary folks- the very folks whose lack of power and privilege compelled them to shoulder the responsibilities that kept our society intact.

If those complaints sound unoriginal, it is only because they are. They were the accepted pieties of Berkeley in the sixties which-for reasons I now understand-I eagerly embraced as my own. Whatever half-truths about the university my complaints may have contained, they served me primarily as a misleading and self-serving explanation of why I fled academic life.

The truth is that I fled because I was afraid-afraid that I could never succeed as a scholar, afraid that I could never measure up to the university's standards for research and publication. And I was right-though it took many years before I could admit that to myself. Try as I may, try as I might, I have never had the gifts that make for a good scholar-and remaining in the university would have been a distorting denial of that fact.

A scholar is committed to building on knowledge that others have gathered, correcting it, confirming it, enlarging it. But I have always wanted to think my own thoughts about a subject without being overly influenced by what others have thought before me. If you catch me reading a book in private, it is most likely to be a novel, some poetry, a mystery, or an essay that defies classification, rather than a text directly related to whatever I am writing at the time.

For Whom God Calls

There is some virtue in my proclivities, I think: they help me keep my thinking fresh and bring me the stimulation that comes from looking at life through multiple lenses. There is non-virtue in them as well: laziness of a sort, a certain kind of impatience, and perhaps even a lack of clue respect for others who have worked these fields.

But be they virtues or faults, these are the simple facts about my nature, about my limits and my gifts. I am less gifted at building on other people's discoveries than at tinkering in my own garage; less gifted at slipping slowly into a subject than at jumping into the deep end to see if I can swim; less gifted at making outlines than at writing myself into a corner and trying to find a way out; less gifted at tracking a tight chain of logic than at leaping from one metaphor to the next!

Perhaps there is a lesson here about the complexity, even duplicity, we must embrace on the road to vocation, where we sometimes find ourselves needing to do the right thing for the wrong reason. It was right for me to leave the university. But I needed to do it for the wrong reason- "the university is corrupt" - because the right reason- "I lack the gifts of a scholar" - was too frightening for me to face at the time.

My fear of failing as a scholar contained the energy I needed to catapult myself out of the academy and free myself for another kind of educational mission. But because I could not acknowledge my fear, I had to disguise that energy as the white horse of judgment and self-righteousness. It is an awkward fact, but it is true-and once I could acknowledge that truth and understand its role in the dynamics of my life, I found myself no longer embarrassed by it.

Eventually, I was able to get off that white horse and take an unblinking look at myself and my liabilities. This was a step into darkness that I had been trying to avoid-the darkness of seeing myself more honestly than I really wanted to. But I am grateful for the grace that allowed me to dismount, for the white horse I was riding back then could never have carried me to the place where I am today: serving, with love, the academy

I once left in fear and loathing. Today I serve education from outside the institution where my pathology is less likely to get triggered-rather than from the inside, where I waste energy on anger instead of investing it in hope. This pathology, which took me years to recognize, is my tendency to get so conflicted with the way people use power in institutions that I spend more time being angry at them than I spend on my real work.

Once I understood that the problem was "in here" as well as "out there," the solution seemed clear: I needed to work independently, outside of institutions, detached from the stimuli that trigger my knee-jerk response. Having done just that for over a decade now, my pathology no longer troubles me: I have no one to blame but myself for whatever the trouble may be and am compelled to devote my energies to the work I am called to do!

Here, I think, is another clue to finding true self and vocation: we must withdraw the negative projections we make on people and situations-projections that serve mainly to mask our fears about ourselves-and acknowledge and embrace our own liabilities and limits.

Once I came to terms with my fears, I was able to look back and trace an unconscious pattern. For years, I had been moving away from large institutions like Berkeley and Georgetown to small places like Pendle Hill, places of less status and visibility on the map of social reality. But I moved like a crab, sideways, too fearful to look head-on at the fact that I was taking myself from the center to the fringes of institutional life and ultimately to a place where all that was left was to move outside of institutions altogether.

I rationalized my movement with the notion that small institutions are more moral than large ones. But that is patently untrue – both about what was animating me and about institutions! In fact, I was animated by a soul, a "true self," that knew me better than my ego did, knew that I needed to work outside of institutional crosscurrents and constraints.

This is not an indictment of institutions; it is a statement of my limitations. Among my admired friends are people who do not have my limits, whose gifts allow them to work faithfully within institutions and, through those institutions, to serve the world well. But their gift is not mine, as I learned after much Sturm und Drang - and that is not an indictment of me. It is simply a truth about who I am and how I am rightfully related to the world, an ecological truth of the sort that can point toward true vocation.

For Whom God Calls

Selfhood, Society, and Service

By surviving passages of doubt and depression on the vocational journey, I have become clear about at least one thing: self-care is never a selfish act- it is simply good stewardship of the only gift I have, the gift I was put on earth to offer to others. Anytime we can listen to true self and give it the care it requires, we do so not only for ourselves but for the many others whose lives we touch.

There are at least two ways to understand the link between selfhood and service. One is offered by the poet Rumi in his piercing observation: "If you are here unfaithfully with us, you're causing terrible damage." If we are unfaithful to true self, we will extract a price from others. We will make promises we cannot keep, build houses from flimsy stuff, conjure dreams that devolve into nightmares, and other people will suffer if we are unfaithful to true self.

I will examine that sort of unfaithfulness, and its consequences, later in this book. But a more inspiring way of understanding the link between selfhood and service is to study the lives of people who have been here faithfully with us. Look, for example, at the great liberation movements that have served humanity so well in eastern Europe, Latin America, and South Africa, among women, African Americans, and our gay and lesbian brothers and sisters. What we see is simple but often ignored: the movements that transform us, our relations, and our world emerge from the lives of people who decide to care for their authentic selfhood.

The social systems in which these people must survive often try to force them to live in a way untrue to who they are. If you are poor, you are supposed to accept, with gratitude, half a loaf or less; if you are black, you are supposed to suffer racism without protest; if you are gay, you are supposed to pretend that you are not. You and I may not know, but we can at least imagine, how tempting it would be to mask one's truth in situations of this sort- because the system threatens punishment if one does not.

But in spite of that threat, or because of it, the people who plant the seeds of movements make a critical decision: they decide to live "divided no more." They decide no longer to act on the outside in a way that contradicts some truth about themselves that they hold deeply on the inside. They decide to claim authentic selfhood and act it out-and their decisions ripple out to transform the society in which they live, serving the selfhood of millions of others.

I call this the "Rosa Parks decision" because that remarkable woman is so emblematic of what the undivided life can mean. Most of us know her story, the story of an African American woman who, at the time she made her decision, was a seamstress in her early forties. On December 1, 1955, in Montgomery, Alabama, Rosa Parks did something she was not supposed to do: she sat down at the front of a bus in one of the seats reserved for whites-a dangerous, daring, and provocative act in a racist society.

Legend has it that years later a graduate student came to Rosa Parks and asked, "Why did you sit down at the front of the bus that day?" Rosa Parks did not say that she sat down to launch a movement, because her motives were more elemental than that. She said, "I sat down because I was tired." But she did not mean that her feet were tired. She meant that her soul was tired, her heart was tired, her whole being was tired of playing by racist rules, of denying her soul's claim to selfhood.

Of course, there were many forces aiding and abetting Rosa Parks's decision to live divided no more. She had studied the theory and tactics of nonviolence at the Highlander Folk School, where Martin Luther King Jr. was also a student. She was secretary of the Montgomery chapter of the National Association for the Advancement of Colored People, whose members had been discussing civil disobedience.

But in the moment she sat down at the front of the bus on that December day, she had no guarantee that the theory of nonviolence would work or that her community would back her up. It was a moment of existential truth, of claiming authentic selfhood, of reclaiming birthright giftedness-and in that moment she set in motion a process that changed both the lay and the law of the land.

Rosa Parks sat down because she had reached a point where it was essential to embrace her true vocation -not as someone who would reshape our society but as someone who

For Whom God Calls

would live out her full self in the world. She decided, "I will no longer act on the outside in a way that contradicts the truth that I hold deeply on the inside. I will no longer act as if I were less than the whole person I know myself inwardly to be."

Where does one get the courage to "sit down at the front of the bus" in a society that punishes anyone who decides to live divided no more? After all, conventional wisdom recommends the divided life as the safe and sane way to go: "Don't wear your heart on your sleeve." "Don't make a federal case out of it." "Don't show them the whites of your eyes." These are all the cliched ways we tell each other to keep personal truth apart from public life, lest we make ourselves vulnerable in that rough-and-tumble realm.

Where do people find the courage to live divided no more when they know they will be punished for it? The answer I have seen in the lives of people like Rosa Parks is simple: these people have transformed the notion of punishment itself. They have come to understand that no punishment anyone might inflict on them could possibly be worse than the punishment they inflict on themselves by conspiring in their own diminishment. In the Rosa Parks story, that insight emerges in a wonderful way. After she had sat at the front of the bus for a while, the police came aboard and said, "You know, if you continue to sit there, we're going to have to throw you in jail."

Rosa Parks replied, "You may do that ... ," which is a very polite way of saying, "What could your jail of stone and steel possibly mean to me, compared to the self-imposed imprisonment I've suffered for forty years-the prison I've just walked out of by refusing to conspire any longer with this racist system?"
The punishment imposed on us for claiming true self can never be worse than the punishment we impose on ourselves by failing to make that claim. And the converse is true as well: no reward anyone might give us could possibly be greater than the reward that comes from living by our own best lights.

You and I may not have Rosa Parks particular battle to fight, the battle with institutional racism. The universal element in her story is not the substance of her fight but the selfhood in which she stood while she fought it-for each of us holds the challenge and the promise of naming and claiming true self.

Michael H Sands

But if the Rosa Parks story is to help us discern our own vocations, we must see her as the ordinary person she is. That will be difficult to do because we have made her into superwoman and we have done it to protect ourselves. If we can keep Rosa Parks in a museum as an untouchable icon of truth, we will remain untouchable as well: we can put her up on a pedestal and praise her, world without end, never finding ourselves challenged by her life.

Since my own life runs no risk of being displayed in a museum case, I want to return briefly to the story I know best-my own. Unlike Rosa Parks, I never took a singular, dramatic action that might create the energy of transformation around the institutions I care about. Instead, I tried to abandon those institutions through an evasive, crablike movement that I did not want to acknowledge, even to myself.

But a funny thing happened on the way to my vocation. Today, twenty-five years after 1 left education in anger and fear, my work is deeply related to the renewal of educational institutions. I believe that this is possible only because my true self dragged me, kicking and screaming, toward honoring its nature and needs, forcing me to find my rightful place in the ecosystem of life, to find a right relation to institutions with which I have a lifelong lover's quarrel. Had I denied my true self, remaining "at my post" simply because I was paralyzed with fear, I would almost certainly be lost in bitterness today instead of serving a cause I care about.

Rosa Parks took her stand with clarity and courage. I took mine by diversion and default. Some journeys are direct, and some are circuitous; some are heroic, and some are fearful and muddled. But every journey, honestly undertaken, stands a chance of taking us toward the place where our deep gladness meets the world's deep need.

As May Sarton reminds us, the pilgrimage toward true self will take "time, many years and places." The world needs people with the patience and the passion to make that pilgrimage not only for their own sake but also as a social and political act. The world still waits for the truth that will set us free-my truth, your truth, our truth-the truth that was seeded in the earth when each of us arrived

For Whom God Calls

here formed in the image of God. Cultivating that truth, I believe, is the authentic vocation of every human being.

DELIVERABLES
REFLECTION PAPER & Questions

1. Where do you stand on the question of vocation?

2. Have you struggled with dual-vacations as brought out in the reading?

3. Do you feel your "Call" is relevant even though you may have accepted your calling at a later stage in life?

4. How much are you willing to sacrifice to fulfill the call upon your life?

Michael H Sands

Chapter 8
An Exercise in Self-Authenticity
The Fear Statement

Michael H. Sands

What Do You Fear Most?
As we wind down this journey towards the inner-self, it has been my personal experience as well as that of being a witness to other minister's struggles that I've found it beneficial to do a simple exercise in self-honesty. Before succumbing to a distorted, grandiose vision of ministry and ministerial accomplishment, it is imperative to begin such a life-altering journey dealing with something that is at the core of Satan's tactic of deceit. This issue, one that serves as a huge impediment to reaching ones inner-being is fear. Therefore, I pose this question to you, blessed reader, "How can one hear God living in an existence shrouded in fear"? I postulate, that it is nearly impossible to do so unless fear is tackled head on. So the million-dollar question and the subject of hits exercise is, What Do You Fear Most?

In the Hebrew text, Isaiah 41:10 speaks these salient words to us:

> do not fear, for I am with you,
> do not be afraid, for I am your God;
> I will strengthen you, I will help you,
> I will uphold you with my victorious right hand

An honest, transparent, answer to this question will be the beginning of your journey towards your inner-self that will negate Satan's tactic of using your fears against you as a means to dissuade and distract you from who and what you are called to be as a minister of the Gospel of Jesus the Christ. Make no mistake, until you confront this question, and can provide to God and yourself an *authentic* answer, your ministry *will* suffer.

Use the following example as a guide. It can be as long or short as necessary to express your thoughts.

Example:

The Fear Statement

What I fear most is "Dying Alone"!
It is this fear that I will have lived my life as an insignificant world citizen with nothing to show, no legacy, and nary a found memory in the minds of those with whom I interacted on this life's journey. Visions in my head of laying despondently alone in a hospital or nursing home bed, sickly, bewildered, depressed, and full of regret in that I find myself buried in a sea of self-pity and angst. No children at my bedside to hold my hand. No children or grandchildren to miss me. No spouse to soothe my aching mind and body with words of comfort to depart with. No deacon to ease my soul, and no pastor to erase the guilt of my humanistic unbelief.

Visions of what I have done to satisfy the God of my creation are overshadowed by thoughts of what I should have done while having the strength and will to do God's. The work I've done is negated by visions of procrastination, skepticism, and a loathsome self-worth. I who have given so much to others, now find myself unappreciated and unloved as a lay in bed wasting away into the ashes and dust my physical body will ultimately return to.

All I can envision is a wasted life God has given me substituted by selfish intent and therefore I am left in misery to suffer the indignations of an unfaithful servant.

The unfortunate last questions in my mind prior to crossing over is; Have I indeed done what God has commanded of me? Do I now doubt all of my life's endeavors and relegate those memories into the category of a meaningless existence. Will the work I've done truly speak for me? Then I am left to eternally wander in the forest as a lost spirit according to the religious beliefs of my ancestral Yoruba people, who believed such a fate awaits those who have not lived the life expected of them and are therefore denied eternity with the Creator.

Thus are the seeds of disillusionment and doubt planted through the wiles of Satan upon even the most faithful among us.

Are you able to admit and confront your fears? If you can't, what makes you think that you can stand before God's people and minister the "Good News" if you cannot apply it to your own spiritual journey? Can you dismiss your first inkling to answer such questions with a resounding, "I don't have any fears…"? or an even more untenable response that uses God as your scapegoat by saying, "God is my …(insert excuse here)"?

Now is the time to get real about whatever that "something" is that lurks within your psyche. In his book, *The Creative Encounter*, Howard Thurman speaks of the *Authentic Self*. He again mimics this theme of self-authenticity in his famous speech The Sound of the Genuine (used as an inspirational reading at the beginning of this book) at a Baccalaureate Service for the graduates of Spelman College in 1980. Now is the time to examine that *Thurmanian* theme and journey towards the genuine, authentic person within, revealing that which you have been hiding behind and has debilitated and truncated your physical and spiritual being all these years. Predictably, most readers will most likely take the path of least resistance and declare all is well, not humbling themselves to the fact that their mind has become a battlefield of contradictions and placations that only serve to defeat the authentic, genuine self rather than transform into the naked, unmasked creation that binds the relationship between self and God.

Yet despite all this, the Hebrew narrative found in Isaiah 41:10 reveals within the first three words, the beginning of your journey to self, DO NOT FEAR! Such a simple concept, such a simple directive, such a simple theme has for most been extremely illusive. For most, our socialization to succumb to our fears began at an early age where humans find that it is easier to protect oneself by letting fear control your reaction than to apply the courage given to us by God to simply NOT FEAR. Granted, fear is a genetic survival mechanism, but the fear to which I refer is a paralyzing fear the stifles the spirit and derails life's possibilities. Have you ever wondered why when angels or even Jesus encounters man, they say "Fear Not" before any pronouncement? They are telling us to ignore our first instinct and open our spirit to Holy revelation which cannot be received as along as the recipient is in a state of fear. Has such a simple instruction become too difficult to follow since we've become so full of philosophical and theological idioms that the sheer simplicity of the command frightens you?

What then do you do to overcome? It's in the next four words… "I AM WITH YOU"! Believe that God is with you! It all comes down to faith!

<u>Deliverable</u>

Write *Your* Fear Statement!

Michael H Sands

CHAPTER 9
THE "CALL" PAPER

Michael H. Sands

All of the readings and exercises encountered to this point have prepared you to write your "Call" paper. I strongly encourage you to share it with your pastor/sponsor. I pray that they would push your writing towards authenticity and frankness rather than writing for others' approval. Please take this seriously as an authentic call paper will reveal the inner-most in you, and failure to be transparent to yourself and God makes your journey in ministry fraught with disappointments.

Use the following outline to complete your paper. Doing so will help you stay focused and ensure that your call paper will be comprehensive. Also, and this is important, the call paper *IS NOT* an autobiographical exercise. Keep your efforts concentrated on those experiences related to your call. (See Attachment 1 – for an abbreviated example of a call paper.)

THE "CALL" PAPER OUTLINE

I: Introduction – 1 Page
- Who are you?
- How did you arrive to this point in life that this decision is now before you?

II: Describe your call experience – 2 to 4 Pages
*Select from **1** of the three types:*
- Direct Call (Meaning God spoke to you directly to you, also referred as a Dialogical Call)
- Indirect Call (You were compelled to ministry through an experience)

For Whom God Calls

- Influenced Call (You felt a call because others, like family, friends, church members, clergy told you that you were called)

III: The Reflective Practitioner - 4 pages

- How has the bible influenced your call. There **MUST BE** a biblical reference...no exceptions.
- What is your Theology (What do you believe)?
- What is your understanding of God at this moment. (R*ESIST* looking this up or seeking a commentary to explain *YOUR* beliefs. Be genuine in what you believe. The goal is to be honest with yourself...not meet the expectations of other people!

IV: Denominational Influences - 2 pages

- What is your understanding of your denomination and how has this influenced you and your ministry journey thus far?

V: What Has God Called ME to do? – 2 pages

- Having declared that you have been called by God, and using your biblical reference to support your calling...What has God *SPECIFICALLY* called you to do?
- What is *YOUR* Ministry? (***Generalizations are unacceptable***)

VI: Plan of Action – 2 to 3 pages

- Outline what steps/objectives you are going to or have taken towards fulfilling the Calling God has placed upon you?
- What resources do you need?
- What is your time table for accomplishing your objectives? (Be Specific!)

VII: Conclusion – 1 to 2 pages

Michael H Sands

- Wrap everything up neatly so the reader can hear **YOUR VOICE SPEAKING**

* I again stress that you share your completed call paper with your pastor for input whenever possible. If you don't have a pastor or mentor you feel comfortable sharing this document with, for a small fee, I will review and provide feedback to you about your paper. I assure you that my critique will be no different than if you were a student in my class. My purpose in reviewing the call paper is to extract the maximum amount of authenticity from your document. I'll do my best to read "in between" the lines. I search for hidden meanings. I also will challenge you when I sense that you are trying to be politically correct, or are avoiding true meaning by hiding behind personal myths. With love, I will provide non-judgmental feedback.

This is my God given gift and I have no motive other than to strip down barriers to your authenticity to help you reach your full God given potential so that you may serve the Triune God with all you heart, mind, and spirit.

For Whom God Calls

Chapter 10
Your Personal Library

Listed below is probably one of the most valuable resources I can provide to new ministers. I have often found in consultation with new ministers, a desire to start a personal library from which to use as a resource for study, sermon preparation, and teaching support. Many have acquired books that in my view are more about the personal opinions of the author rather than an objective scholarly resource. I have nothing against resources published by those whose narratives provide valuable think pieces and inspiration. For serious study however, I strongly recommend that at a minimum those inspirational books be supplemented with some of the ones I've listed here. The list is not all inclusive, but it is organized categorically to help as a guide for texts that have proven to be invaluable throughout my years of study for those just beginning their ministerial walk. Even the Biblical translations themselves vary in accuracy to the original text.

Recommended Biblical Translation

<u>New Revised Standard Version (NRSV)</u>: Though not perfect, it is recognized by many scholars today as the best English language translation for serious in-depth study. (Gorman 2009, p.45) Though you may choose to use a translation that you feel more comfortable with, or tradition has taught you is the only "valid" translation, the NRSV is accepted as the bible translation of choice in many seminaries and academic settings.

Bibliography for the Readings in this Book

In my classroom courses, students are required to buy their books. The readings in this book were extracted from those books. Unfortunately, these excerpts in this book only giving you a glimpse of their rich content. I highly encourage you to purchase these books so that you can benefit from a more comprehensive understanding of the subject matter. This will further assist you in your ministry journey.

Akbar, Na'im. *Breaking the Chains of Psychological Slavery.* Tallahassee, FL: Mind Productions & Associates, ©1996.

Cetuk, Virginia Samuel. *What to Expect in Seminary: Theological Education as Spiritual Formation.* Nashville: Abingdon Press, 1998.

Palmer, Parker J. *Let Your Life Speak: Listening for the Voice of Vocation.* San Francisco: Jossey-Bass, 2000.

Pitt, Richard N. *Divine Callings: Understanding the Call to Ministry in Black Pentecostalism.* New York: New York University Press, 2012.

Whelchel, L H. *The History and Heritage of African-American Churches: A Way Out of No Way.* St. Paul, Minn.: Paragon House, 2011.

Wimberly, Edward P. *Recalling Our Own Stories: Spiritual Renewal for Religious Caregivers.* The Jossey-Bass Religion-in-practice Series. San Francisco, CA: Jossey-Bass Publishers, 1997.

General Library Collection

The following books are just a sample of the books in my personal library that I have accumulated over the years. I found these particular texts to be most beneficial to new/beginning ministers. Though their content can be challenging at times, especially to many embedded theologies, the task of finding a good mentor would be particularly helpful when you have questions about what you encounter as you engage these texts.

Ministry in the African American Context

Akbar, Na'im. *Know Thyself*. Tallahassee, FL: Mind Productions & Associates, 1999.

Ani, Marimba. *Let the Circle Be Unbroken: The Implications of African Spirituality in the Diaspora*. New York: Nkonimfo Publications, 1997.

Bogle, Donald. *Toms, Coons, Mulattoes, Mammies, and Bucks: An Interpretive History of Blacks in American Films*. 4th ed. New York: Continuum, 2001.

Burrell, Tom. *Brainwashed: Challenging the Myth of Black Inferiority*. New York, NY: Smiley Books, 2010.

DeGruy, Joy. *Post Traumatic Slave Syndrome: America's Legacy of Enduring Injury and Healing*. Portland, OR: Joy DeGruy Publications, 2005.

Du Bois, W E B. *The Souls of Black Folk*. Dover Thrift Editions. New York: Dover, 1994.

Earl, Riggins Renal. *Dark Symbols, Obscure Signs: God, Self, and Community in the Slave Mind*. Knoxville: University of Tennessee Press, 2003.

Fanon, Frantz. *Black Skin, White Masks*. Get Political. New York: Grove Press, 2008.

Mullane, Diedre, ed. *Crossing the Danger Water: Three Hundred Years of African American Writing*. New York: Anchor Books, 1993.

Rudisel, Christine, and Robert Blaisdell, eds. *Slave Narratives of the Underground Railroad*. Dover Thrift Editions. Mineola, New York: Dover Publications, Inc., 2014.

Thomas, William Hannibal. *The American Negro: What He Was, What He Is, and What He May Become; a Critical and Practical Discussion*. London: The Macmillan Company, 1901.

Russell-Cole, Kathy, Midge Wilson, and Ronald E. Hall. *The Color Complex: The Politics of Skin Color Among African Americans*. New York: Anchor Books/Doubleday, 1993.

Walker-Barnes, Chanequa. *Too Heavy a Yoke: Black Women and the Burden of Strength*. Eugene, OR: Cascade Books, 2014.

Wilkerson, Isabel. *The Warmth of Other Suns: The Epic Story of America's Great Migration*. New York: Random House, 2010.

West, Cornel. *Race Matters*. New York: Vintage Books, 1994

Christian Education

Browning, Robert L., ed. *The Pastor as Religious Educator*. Birmingham, Ala.: Religious Education Press, 1989.
McKinney, Lora-Ellen. *Christian Education in the African American Church: A Guide for Teaching Truth*. Valley Forge, PA: Judson Press, 2003.
Tye, Karen B. *Basics of Christian Education*. St. Louis, Mo.: Chalice Press, 2000.

African American Worship

Costen, Melva Wilson. *African American Christian Worship*. Updated Edition. Nashville, TN: Abingdon Press, 2007.
McKinney, Lora-Ellen. *Total Praise: An Orientation to Black Baptist Belief and Worship*. Valley Forge, PA: Judson Press, 2002.
Rognlien, Bob. *Experiential Worship: Encountering God with Heart, Soul, Mind, and Strength*. Colorado Springs, CO: NavPress, 2005.
Segler, Franklin M., and C Randall Bradley. *Christian Worship: Its Theology and Practice*. 3rd ed. Nashville, Tenn.: B & H Pub. Group, 2006
Segler, Franklin M., and C Randall Bradley. *Understanding, Preparing For, and Practicing Christian Worship*. 2nd ed. Nashville, Tenn.: Broadman & Holman, 1996.
Talbot, Frederick Hilborn. *African American Worship: New Eyes for Seeing*. Eugene, OR: Wipf & Stock, 2007.
White, James F. *A Brief History of Christian Worship*. Nashville: Abingdon Press, 1993.
Witvliet, John D. *Worship Seeking Understanding: Windows Into Christian Practice*. Grand Rapids, Mich.: Baker Academic, ©2003.

Theology/Theology in the African American Context

Andrews, Dale P. *Practical Theology for Black Churches: Bridging Black Theology and African American Folk Religion*. Louisville, KY: Westminster John Knox Press, 2002.

Baltazar, Eulalio R. *The Dark Center: A Process Theology of Blackness*. New York: Paulist Press, 1973.

Barth, Karl. *Evangelical Theology: An Introduction*. Grand Rapids, Mich.: Eerdmans, 1979, 1963.

Coleman, Will. *Tribal Talk: Black Theology, Hermeneutics, and African/American Ways Of "Telling the Story."* University Park: Pennsylvania State University Press, 2000.

Cone, James H. *Said I Wasn't Gonna Tell Nobody: The Making of a Black Theologian*. Maryknoll, NY: Orbis Books, 2018.

Cone, James H., and Gayraud S. Wilmore, eds. *Black Theology: A Documentary History*. 2nd ed. Vol. 2. Maryknoll, N.Y.: Orbis Books, 1993.

Cone, James H., and Gayraud S. Wilmore, eds. *Black Theology: A Documentary History*. 2nd ed. Vol. 1. Maryknoll, N.Y.: Orbis Books, 1993.

Grant, Jacquelyn. *American Academy of Religion Academy Series*. Vol. 64, *White Women's Christ and Black Women's Jesus: Feminist Christology and Womanist Response*. Atlanta, Ga.: Scholars Press, 1989.

Musser, Donald W., and Joseph L. Price. *A New Handbook of Christian Theologians*. Nashville: Abingdon Press, 1996.

Riggs, Marcia, and James Samuel Logan. *Ethics That Matters: African, Caribbean, and African American Sources*. Minneapolis: Fortress Press, 2012.

Roberts, J Deotis. *Bonhoeffer and King: Speaking Truth to Power*. Louisville, Ky.: Westminster John Knox Press, 2005.

Robinson, Elaine A. *Race and Theology*. Horizons in Theology. Nashville: Abingdon Press, 2012.

Taylor, Robert Joseph, Linda M. Chatters, and Jeffrey S. Levin. *Religion in the Lives of African Americans: Social, Psychological, and Health Perspectives*. Thousand Oaks: Sage Publications, 2004.

Thurman, Howard, Walter E. Fluker, and Catherine Tumber. *A Strange Freedom: The Best of Howard Thurman On*

Religious Experience and Public Life. Boston: Beacon Press, 1998.

Webster, John, ed. *The Oxford Handbook of Systematic Theology*. Oxford Handbooks. Oxford: Oxford University Press, 2007.

Church History

Bettenson, Henry, and Chris Maunder, eds. *Documents of the Christian Church*. New Edition. Oxford: Oxford University Press, 1999.

Eusebius. *The History of the Church from Christ to Constantine*. Translated by G A. Williamson. Penguin Classics. London: Penguin Books, ©1989.

González, Justo L. *The Story of Christianity*. 2nd ed. Vol. 1. New York: Harper One, 2010.

González, Justo L. *The Story of Christianity*. 2nd ed. Vol. 2. New York: Harper One, 2010.

African Religion & Cosmology

Ani, Marimba. *Yurugu: An Afrikan-Centered Critique of European Cultural Thought and Behavior*. Washington, DC: Nkonimfo Publications, 2007, 1994.

Bunseki, Fu-Kiau. *African Cosmology of the Bântu-Kôngo: Tying the Spiritual Knot*. 2nd ed. Brooklyn, NY: Athelia Henrietta Press, Pub. in the name of Orunmila, 2001.

Diop, Cheikh Anta. *The African Origin of Civilization: Myth or Reality*. New York: L. Hill, 1974.

Magesa, Laurenti. *African Religion: The Moral Traditions of Abundant Life*. Maryknoll, NY: Orbis Books, 1997.

Ptahhotep, Asa G. Hilliard, Larry Williams, and Nia Damali. *The Teachings of Ptahhotep: The Oldest Book in the World*. Atlanta, Ga.: Blackwood Press, 1987.

African American Religion and Church History

DuBois, W.E. Burghardt. *The Negro Church: Report of a Social Study Made under the Direction of Atlanta University; Together with the Proceedings of the Eighth Conference*

for... Held at Atlanta University, May 26th, 1903. Atlanta: Create Space Independent Publishing Platform, 1903.
Lincoln, C Eric, and Lawrence H. Mamiya. *The Black Church in the African-American Experience.* Durham: Duke University Press, 1990.
Raboteau, Albert J. *Canaan Land: A Religious History of African Americans.* Oxford: Oxford University Press, ©2001.
Raboteau, Albert J. *Slave Religion: The.* Updated Edition. Oxford: Oxford University Press, 2004.
Sernett, Milton C., ed. *African American Religious History: A Documentary Witness.* 2nded. The C. Eric Lincoln Series on the Black Experience. Durham: Duke University Press, 1999.
Whelchel, L H. *My Chains Fell Off: William Wells Brown, Fugitive Abolitionist.* Cambridge, MA: Schenkman, 1983.
Whelchel, L H. *Hell Without Fire: Conversion in Slave Religion.* Nashville: Abingdon Press, 2002.

Baptist and Black Baptist Church History

Fitts, Leroy. *A History of Black Baptists.* Nashville, Tenn.: Broadman Press, 1985.
Goodwin, Everett C. *The New Hiscox Guide for Baptist Churches.* Valley Forge: Judson Press, 1995.
Maring, Norman H. *A Baptist Manual of Polity and Practice.* 2nd ed. Valley Forge, PA: Judson Press, 2012.
Torbet, Robert G. *A History of the Baptists.* 3rd ed. Valley Forge: Judson Press, 1963.

The Contemporary Black Church

Abrams, Andrea C. *God and Blackness: Race, Gender, and Identity in a Middle Class Afrocentric Church.* New York: NYU Press, 2014.
Billingsley, Andrew. *Mighty Like a River: The Black Church and Social Reform.* New York: Oxford University Press, 1999.
Davis, Reginald F. *The Black Church: Relevant or Irrelevant in the 21st Century?* Macon, Ga.: Smyth & Helwys Pub., 2010.

Evans, Joseph. *Lifting the Veil Over Eurocentrism: The DuBoisian Hermeneutic of Double Consciousness*. Trenton, New Jersey: Africa World Press, 2014.

Fluker, Walter E. *The Ground Has Shifted: The Future of the BlackChurch in Post-Racial America*. Religion, Race, and Ethnicity. New York: New York University Press, 2016.

Franklin, Robert Michael. *Another Day's Journey: Black Churches Confronting the American Crisis*. Minneapolis: Fortress Press, 1997.

Ginwright, Shawn A. *Black Youth Rising: Activism and Radical Healing in Urban America*. New York: Teachers College Press, 2010.

Kinnaman, David, and Gabe Lyons. *Unchristian: What a New Generation Really Thinks About Christianity-- and Why It Matters*. Grand Rapids, Mich.: Baker Books, 2007.

Paris, Peter J. *The Social Teaching of the Black Churches*. Philadelphia: Fortress Press, 1985.

Price, Emmett George, ed. *The Black Church and Hip Hop Culture: Toward Bridging the Generational Divide*. African American Cultural Theory and Heritage. Lanham, Md.: Scarecrow Press, 2012.

Smith, R Drew, ed. *Black Churches and Local Politics: Clergy Influence, Organizational Partnerships, and Civic Empowerment*. Lanham, Md.: Rowman & Littlefield Publishers, 2005.

Biblical Reflection and Exegesis

Alter, Robert. *The Art of Biblical Narrative*. New York: Basic Books, 2011.

Brown, Raymond E., Joseph A. Fitzmyer, Roland E. Murphy, and Carlo Maria Cardinal Martini, eds. *The New Jerome Biblical Commentary*. Englewood Cliffs, NJ: Prentice-Hall, 1990.

Buttrick, George Arthur, ed. *The Interpreter's Bible: In The King James and Revised Standard Versions with General Articles and Introduction, Exegesis, Exposition for Each Book of the Bible; In Twelve Volumes*. Vol. 11. New York: Abingdon Press, 1955.

For Whom God Calls

Coogan, Michael David, Marc Zvi Brettler, Carol A. Newsom, and Pheme Perkins. *The New Oxford Annotated Bible: New Revised Standard Version*. 4th ed. Oxford England: Oxford University Press, 2010.

Dibelius, Martin, and Hans Conzelmann. *The Pastoral Epistles: A Commentary On the Pastoral Epistles,*. Hermeneia--a Critical and Historical Commentary on the Bible. Philadelphia: Fortress Press, 1972.

Green, Jay P., ed. *The Interlinear Bible: Matt. - Rev..* Vol. 4. Grand Rapids, MI: Baker Book House, 1981.

Harvey, Van A. *A Handbook of Theological Terms*. New York, NY: Touchstone Book Simon & Schuster, 1997.

Hayes, John H., and Carl R. Holladay. *Biblical Exegesis: A Beginner's Handbook*. 3rd ed. Louisville, KY: Westminster John Knox Press, 2007.

Evans, Craig A., and Stanley E. Porter, eds. *Dictionary of New Testament Background: A Compendium of Contemporary Biblical Scholarship:* Downers Grove, IL: Inter Varsity Press, 2000.

Farmer, William Reuben. *The International Bible Commentary: A Catholic and Ecumenical Commentary for the Twenty-First Century*. Collegeville, MN: Liturgical Press, 1998.

Gorman, Michael J. *Elements of Biblical Exegesis: A Basic Guide for Students and Ministers*. revised and expanded ed. Grand Rapids, Mich.: Baker Academic, 2010.

Green, Jay P. *The Interlinear Bible: Hebrew/English*. Grand Rapids, MI: Baker Book House, 1983.

Marshall, I Howard, and Philip Towner. *A Critical and Exegetical Commentary On the Pastoral Epistles*. The International Critical Commentary. Edinburgh: T & T Clark, 1999.

Mounce, William D. *Word Biblical Commentary*. Vol. 46, *Pastoral Epistles*. Nashville: TN. Nelson, 2000.

Pritchard, James B., ed. *Ancient Near Eastern Texts Relating to the Old Testament*. 2nded. Princeton, NJ: Princeton University Press, 1955.

Quinn, Jerome D. *The Anchor Bible*. Vol. 35, *The Letter to Titus: A New Translation with Notes and Commentary and an Introduction to Titus, I and Ii Timothy, the Pastoral Epistles*. New York: Doubleday, 1990.

Soulen, Richard N., and R Kendall Soulen. *Handbook of Biblical Criticism*. 3rd ed. Louisville: Westminster John Knox Press, 2001.

Stuart, Douglas K. *Word Biblical Commentary*. Vol. 31, *Hosea-Jonah*. Grand Rapids, Michigan: Zondervan, 2014.

Webster, John, ed. *The Oxford Handbook of Systematic Theology*. Oxford Handbooks. Oxford: Oxford University Press, 2007.

For Whom God Calls

Chapter 11
Next Steps

    Hopefully, you've engaged the previous chapters with humility, honesty, and integrity. So naturally, your next question might be, What's Next"? Answering that question depends on what issues you encountered in the material. It would be too easy for me to suggest a plan-of-action for you to follow like a roadmap, but unfortunately or fortunately, every person is unique. I recommend certain classes should naturally follow an introduction to ministry, and if you were a part of my ministry training regimen, there would be. But what comes next *for you* is hard to quantify using a universally applicable plan where I don't interact with you regularly.
    Therefore, my suggestion is to grab a pillow, find a quiet place where you won't be disturbed, throw that pillow on the floor, get down on your knees (if able), and have a long conversation with God. I used the term "conversation" for a reason. Similar to when Howard Thurman refers to the genuine self, you likewise need to strip yourself of your internal and external facade and get down to the *real you* when coming before God. It is my sincere belief that such an exercise places you in a posture where God will listen to the authentic you, the you God intended.
    During this conversation with God, confront yourself with what the readings and exercises have revealed to you. One such example, and one that has far-reaching consequences if not dealt with candidly, is your motivation for entering ministry. Have you asked yourself why? Have you asked yourself what benefit you bring to God's people? Have you confronted possible ulterior motives for entering ministry that serve yourself, please others, or fulfills expectations from some outside stimulus?
    To further clarify what I mean, have you ever gotten that "Gut" feeling deep inside that something isn't right that you're getting ready to do, or get into a situation that you know you shouldn't, but because of the perceived benefit you did it anyway? How many times when faced with a scenario like this have you listened to your "gut" and made a decision that you discovered was

the right one? Unfortunately, many choose to surrender to whims that are counter to their intuition only to suffer grave consequences. It takes a faithful person to ignore these potential mishaps and listen to the spirit within.

Similarly, one can get caught up in making a commitment to ministry based on pressures from external influences that are counter to what you truly feel inside. For example, you're going into ministry because your mother or father is a minister and you're to follow in their footsteps. Maybe someone approached you and "prophesized" that you would be a great preacher one day, and you believe that you're fulfilling that prophesy. Perhaps you survived some traumatic experience, and you took that as a sign that God wants you to be a minister of the Gospel. *To clarify, I'm not saying that any of these scenarios can't be genuine calls from God.* My point is, are *you* making the call determination, or has God truly spoken to you and compelled you to be a minister of the Gospel?

The scenarios are endless when it comes to ulterior motives to justify the call to ministry. Therefore, the conversation with God demands an unabashed, down-and-dirty, tear-producing, scream and shout conversation with God. Have faith that such a genuine encounter with God will elicit a response from God and be willing to accept the answer God provides. This is when courage, faith, and humility come in. If God answers, for example, "be a member, not a leader", then what? What do you do if you've convinced your family, people in your church, the pastor, and yourself that you're going to be a minister but God's answers, *NO!* Your choice should be to remain true to yourself. Unfortunately, people enter ministry despite being told, no.

If your call is not of God, you'd be fooling yourself. Believe it or not, others in ministry, like your pastor and fellow associates, sense the genuineness of your calling. It's something called empirical evidence (and often kept a contentious secret, especially in the Black Baptist church). What are you exhibiting that demonstrates a genuine call to be a minister of the Gospel? Here's a simple test. When was the last time you read your bible when you weren't preparing to preach or teach? When was the last time you volunteered to help in the church yet declined for no good reason other than being inconvenienced? When was the last time

For Whom God Calls

you reached out to someone in need? When was the last time you did something nice for a stranger; unsolicited? When was the last time you prayed for someone or comforted someone who was hurting? Enough said!

After wrestling with your conversation and let's suppose God has confirmed your call, then the question becomes, what has God specifically called you to do? I always stress to students the need to answer that question. I am firmly in the camp of God calling people to specific ministries and not general call declarations. I always push back on young ministers who declare God has called them to preach. My response to such a declaration is to ask associates where, when, and how you should preach? Too often I encounter associate ministers who are frustrated because they say they are called to preach but don't get the opportunity to preach in their church setting. I respond with my own experience during my early ministry training in Mississippi.

A pastor on my ordination catechism routinely stood outside on the sidewalk with a portable microphone and preached like he was before a congregation of thousands. Unphased by his surroundings, he preached to passing cars and pedestrians as they passed by. He had no regard for an "audience" but preached the Word of God with all his heart! He did this at least twice a week! My pastor then said to me, if you want to preach, nothing is stopping you. If God has called you to preach, no one can stop you. Go out on a corner and preach! What I get when I tell ministers this story is a terse smile. But the truth is when they say they want to preach, they want to preach in "prime time," 11 am on Sunday with a full choir behind them and a shouting congregation in front of them hurling "Amens" at the pulpit.

I wouldn't deny having these imagines implanted in your psyche, and if that is a vision God has given you, then it is up to you to make it a reality! Fulfillment of your call takes action on your part, not some imaged scenario where the pastor regularly "puts you up" because you're so wonderful! It's not going to happen! My advice is to narrow down your specific ministry and pursue what God has given you to fulfill.

For example, if your calling is Youth Ministry, then get involved with the youth. If it's ministering to the homeless, get involved with homeless shelters. If it's ministering to the incarcerated, get involved with the prison system. None of these entities is going to seek you out somehow miraculously. The fundamental principle I see in Jesus' message is, "Go!" You want to minister to battered women, then find them and minister to them. Nobody's going to knock on your door and ask you. Even if your call is to serve inside the church walls, be proactive and find something to do in the church. Don't wait for the pastor to come and ask you to help. In other words, if God has placed a call in you to 'go forth", then go!

Once you've gained clarity, then it's time to begin a theological self-assessment and address those shortcomings and barriers to accomplishing your ministerial call. For example, if God has called you to minister to youth, Don't spend countless hours studying the theological principles of Kant! Instead, absorb, learn, practice all you can about youth in your ministry applicable to your setting. If you find yourself having to force yourself, you might consider that your selected ministry is not your "called" ministry. I advise that you not wallow in frustration doing something counter to what God has called you to do.

I wish you all the success in the ministry that God has in store for your life's journey. I reiterate that this journey in ministry is fraught with challenging moments and will take the "faith of a mustard seed" to put you where God wants you to be. Let us keep each other in prayer that we accomplish God's calling for the *Glory of God,* and may you find peace in God's directions.

AMEN

For Whom God Calls

ATTACHMENT 1
SAMPLE CALL PAPER

What follows is an abbreviated call paper to use as an example for your own call paper. It is provided not for your critique, but to help guide you through the process of putting to paper the impetus for your decision to become a minister of the Gospel of Jesus the Christ. What is asked of you is much longer, so feel free to provide more details of your journey. However, it is not an autobiography so it shouldn't being with, "I was born...!" Also, it is not necessary that you cite references similar to the sample, However, it would help to know where your influences came from.

Introduction

The call to ministry is a profound personal experience that has many life-long ramifications. It is literally a change in ones understanding of themselves and their walk with God. In the following pages, I will describe "The Call", my journey to the ministry in two phases. Phase I will be a description of my call. Phase II will be a reflection on how the Bible influenced my call, my theology, and my denominational influences.

Phase I: Describing Your Call

The "Call" can be defined as a person's "motivation for ministry."[1] Using this definition, I agree that there was a definite call on my life to enter the ministry. Although my call to ministry was freighting in a sense, it did not result in immediate submission. Cetuk describes her motivation as a presence overtaking her that led to an inner realization that "God wanted her to be an ordained minister".[2]

Michael H Sands

I would classify my calling as a "Dialogical Call." By dialogical I mean that my call came directly from God through Jesus.[3] Like Saul on the Damascus road, Christ came to me and confronted me as to what was I doing with my life and he then told me I was to preach His message to the lost. Like Cetuk, witnessing my pastor in the pulpit and their daily routine reaffirmed the clear message given to me by Jesus that serving Him as a Pastor was my calling.[4] I befriended a local Pastor and ultimately joined his church. On a beautiful Sunday afternoon in April, I went to his study before service and told him my story and how I believed I was sent to him to start my ministerial walk. He asked that I declare this in front of the congregation. I did so when he opened the doors of the church. In front of the congregation he began to weep openly and stated that God had already confirmed to him the reason I was there and that he was only waiting for me to submit to my call. This same Pastor licensed and ultimately ordained me in 2002.

My call was based on the motivation to serve God's people similar to Cetuk's observation that seminary students "want to make the world a better place and to spread the gospel message of love, justice, and reconciliation."[5] I was licensed and ordained in recognition of my service to the church. I gave and continue to give of myself tirelessly, not for the purpose of achieving some goal, but only to do my part in encouraging the subaltern and in thanks to what God has done for me.

Wimberly presents the concept of Perfectionism. Specifically, as it applies to me, the "perfection of empathy."[6] Wimberly goes on further to explain that this type of empathy is a trap that many ministers fall into from thinking that they can empathize with their parishioners and keep their own identity intact.[7] I do agree wholeheartedly with his observations, and I admit that I am a very strong empathizer and is how I feel most comfortable when ministering to all types of people. Unlike Wimberly's conclusion on this topic however, I *can* keep my individuality intact.[8] I have the ability to place myself in the shoes of individuals because I have experienced many similar situations in my life. However, after ministering, I can step away and sleep comfortably! This is one of my gifts from God and it is my belief that the reason He allowed me to experience so much pain and suffering was so I could empathize with His people without "Sucking the life out of myself."[9]

Phase II: The Reflective Practitioner

How has the Bible influenced my call:

What comes immediately to mind is the story of David and Uriah. The scripture tells of how David was one after Gods own heart. David had everything he could ever want or need and God greatly blessed him. But…the passions of the world, symbolized by Bathsheba, led David to deceitfully murder Uriah to cover his sin in satisfaction of his lust.[10] Though I have not physically killed anyone, I too succumbed to the lusts of the world and sinned greatly before the Lord. Even while I was in my sin, God saw fit to rescue me and place me before His people. My viewpoint that anyone can be forgiven for their transgressions is the foundation of my compassion towards people. If God forgave David, and forgave me, He will forgive those strangled by guilt. Because of his sin, David was denied the honor of building God's temple.[11] My life mirrors the same denial of potential. With the gifts God has given me, I could have been a great political leader through elected office because my passion for justice is so strong. However, because of my past, I will never be able to hide my sin from worldly scrutiny so like David, God has denied me my full potential. However, God has opened other doors as a sign that I can still be of service to Him and His people.

My Theology:

My theology is uncomplicated. I believe in the Holy Trinity. I believe that Jesus is the Christ, born of a virgin, was crucified, and rose on the third day in propitiation for the sins of mankind. I believe in my very soul that God is a forgiving God and that He allows us to stumble and fall, but provides His grace and mercy to stand again. If it were not for this belief I would not be here. I have no ego to destroy; God has taken that, so I treat everyone with love and compassion. I am no saint, but I live each day in the hope that someone I encounter will witness the glory of

Michael H Sands

God through me. I complain not for what I do not have, and believe that my final reward is on the "other side." People don't understand me for they view me as an impossibility, that I can't be as I say. My actions speak otherwise and I have a God given influence over people to let them see the God in me so that they can share in His glory. Accepting my call has changed me into a person unrecognizable by my family, former friends, and peers. The call to preach Gods word saved my like.

Denominational Influences:

     I am Baptist and therefore was brought up in churches that had no centralized binding governing body. However, there are some accepted consistencies as far as the ministry is concerned. In order to become ordained, a person must first become licensed. Licensing requirements vary somewhat from church to church depending on the pastor. My track to ordination began with a special afternoon trial sermon service that was witnessed by a group of invited ordained ministers. These ministers conferred afterwards to decide if my sermon exhibited enough evidence to grant a license to preach. After agreement was reached to grant the license, the pastor brought the decision before the church with a motion to grant license. The license, once granted, is then held by the church indefinitely until such time the Pastor deems you fit for ordination.   However, the license can be revoked at any time for malfeasance. Other Baptist churches I have served in require a year after the trial sermon to become eligible for licensure. Similar to my process, once the license is conferred, the ordination time frame is at the discretion of the Pastor. For me, licensure and my eventual ordination were great honors that I did not strive to achieve. I was too humble to ask about it and it only came up in conversions initiated by the pastor. With all the emphasis given to ordination, the most controversial decision is Pastorship. Becoming a pastor can be a very political process where many pastors act as gatekeepers.   Though many pastors have told me that I will "one day" make a great pastor, the only way they would ever endorse me for a pastoral opportunity is if I was a seminary graduate. Its humbling to admit, but one of my primary reasons for coming to seminary is to "fill that square" on a path to Pastorship.

However, this seems to be a Northern phenomenon since in the deep rural south, seminary is jokingly referred as the "cemetery."

Conclusion

In the previous pages I have attempted to outline my "call" in order to clarify for the reader as well as myself the legitimacy of Gods call on my life. Regardless of a consensus with my call experience and subsequent choices, I am here in seminary now to fulfill what God has called me to do. I am reminded of a scene from the Color Purple were Celie says, "I'm poor, black, and I may even be ugly, but dear God I'm here, I'm here."[12] I too feel the same. I might have let God down, I may not be the smartest, and I may have made serious mistakes in my life, but thank God, I'm here!

Notes

1. Edward P. Wimberly, *Recalling Our Own Stories: Spiritual Renewal for Religious Caregivers* (San Francisco, CA: Jossey-Bass, 1997), 1.
2. Virginia Samuel Cetuk, *What to Expect in Seminary: Theological Education as Spiritual Formation* (Nashville, TN: Abingdon Press, 1998), 15.
3. Temba L. Mafico, *The Devine Call and the Human Response* (Lecture Handout, Interdenominational Theological Center, Atlanta, GA, October 17, 2011), 1.
4. Virginia Samuel Cetuk, *What to Expect in Seminary: Theological Education as Spiritual Formation* (Nashville, TN: Abingdon Press, 1998), 15.
5. Ibid., 52.
6. Edward P. Wimberly, *Recalling Our Own Stories: Spiritual Renewal for Religious Caregivers* (San Francisco, CA: Jossey-Bass, 1997), 6.
7. Ibid.
8. Ibid., 7.
9. Ibid.
10. 2 Samuel 11: 3 – 12:10. (New Revised Standard Version)

11. 1 Chronicles 17: 4.
12. *The Color Purple.* DVD. Directed by Stephen Spielberg, 1989.

Bibliography

Cetuk, Virginia Samuel. *What to Expect in Seminary: Theological Education as Spiritual Formation.* Nashville, TN: Abingdon Press, 1998.

Temba L. Mafico, Temba L. *The Devine Call and the Human Response.* Atlanta, GA: 2011.

Walker, Alice. *The Color Purple.* New York, NY: Houghton Mifflin Harcourt, 1992.

Wimberly, Edward P. *Recalling Our Own Stories: Spiritual Renewal for Religious Caregivers.* San Francisco, CA: Jossey-Bass, 1997.

For Whom God Calls

Notes

Inspirational Reading

1. This text is based on excerpts from Dr. Howard Thurman's Baccalaureate Address at Spelman College, May 4, 1980, as edited by Jo Moore Stewart for The Spelman Messenger Vol. 96 No. 4 (Summer 1980), 14-15. This text has been adapted from a transcription of an audiotape of Dr. Thurman's baccalaureate address.

2. Dr. Thurman paraphrased this story from the Gospel According to Mark 5:1-13.

3. Catherine Cate Coblentz with illustrations by Janice Holland, Blue Cat of Castle Town (London : Longmans, Green & Co., 1949).

4. Italics not in the original. Emphasis added for clarity of reading.

5. Italics not in the original. Emphasis added for clarity of reading.

6. The poetry cited appears to have been composed by Thurman himself.

7. Thurman is quoting from the creation story in Genesis 1:26. The final words of Dr. Thurman's address —"Don't defy Him. Don't defy Him. Your arm might wither"— have been deleted from this text for the sake of clarity. In context, those words play upon the poetry of James Weldon Johnson, the author of God's Trombones, a volume of poetic texts based on the tradition of African-American preaching.

Chapter One

1. William T. Sherman, Memoirs of General William T Sherman (Bloomington: Indiana University Press, 1957), 96-99.

2. W. P. McClutchey, November 15, 1952, Wylie and Mineva McClatchey family papers, Georgia Department of Archives and History, Atlanta, Georgia, Andrew Billingsley, *Mighty Like a River: The Black Church and Social Reform*, (New York: Oxford University Press, 1999), 22-23.

3. *Marietta Daily Journal*, May 3, 1960. When Mother Dicey and other Blacks were allowed to join First Baptist Church of Marietta, Georgia, there were some Whites who raised the question as to whether Blacks had souls. Despite the dangers, the enslaved exhorter, Ephraim Rucker, was determined to proclaim the gospel regardless of the consequences. Once Rucker was brutally whipped, but despite the beating he resolved to lead the enslaved Blacks in a private prayer meeting, which was discovered, and he was whipped yet again even while the wounds from the first lashing were still healing.

4. Celestine Sibley, "*Restoring Zion in Cobb County,*" *Atlanta Journal Constitution*, September 25, 1985. Church attendance was often more appealing to the enslaved than to the slaveholders. The enslaved attended the First Baptist Church of Marietta in such large numbers that the church leaders considered extending the gallery or cutting open a window in the front of the church to accommodate the increased number of Blacks. Blacks eventually grew restless and eager to form their own church. Rucker Ephraim, property of the Dobbs family, petitioned to perform marriages to "persons of color. "The church minutes indicate that the White members felt it was " inexpedient at the present time for Ephraim to marry persons of his own color," but they permitted him to preach in prayer meetings when called on by the watchman or slave overseer.

In 1855, the Black members of First Baptist petitioned the White members to allow them to organize their own church. For some reason, Rucker Ephraim, who had been a strong advocate of an independent church, asked the White pastor to drop the petition. This infuriated the Black church members, and they voted him out of the church on April 1, 1855; however, they restored his membership two months later.

In April 1856, the First Baptist Church convened a church conference to find out why the Blacks had boycotted communion on the previous Sunday. The Blacks stated in their response that "they did not feel prepared to take communion as their minds were rather frustrated about the alteration made relative to their occupying a portion of the altar and they thought they would wait until another

For Whom God Calls

time. "The Blacks assured the church that "they did not think of rebelling against the church and were sorry the church thought so." The Marietta Daily Journal, Saturday, May 17, 1986, 7Al.

In May of 1856, First Baptist Church voted to grant the Blacks their request to secure their own place of worship, while the Whites would continue as members of the First Baptist Church. The White church was reluctant to relinquish control over the Black members. The church appointed a committee "to assist the black members in procuring a lot and drawing up rules by which they will be governed."

The Black congregation petitioned the White overseers and deacons for church officials of their own color, and this request was granted by the ordaining of Joshua, the property of Mrs. D.A. Campbell, and Richard, the property of the estate of Dr. S. Smith, as deacons. Also Rucker Ephraim was appointed to preach to the Black members.

In 1862, there were twice as many Black members as there were Whites. During the Civil War the disparity between the Black and White members increased because many White men enlisted in the Confederate Army, a circumstance that inadvertently gave the Blacks more freedom to govern themselves. During the war, First Baptist Church was used as a hospital, and the Blacks worshipped in a separate facility. At first they remained an appendage of the White church until the arrival of the Union General William T. Sherman, who literally set the captives free. (The Marietta Daily journal, Saturday, May 17, 1968, 6A-8A.) On April 8, 1866, Zion Baptist Church was formally organized with Ephraim B. Rucker serving as the first pastor. Ruth W. Miller, First Family Memoirs *(A 150-Year History of First Baptist Church* [Marietta, Georgia, 1985], 27.)

5. Billingsley, 23; Gregory D. Coleman, We're Heaven Bound (Athens: C. of Georgia Press, 1992.) This book describes the illustrious history of Bethel A.M.E. Church, and the production of the plays which became major social events at the church on Sweet Auburn Avenue in Atlanta, Georgia. For a vivid description of the capture of Atlanta, see William T. Sherman, Memoirs of General William T. Sherman, *Memories of General William T. Sherman*, Volume II, 96-136. The two pioneering Black churches in Atlanta were the Bethel A.M.E. Church and Friendship Baptist

Church; they respectively gave birth to Morris Brown College and Spelman College. These churches also laid down the economic foundations for a vibrant Black professional class in Atlanta. Both leased property to the Atlanta Board of Education to ensure that Black children would have public schools to attend. (Jerry John Thornberry, *The Development of Black Atlanta*, 167.)

6. Ibid. After being liberated from the control of the White church, the jubilant Blacks named their side of town Sherman town to honor the man who led the Union troops. (Cathy Tyler, "Church History Recorded, "*The Daily News*, Stone Mountain, Georgia, January 31, 1992.)

7. Sara Louis Gray, *Baptist Heritage: Bethlehem Baptist Church of Christ, 1823- First Baptist Church, 1973* (Covington, Newton County, Georgia), 24.

8. Ibid. 25.

9. Billingsley, 23.

10. Gray, 25. Sara Louis Gray's history of Bethlehem Baptist Church noted the first enslaved male to join the White First Baptist Church. The enslaved was named Brother Glasgow, and he was the property of Mr. Mathew Smith. His membership was facilitated by a letter from the slave master and the first enslaved member by conversion or profession of faith was Celia, the property of Mr. Carey Wood. The professors of Oxford, which was not too far from the church, permitted their slaves to attend Bethlehem Baptist Church. An old enslaved preacher known as Brother Jerry was permitted to preach to the enslaved as long as it was done under White supervision. (Gray, 12.)

11. Sherman, 180-181.

12. Billingsley, 24.

13. Billingsley, 24; Ira Berlin, et al., *Free At Last: A Documentary History of Slavery, Freedom and the Civil War*(New York: The New Press, 1992), 310. After the emancipation, these religious leaders were well aware of the need for fostering a sense of community and the most formidable and effective institution that
the formerly enslaved had developed was the independent Black churches-to which the freedmen now turned for leadership. The proliferation of newly independent Black churches was a natural consequence of emancipation. Immediately following the abolition

of slavery, urban Blacks moved quickly to seize control of their own religious institutions. Reconstruction dictated a time for consolidation and transformation of religious and cultural institution for Blacks. The "Invisible Institution" of the rural south now emerged into the full light of day. Eric Foner, *Reconstruction America's Unfinished Revolution,* 1863-1877 (New York: Harper and Row Publishers, 1988), 88-90.

The emancipation freed the Blacks with a promise of material provisions, but that promise would not be fulfilled. And worse still, the defamatory image of Black people and trauma to their collective psyche was not addressed. The theological, anthropological, medical, and economic justifications for slavery and racism were developed and promoted by White clergy, physicians and university professors in the leading ecclesiastical and academic institutions of America and Europe. In the aftermath of the collapse of southern slaveholding those justifications were not rebutted. Indeed, arguments for the intellectual and moral inferiority of people of African descent continued well into the twentieth century, and they were not widely challenged until the 1960s. All of the mainline White denominations urged Blacks to remain within their folds but as subordinated members. White minsters and church officials continued to promote the inferior status of Blacks with segregated seating in churches and exclusion from church administration. (Foner, 89; H. Shelton Smith, *In His Image But: Racism in the Southern Religion* (1780-1910) (Durham: Duke University Press, 1972), 209-213.

    14. Sherman, 243-252.

    15. Ibid.

    16. Ibid. These religious leaders who conferred with Stanton and Sherman were well aware of the fact that freedom without land left them in a vulnerable and destitute condition not much better than their previous condition of servitude. It was on the issue of land tenure that the real struggle for Black freedom would be won or lost. The freedmen sagaciously realized that gaining immediate control of their destiny hinged upon the ownership of land. Without land, they would have lives of dependency, subservience, and poverty. Donald L. Grant, *The Way it Was the South: The Black Experience in Georgia* (Athens: University of Georgia Press, 1993), 93.

17. Billingsley, 23.
18. Ibid.
19. Ibid.
20. Ibid., 29. Vincent Harding, *There Is a River* (New York: Vintage Book 1983), 258-276.
21. James M. McPherson, *The Negro's Civil War* (New York Vintage Books 1965), 300.
22. Willie Lee Rose, *Rehearsal for Reconstruction* (New York: Vintage Book 1964), xiii. W.E.B. DuBois, *Black Reconstruction in America, 1860-1880* (New York. Atheneum, 1972), 3-16. DuBois provides an insightful study of one of the most fascinating periods in American history. He gives a meticulous interpretation of "twenty years of fateful history with especial reference to the efforts and experiences of the Negroes themselves. "DuBois attempted to correct a gross imbalance in telling the story of Reconstruction, as the works of White scholars had previously focused on presenting the side of the former slaveholders, and they
largely ignored the story of those who were enslaved and oppressed. The thesis of this undervalued book is: "How black men coming to America in the sixteenth, seventeenth, eighteenth and nineteenth centuries became a central thread in the history of the United States, at once a challenge to its democracy and always an important part of its economic history and social development." (DuBois, 3.)
23. *Journal of the General Conference of the Methodist Episcopal Church, 1844, 63*, 64, 66, 143, 148; John N. Norwood, *The Schism in the Methodist Episcopal Church, 1844* (New York: Alfred, 1923). This book provides an account of the divisiveness over the question of slavery in the church.
24. *General Conference of the Methodist Episcopal Church Minutes 1868*, 373, 238, 241. Joel Williamson, *After Slavery: The Negro in South Carolina During Reconstruction 1866-1877* (Chapel Hill: The University of North Carolina Press, 1965), 180-181.
25. Othal H. Lakey, The *History of the C.M.E. Church* (Memphis: C.M.E. Publishing House, 1985), 179-182. Love Henry Whelchel, *Hell Without Fire*, 93-109.

26. Walter L. Fleming, *Documentary History of Reconstruction* (Cleveland, Ohio: The Arthur H. Clark Company, 1907), 233-234. Emory Stevens Burke, ed., *The History of American Methodism*, 3 vols. (Nashville: Abingdon Press, 1964), 11, 65-85. Robert Cruden; *The Negro in Reconstruction* (Englewood Cliffs: Prentice Hall, Inc., 1969), 36. *Testimony from Report of the Joint Committee on Reconstruction*, 1866, Parts II, III, and IV; Hunter Dickinson Farish, *The Circuit Riders Dismount* (Richmond: The Dietz Press, 1938), 174. Martin Luther King, Jr., would later speak of the folk wisdom expressed by southern Blacks as their "ungrammatical profundity." Stephen B. Oates, *Let the Trumpet Sound: The Life of Martin Luther King* (New York: Harper and Row, Publishers, 1982), 77.

27. Grant, 267.

28. Ibid.

29. DuBois, 637-699. "The first great mass movement for public education, at the expense of the state, in the South, came from Negroes. Prior to the Civil War there were advocates for better education in the South, but few had been listened to. Schools for indigents and paupers were supported, here and there, and more or less spasmodically. Some states had elaborate plans, but they were not carried out. Public education for all at public expense was, in the South, a Negro idea." (DuBois, 638.)

30. C. Eric Lincoln and Lawrence Mamiya, *The Black Church in the African American Experience*, 92-93.

31. Foner, 92-93.

32. Grant, 113-116, 267; Lakey, 263; Whelchel, 103.

33. Mary Frances Berry and John Blassingame, *Long Memory: The Black Experience in America* (New York: Oxford University Press, 1982), 108.

34. Grant, 112.

35. Ibid., 257.

36. Foner, 329, 426; Lincoln and Mamiya, 204, 217; George Brown Tindall, *South Carolina Negroes*, 1877-1900 (Columbia: University of South Carolina Press, 1952), 14.

37. DuBois, 387; Alrutheus Ambus Taylor, *The Negro in South Carolina During Reconstruction* (New York: A.E.E. Press, 1924), 107.

38. Foner, 534.

39. Tindall, *South Carolina Negroes, 1877-1900*, (Columbia, SC: University of South Carolina Press),154-156; Rayford W. Logan and Michael R. Winston, *Dictionary of American Negro Biography* (New York: W.W. Norton and Company, 1982), 84-85.

40. Logan and Winston, 523; Foner, 352-353; DuBois, 449,450, 594-595.

41. Ibid.

42. DuBois, 638.

43. Foner, 27, 426; DuBois, 393, 395; Criden, 88; Lerone Bennett, *Before the Mayflower: A History of Black America* (Chicago: Johnson Publishing Company, 1987), 231, 481; Logan and Winston, 89-90; Richard Bryant Drake, *"The American Missionary Association and the Southern Negro, 1861-1888"* (A Thesis: Emory University, 1957), 221.

44. DuBois, 637-667; Janet Duitsman Cornelius, *While I Can Read My Title Clear*, 85-104; Whelchel, 48-62; Raboteau, 96 150; Drake, 9, 31; Thornberry, 183, 140, 150. With gunfire at Fort Sumter signaling the beginning of the Civil War, a war to save the Union that was unintentionally transformed into a war to free the slaves, Northern abolitionists began to redirect their efforts toward protecting those Blacks who were seeking refuge in the Union Army from their former slaveholders. Several benevolent societies sprang up ostensibly to aid the Negro, and the foremost among these was the American Missionary Association (AMA). The AMA comprised erudite Northerners trained at leading northern universities such as Harvard, Yale and Princeton. These missionaries also went to the South after the Civil War as they attempted to release the freedmen from the influences of the slaveholding South by indoctrinating them into the cultural hegemony of the White North. These Northern missionaries came south with a mission and a paternalistic attitude. They considered that the Blacks would now accept their leadership and direction in the churches and schools that would be set up for them. The administration and faculties at the schools established by the missionaries were primarily made of White Northerners. According to Thomas Chase, an AMA faculty member at Atlanta University, "It should be the policy of the AMA to make haste slowly in this direction and as a rule employ only such colored

teachers and preachers as we make in our institutions and feel that we can trust and rely upon." (Richard Drake, 179-180.) The AMA missionary workers played a key role in cultivating cliquish dispositions among the Black elite in Atlanta. Influential AMA teachers such as Thomas Chase, Horace Bumstead, and Edmund Asa Ware had all attended Ivy League schools, and they wanted educators and ministers serving in Black churches and schools to receive the benefit of the elitist values which they espoused. Through their funding capacity, the AMA exercised effective control over a number of the colleges that were set up for Blacks, and they also financed the early development of the historic First Congregational Church, which was attended mostly by Black professionals. Indeed, as long as the church received AMA monies it accepted the appointment of White ministers. In 1894, the church became self-supporting and the members forthwith proceeded to vote for the appointment of a Black pastor.

The legacy of elitism cultivated among Blacks included the formation of exclusive social gatherings and Eurocentric-style worship services, which tended to limit both the growth of their churches and the extent of community services provided by those churches. (Jerry Thornberry, *The Development if Black Atlanta*, 180-181.) Henry L. Morehouse, president of the AMA stated without apology that the goal of the organization was to indoctrinate "America in the Negro," by which he meant the "American ideal of citizenship, of church membership, of family life, etc., incorporated in the Negro character." The goal of these White educators was to create White men and women inside black skins. [James M. McPherson, *The Abolitionist Legacy* (New Jersey: Princeton University Press, 1975), 184.] The historic Morehouse College in Atlanta is named in honor of Henry L. Morehouse, first president of the AMA. His philosophy and attitude about the role of the Negro and the purpose of education for Negroes speaks volumes about the original mission of Morehouse College and a number of other postbellum historically Black colleges and universities-to produce graduates who would seek to assimilate as far as possible into the larger society, and who would have no inclination whatsoever to develop autonomous agency in the interests of their own community.

45. Thornberry, 12, 1977, 154-156, 178-184.

46. Lincoln and Mamiya, 7-10.
47. W.E.B. DuBois, *The Negro Church* (Atlanta: The Atlanta University Press, 1903), 1-7.
48. Brooks, 29-32.
49. Edward Madal, A Right to the Land· Essay on the Freedmen's Community (Westport, Conn.: Greenwood Press, 1977), 77.
50. Ibid., 78.
51. Ibid.
52. Ibid., 79.
53. Ibid., 8.
54. Report if the joint Committee on Reconstruction, 39th Congress, 1st Session, Vol. 11, 1:52-53.

Chapter Four

1. Fact Book on Theological Education for the Academic Year 1995-1996 (Pittsburgh: The Association of Theological Schools in the United States and Canada), 48.
2. Lynn Rothstein, *Consortium for Institutional Research at Theological Schools Entering Student Questionnaire 1994* (Pittsburgh: The Association of Theological Schools and the Consortium Institutions, 1994), 6.
3. ATS Fact Book 1995-1996, 46.
4. Ibid., 27.
5. Laypeople serving as supervisors of students in the broadest sense of the word is a widespread practice in theological education today. Called various things (Teaching Church Committee, Lay Training Committee, and so forth), the committee serves to give students both a broader source of feedback and evaluation and an arena in which to talk regularly with trusted laypeople about issues of importance in ministerial formation.
6. The ATS Fact Book 1996-1997 notes that of 63,618 students enrolled in accredited theological schools in 1996, 41 percent (27,876) were in Master of Divinity programs, making that the degree with the highest portion of students (p. 34).
7. Philipp Melanchthon, *The Apology of the Augsburg Confession, in The Book of Concord: The Confessions of the Evangelical Lutheran Church*, trans. and ed. Theodore G. Tapper!

(Philadelphia: Muhlenberg, 1959), 269.

8. Martin Luther, *"A Treatise on Christian Liberty,"* trans. W. A. Lambert, in Works of Martin Luther, vol. 2 (Philadelphia: Muhlenberg, 1943), 333.

9. Bertram Lee Woolf, *Reformation Writings of Martin Luther* (London: Lutterworth, 1952), 275, quoted in William Robinson *Completing the Reformation: The Doctrine of the Priesthood of All Believers* (Lexington, Ky.: The College of the Bible, 1955), 11.

10. Webster's New World Dictionary of the American Language, College Edition (New York: The World Publishing Company, 1960), 1633.

11. Gustaf Wingren, *Luther on Vocation* (Philadelphia: Muhlenberg, 1957), 124.

12. Bertram Lee Woolf, *Reformation Writings of Martin Luther* (London: Lutterworth, 1952), 276.

13. Cyril Eastwood, *The Priesthood of All Believers: An Examination of the Doctrine from the Reformation to the Present Day* (London: The Epworth Press, 1960), 60.

14. Martin Luther, *"The Babylonian Captivity of the Church"* trans. A. T. W. Steinhaeuser, in Works of Martin Luther, vol. 2 (Philadelphia: Muhlenberg, 1943), 279.

15. Presbyterian Church (USA) *Book of Order* (Louisville: Office of the General Assembly, 1994), G-6.0101-102, G-6.0105.

16. *The Book of Discipline of The United Methodist Church* (Nashville: The United Methodist Publishing House, 1996), 301.

17. *Candidacy Manual for the Evangelical Lutheran Church in America* (Chicago: Division for Ministry, 1995), 11.

18. Denominations vary in the length of time one must be a church member before beginning the ordination process. The Evangelical Lutheran Church in America, the United Church of Christ, and The United Methodist Church all require a minimum of one year membership. The Presbyterian Church (USA) requires a six-month minimum membership prior to beginning the process. All denominations assume active participation in the life of the congregation. In these churches, along with the Episcopal Church and the churches comprising the Baptist tradition, the local congregation must give assent and support to the candidacy of a

particular person. If such support is not given, the person seeking ordination will not be permitted to continue in the process.

In addition, denominations vary on the degree to which they are involved in a student's enrolling in seminary. United Methodist candidates apply to seminary independently of any movement through the ordination process. In the Evangelical Lutheran Church, however, students require the support of the Candidacy Committee before beginning their theological studies (*Candidacy Manual*, 8.)

19. Presbyterian Church (USA), *Book of Order*, G-14.0302, G-14.0304.

20. "Entrance Procedures into Licensed and Ordained Ministry," In The Book of Discipline of The United Methodist Church (Nashville: The United Methodist Publishing House, 1996), 305.

21. Ibid., 304.

22. Evangelical Lutheran Church in America, *Candidacy Manual*, 12.

Featured Readings Bibliography

Akbar, N. (1996). *Breaking the Chains of Psychological Slavery* (1st ed.). Mind Productions & Associates.

Cannon, K. G. (2007). *Teaching Preaching: Isaac Rufus Clark and Black Sacred Rhetoric* (1st ed.). Continuum.

Cetuk, V. S. (1998). *What to Expect in Seminary: Theological Education as Spiritual Formation*. Abingdon Press.

Crossings Reflection #4 "The Sound of the Genuine" Rev. Dr. Howard Thurman (1899–1981). (n.d.). The University of Indianapolis. https://www.uindy.edu/eip/files/reflection4.pdf

Pitt, R. N. (2012). *Divine Callings: Understanding the Call to Ministry in Black Pentecostalism*. NYU Press.

Whelchel, L. H. (2011). *The History and Heritage of African American Churches: A Way Out of No Way*. Paragon House.

Michael H Sands

As a service to individuals who don't have a pastor or mentor you feel comfortable with sharing your call paper, or you would like a non-biased review of your call paper prior to submitting to your pastor or mentor, or for your own edification, I will review your call paper for a small fee. If interested, please send a message stating that you purchased the book and would like me to review your call paper. I will send you an invoice and submission instructions.

Please send inquiries to:
ministermikesands@yahoo.com.

For Whom God Calls

www.ingramcontent.com/pod-product-compliance
Lightning Source LLC
Chambersburg PA
CBHW071430070526
44578CB00001B/51